THE GREAT DAYS OF THE
GWR

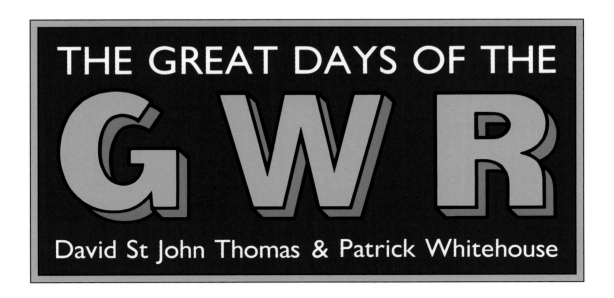

THE GREAT DAYS OF THE
G W R

David St John Thomas & Patrick Whitehouse

BCA
LONDON · NEW YORK · SYDNEY · TORONTO

Frontispiece *One of Newton Abbot's Bulldog class 4-4-0s kept specially for pilot duties over the South Devon banks double heads a Castle past Stoneycombe quarry on the westward ascent of Dainton.*

From a painting by G. F. Heiron

A railcar in cider country. Steens Bridge, the penultimate station en route from Worcester to Leominster via Bromyard with a GWR railcar waiting time with the 4.30pm ex Worcester, shown in the timetable as 3rd class only. The date is summer 1952. This was a fine example of a Great Western country station still providing passenger comforts – for example a coal fire in the waiting room in the winter; with sometimes hours on their hands between trains the staff took practical pride in their station – they were not only gardeners but topiarists too. The section from Bromyard to Leominster closed on 19 September 1952 and Worcester-Bromyard on 7 September 1964.

This edition published 1991
by BCA by arrangement
with David St John Thomas Publisher

CN 1874

Printed and bound in Great Britain
by Butler & Tanner Ltd, Frome

CONTENTS

1 INTRODUCTION 9
Broad Gauge Footplate Trip 27
2 AN ALIEN VIEW 33
Topdog, Underdog 42
3 THE SEASONAL GREAT WESTERN 47
The Railcars 54
4 A DAY IN THE LIFE OF 'A' SHOP 57
Great Western London 65
5 A TALE OF FOUR CASTLES 73
Great Western Cross Country 84
6 THE SEA WALL 89
Locomotive Sheds and Allocation January 1938 101
7 FIVE LOCOMOTIVE BIOGRAPHIES 109
A Busy Weekend at Cardiff 129
South Wales 135
8 FAST WORK IN THE MARCHES 139
No 2937 Clevedon Court 146
9 SNOW HILL DAYS 149
Snow Hill's Signalling 159
10 HOW CUT OFFS MADE THE WESTERN GREAT 161
Taunton 169
11 THREE WEST COUNTRY JOURNEYS
(Early 1950s) 173
Engineering Instructions 180
12 CAMBRIAN HOLIDAY 1937 183
Aberystwyth to Carmarthen 194
One Man's View 197
13 THREE OFFICIALS 201
Wartime Branch Line 208
14 A BUSINESS TRIP WINDSOR TO
SHREWSBURY 1920 211
Commuters and Steam 1957–64 219
ACKNOWLEDGEMENTS 222
INDEX 223

When the Great Western was great, railways were the leaders in public transport; they were evocative, often colourful and accepted universally as a permanent feature of the landscape as well as the travel scene. No wonder, then that small boys had ambitions to be engine drivers and that coloured postcards were on hand, in stationers, shops and on railway stations, to capture the atmosphere and the ambience. In those days, and indeed into early BR times colour photography was neither readily available nor practicable for the amateur and artists impressions, often painted over black and white photographs were the norm. These cards and the colour plates appearing in such journals as the Railway Magazine and the Locomotive, were (and still are) for the most part, the only examples of the then day to day railway scene available; they brought it to life dramatically.

Entitled 'A Broad Gauge Flier near Uffington' this Locomotive Publishing Co's card was not as popular as many showing the more modern scene but we must be grateful for it's production as this is one of very few showing Brunel's 7ft 0¼ins gauge. It is identifiable as a down express from the position of the bars on the telegraph poles as they were always fitted to the up side. It dates from the Edwardian era (or early George V) as the postage stamp used was ½d, less than a quarter of today's penny.

GREAT WESTERN EXPRESS

A Valentine card showing one of Churchward's double framed 4-4-0s, probably a Bulldog emerging from Parsons Tunnel adjacent to the beginning of the sea wall stretching to Teignmouth. The scene is before the change of coach livery to maroon (between 1905 and 1909). The engine carries no number on the bufferbeam and its train is made up of one hundred per cent clerestory stock.

'The Flying Dutchman', one of Raphael Tuck and Sons 'Oilette' cards in their Famous Expresses series. The train is a Paddington–

"Flying Dutchman" G.W.R.
NEAR SLOUGH.

Birmingham one headed by City class No 3433 City of Bath (later No 3710). Again this is a down train and the photograph was taken near Slough. This was a special issue of the card which is stamped on the bottom with Tuck's trade mark plus the words 'Proof Limited to 1000 copies' in gold script. The scene on the postcard has been doctored as by the 1900s the line from Paddington to Reading was all four track.

PADDINGTON STATION. G.W.R.

Paddington station in the Edwardian age looking outward from the buffers. Lighting even then was by electricity – from the look of the globes, probably carbon-arc lamps. Despite enlargement and modernisation the scene is recognisable today. Locomotive types which can be identified are (L to R) a 2-4-0T (Metro), a 2-4-0 with domeless Belpaire boiler and a large wheeled double framed 4-4-0, probably a City. A Tuck Oilette card, London Railway Stations series.

4-4-0s Nos 7 Armstrong and 8 Gooch backing out of Paddington in 1910 after working an up express. These were two of the four earliest 7ft 4-4-0s built in 1894 and were nominal rebuilds of 2-4-0 tandem compounds, No 7 standard gauge and No 8 a broad gauge convertible. Armstrong has been rebuilt with a standard No 2 boiler whilst Gooch still retains the original. Both were withdrawn during 1929, No 7 in September and No 8 in April. LPC card.

A representative of the 2221 class 4-4-2Ts built between 1905 and 1912 for the more important outer-suburban trains to and from Paddington. The class had a relatively short life and was extinct by September 1935 being superceded by the 61XX 2-6-2Ts. The locomotive on the original card bears an incorrect number but the train is typical of the immediate pre 1914 era. (The card may be based on a photograph by F. E. Mackay). LCC Reward card from LPC series.

1
INTRODUCTION

THAT the public spent over a million pounds on our *GWR 150* shows that the subject is popular but does not give an automatic reason for another volume. The justification for this is the new material that comes to light (literally hundreds of former employees wrote in about their personal experiences after publication of *GWR 150*) and there is a constant reassessment as to how Great the railway really *was*. Interest today is naturally centred on the 1930s and thereafter, in other words in living memory, and free from the necessity of even sketching the earlier history we here unashamedly concentrate on portraits of what older readers could have seen for themselves – and younger ones heard tell of from the previous generation. We have tried to portray the railway as a whole – not of course setting out to catalogue it but to catch all its various moods and tempos in the rural back of beyond as well as cities, on very everyday as well as the famous trains.

Why the Great Days? The truth is that during much of its history the GWR did not live up to its name. After a splendid start with Brunel's uniquely great main line from Paddington to Bristol and the world's fastest train taking full advantage of the seven foot gauge, enterprise languished and places such as Bridgwater in Somerset and Plymouth celebrated the opening of their second, rival line with greater enthusiasm than they welcomed the first ever steam engine decades earlier. Only after the abolition of the broad gauge did the GWR finally become a great railway but even then its conservatism held back its innovation and, while the traditions that were to serve it so well had now been firmly established, they were not to be fully exploited until after 1923. It was undoubtedly the fact that alone of the four major railways of the Grouping era (1923–47) the Great Western retained its identity that resulted in its ultimate greatness.

A great tradition of continuity was astutely combined with powerful innovation and an imaginative publicity machine to make the Great Western probably the most loved commercial organisation in the entire history of the Western world. A tall claim, you may think, but try to name a rival candidate that has had so much written and said about it, of which so much has been preserved decades after it ceased to be. Certainly nowhere in the world at any time has a large employer been so revered as was the GWR in its heyday. It was assumed that sons would wish to follow fathers and grandfathers in its service, as worthwhile and as secure an employment that was open to most men. This of course is familiar territory and must not be dwelt upon for long, but (just to quote one example) between the wars the Great Western held a safety record

Comparison. In 1903 the Great Western Railway purchased a 4 cylinder compound 4-4-2 similar to a standard class of the Northern Railway of France. It was numbered 102, named La France *and painted black with red and white lining. Two larger French 4-4-2s were delivered in 1905. The engines were purchased to run alongside Churchward's then new two cylinder and four cylinder Atlantics for technical comparisons.* La France *and the Swindon built engines were used turn and turn about on West of England expresses to and from Paddington. A down train, probably the 10.10 am Paddington to Penzance, is seen passing Subway Junction, Westbourne Park during 1904 or 1905. The stock consists of five clerestory roof corridors plus a 'Dreadnought' tri-composite restaurant car fourth from the engine. The signals, instead of the normal stripes on the arms, have letters denoting the line to which they apply, e.g. ML, to EL.*

The same train, this time behind Churchward 4-4-2 No 171 Albion, *a two cylinder locomotive later converted to a Saint 4-6-0. The 'Dreadnought' coach is just discernible. This photograph is taken from a Tuck 'Oilette' coloured postcard (reproduced in our companion volume 'Great Days of Express Trains') and the setting is probably deliberately anonymous but likely to represent the four tracks between Paddington and Reading. The signature is 'F. Moore' a pseudonym for one of several artists employed by the Locomotive Publishing Co.*

Churchward's designs were to revolutionise Great Western locomotive practice and performance from the early 1900s and onwards for twenty years. The Saints and Stars were the leading contenders with the County 4-4-0s – for all their rough and ready characteristics – hard at work on secondary expresses on such routes as Birmingham to Bristol via Stratford upon Avon, the North to West trains and the Weymouths. These cards represent a cross section of the classes and routes concerned.

No 3807 County Kilkenny built in 1906 heads a train of toplight maroon painted stock en route from Paddington to Weymouth. An LPC card.

No 2902 Lady of the Lake built in 1906 with an up six coach Birmingham express on the joint line with the Great Central near Ruislip. Again the stock is maroon dating the card between 1910 and 1914. This as an LPC original later reprinted by Ian Allan Ltd.

A Valentine card, one of a series showing night scenes. The train is on the then single line section running along the sea wall near Dawlish. The caption reads 'GWR, Plymouth Express' – in spite of the single headlamp shining over the top of the smokebox. The original photograph was probably taken around 1905, the locomotive a Saint class 4-6-0, possibly No 100 William Dean renumbered 2900 in 1912, with the stock still in chocolate and cream. The train is a long one – up to ten vehicles are visible.

An unusual 'local view' card entitled 'Dinner Hour GWR works Swindon'. There is no indication of the publisher but the postmark is, appropriately Swindon, 1.30PM. AP29.04.

Topdog, underdog. Where the GWR shared a station with another company the predominant colour of engines was usually Swindon green. This was certainly the case at Worcester Shrub Hill as can be seen on the accompanying postcard reproduction (LPC and later their 'Alphalsa' associate) taken from a photograph looking north. The Great Western trains appear to be local ones with an Armstrong double framed 0-6-0 on the left and a unknown locomotive in the bay on the right. The Midland's Johnson 0-6-0 could well be at the head of a Birmingham to Bristol excursion as the train is long and the engine carries class A headlamps as well as the reporting number 170.

Another 'local view' card, this time in a Valentine series entitled 'The Station, Llangollen'. Today the Ruabon–Dolgelly line is long gone but fortunately the station is intact as part of a splendid piece of railway preservation. It is now the terminus of a line proceeding westward towards Corwen.

Shrub Hill Station, Worcester.

The Station, Llangollen

Edwardian progress. The new Snow Hill station (completed 1912) just into King George V's reign. Platform 7 (left) and 11 (right) are the main up departure platforms with a London express ready to leave – note the destination board held in brackets on the second clerestory roofed coach and the newer Churchward toplight vehicles to the rear of the train. It is just coming up to 4.00pm – a London departure time for decades. The platform train destination board is just under the 'Refreshments' sign, later it was moved to stand adjacent to the steel column in the foreground. The station reconstruction is not quite complete – platform 11 does not appear to be in use, note the cross on the signal arm. The numbering of platforms 11 and 12 was soon reversed and this end became No 12.

better than that attained by any other system of whatever transport mode before or since. This again was undoubtedly largely due to the combination of tradition and continuity. Everyone knew the *Great Western way* of doing things, which avoided the waste and confusion that are so common in railway history. Of course the liberal spending on safety, including the world's first automatic train control (ATC, though in fact it was really only automatic warning) was enormously helpful but we have seen all too clearly in recent times that investment alone does not create an esprit de corps. The point was made in *GWR 150* that when the railway changed its rules or introduced something brand new, it did so carefully and almost always successfully, so that the staff genuinely believed something different would be something better.

There is no doubt that in pursuing its individual brand of tradition and progress the railway became steadily more unique, differing from the others in a whole catalogue of ways. Not everybody worshipped it. Some found it increasingly irritating, and their anger has hardly subsided today. For the sake of balance we include a chapter called An Alien View. And to demonstrate a touch of the earlier greatness, this introduction is followed by our first shorter 'filler' on a footplate journey on the world's fastest train in broad gauge days.

But as already stated most of our content is on the ultimate Great Days well within living history, when the GWR triumphed in its unique

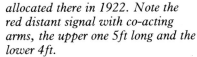

3232 class 2-4-0 No 3247 on a secondary express c1922 – as the stock is variously crimson lake and chocolate and cream. The date is certainly not later than 1925 as No 3247 was withdrawn in October of that year. The location may be near Oxford as the locomotive was allocated there in 1922. Note the red distant signal with co-acting arms, the upper one 5ft long and the lower 4ft.

The Great Western ran an exclusive postal train between Paddington and Penzance and vice versa. The up train is seen here just east of Marazion, the first station out of Penzance, on the single line between Marazion and St. Erth – with the exception of the Royal Albert Bridge, the penultimate section of the Paddington–Penzance main line to be doubled. The locomotive is Star class 4-6-0 No 4011 Knight of the Garter and the year 1926. This is one of the TPOs on which letters could be posted whilst the train was standing at stations. The up Penzance TPO still runs and letters can still be posted directly into the sorting carriage. Originally such letters had to bear an extra ½d stamp but since the introduction of two tier postage all that is required is the appropriate first class rate.

Railcar in the Forest of Dean. AEC railcar No 7 built for the GWR in 1935 stands at Coleford terminus (closed to passengers on 8 July 1929) having worked a Birmingham Locomotive Club excursion from Snow Hill in 1950. There were two termini at Coleford the second, from Monmouth, having been closed to passenger traffic since 1 January 1917. The BLC trip covered all lines in the Forest of Dean then open; a fascinating tour of the Forest's extensive network of lines.

Saturday relief. One of Churchward's Moguls 43XX Class No 7308 in early BR plain black takes westbound No 980 past Reading West Main Box. There are at least 12 'blood and custard' bogies behind the tender.

Previous page, above *Worcester Castle. A down Paddington–Worcester–Hereford express headed by a filthy No 7023* Penrice Castle *near Chipping Camden in the summer of 1963 eighteen months before the demise of steam on the Western Region. At that time engines, even if in good mechanical order, were unkempt by rule rather than exception. The Paddington–Worcesters, including the 'Cathedrals Express' were the last express trains regularly allocated to Castles (the Kings had by then all been withdrawn) and No 7023 was one of the contenders for the epic Paddington–Plymouth–Paddington high speed run of 9 May 1964.*

Previous page, below *Two's company. Swindon shed 9 May 1964. On the left is No 7022* Hereford Castle *acting as standby engine in case No 5054* Earl of Ducie *failed on the run from Bristol. This was the vital last leg of the high speed steam run back to Paddington. No 5054, a single chimney Castle, was the engine chosen to attempt the magic 100 mph – sadly it just missed the mark at 94 mph. It is easy to reflect that a double blast pipe locomotive may have done that little bit better. On the right is ex LMS Princess Coronation Pacific No 46251* City of Nottingham *which had worked a special train for the Railway Correspondence and Travel Society from Nottingham. It was quite a day.*

Below *The classic Great Western photograph of all time. The Cornish Rivera Express 10.30 am Paddington–Penzance approaching Southcote Junction, Reading hauled by King class 4-6-0 No 6027* King Richard I *in April 1938. (This may have been a Sunday train as there is no evidence of the 1935 Centenary stock in the train's formation.)*

continuity, ever reliably provided green locomotives followed by chocolate-and-cream coaches, ran the world's fastest and longest non-stop trains and made healthy profits from publicising itself, its numerous books for 'Boys of All Ages' still being collector's pieces.

Many people of course knew it as the holiday line and looked forward to their journey to the seaside as one of life's annual thrills. Great and varied were the facilities provided to cope with the traffic on those legendary summer Saturdays when through trains and carriages ran to many extra destinations; the railway was clearly serving its customers and staff felt they had earned their wages. But the Great Western was a seasonal line in many other ways. There was hardly a branch line where the kind and amount of activity was not affected by the season – which meant both time of year and the actual weather. No wonder that Great Western men were very conscious of seasonal changes and weather patterns. Many were astute forecasters. The Seasonal GWR is the title of one of our main chapters, while those on Cambrian Holiday 1937 and the Sea Wall capture a touch of the magic of the holiday business.

West Country bound. With home and distant 'off' a down Wolverhampton to Kingswear express (via the North Warwick and Honeybourne–Cheltenham lines) passes through Exeter (St. Thomas) in the early 1930s behind Castle class No 5020 Trematon Castle, *new in July 1932 to Laira shed (LA).*

17

*Star class 4-6-0 No 4061
Glastonbury Abbey rests
peacefully on the middle road
between platforms 7 and 9 of
Bristol Temple Meads station in
1935. Note the absence of brass
beading on the splashers. This
adornment common to all GWR
named engines pre World War I
and to classes built new after that
period, was removed during
hostilities to make a token
contribution to the war effort. To
ensure continuity all members of the
batch built in 1922 emerged from
Swindon works in the same
condition. No 4061 was then
allocated to Bristol Bath Road shed
(then number 22) whose cleaners
had clearly done an excellent job.
The single red lamp on the buffer
beam shows it to be a light engine
and the recently coaled tender
indicates that the engine is likely to
be waiting for a West to North or
Weymouth express, very much Star
perquisites at the time. An historical
note is added to the scene by the
poster advertising the Midland and
Great Western Commercial Hotel
on platform 9. The station
rebuilding began in the early 1930s
is almost compelte.*

*The funeral of King George VI on
15 February 1952 brought
considerable extra traffic to the
Western Region. In addition to the
funeral train itself there were
numerous specials for visiting heads
of state and guests from Paddington
to Windsor and return. Train No 6
is seen on the Windsor branch near
Slough headed by Castle class 4-6-0
No 7004* Eastnor Castle.

Not surprisingly, Great Western locomotives – still probably the most modelled in the world – still attract great interest. We take a number of real-life looks at locomotive performance and journeys on a variety of trains; it is surely important to recall just what train travel used to be like, generally more genteel but undoubtedly more varied and slower than we take for granted today. The contemporary business traveller is ever re-astonished at how few crack trains there were, how great the gap between the best and the others and how late in the morning it was before things really got humming. We also look at locomotives from the unusual aspect of individual lives: just how machines were used around the system when new, middle aged and elderly. A feature that comes out time and time again is that while the GWR was far from a wasteful railway it always preferred to have adequate motive power and other facilities than to risk turning traffic away.

Then we have an opportunity to remember the men of the GWR in its great days – the office officials as well as those performing out on the road. What a breed they were, owing (it often seemed) their first allegiance to the Great Western, the Sovereign State, ahead of their families who were anyway dependent on that State, certainly ahead of Great Britain their nation. They thought, talked, acted their lives the Great Western way, proud to be part of it even if they were sometimes critical of details, never doubting their superiority over the employees of other railways. And the point has been made before that the GWR did see itself as the chosen line, did sincerely believe its ways were the best. It ever emphasised it was not just a railway, moreover. With its own telephone and policing, docks and ships, hotels and in its last years plans for holiday camps, its buses that Parliament insisted it gave up, but its continuing enormous road goods fleet and before World War II, its aeroplanes in chocolate and cream, its farms, mine, special whiskey and biscuit collection, magazine and jig-saw puzzles, housing, education and first aid programmes, its patronising co-operation with local authorities over tourism and other issues, its own lingo for telegraphic messages, unique electric plug sizes and specifications for everything from gas meters to tea cups, its nursery that helped beautify station gardens, pension and holiday schemes far ahead of those of other railways – it indeed *was* a nation within a nation.

The contrast between say the Cornish fishing villages and South Welsh mining ones could not have been greater, yet their Great Western stations shared the same paint, the same signals, the same daily time signal from Swindon. A visit from the prime minister would bring little more excitement than that from the superintendent of the line, while if royalty arrived much of the interest would centre on how the GWR conveyed them. The district superintendent was seen as one of the most important citizens of his area as were most stationmasters in their individual towns. When they moved on or retired there was often a collection and a lunch organised by the chamber of commerce. Retired stationmasters long treasured such 'memorials'.

That there was a distinctive way (or specification) of doing just about everything might have been ridiculous had it not worked so well.

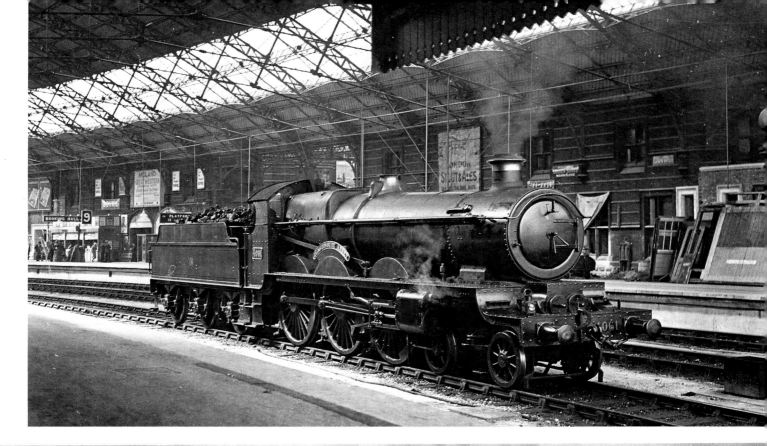

King class 4-6-0 No 6005 King George II *climbing out of Leamington Spa with the 10.00 am from Birmingham Snow Hill to Paddington in October 1958. Apart from the BR Mark I coaches the scene is very much Great Western with 'Reading' lower quadrant signals and a permanent speed restriction indicator referring to the down platform (25 mph) and down through line (40 mph).*

Stability, continuity, a conservative approach coupled with a genuine desire to improve, an ability to back-track on the rare occasions things went wrong, they all contributed to the machine being exceedingly well polished, its parts intimately known. In our *LNER 150* the point was made that on that line young trainees who wanted to get ahead were forever filling up notebooks with knowledge they had gleaned from manuals or colleagues. Many fewer written notes from GWR men are discovered for on the GWR you were more apt to learn orally, to *imbibe* the special way of doing things. It was not that GWR men did not care: they squirrelled away timetables, route maps, rule books, special notices on a prodigious scale: probably a hundred times more GWR than LNER material has survived (just from the Grouping years). But many young recruits knew most of the rules, taught by dad, uncle, or a friendly porter or signalman, well before joining the company's service. Freemasonry had nothing on Great Westernry!

The pride in the railway was its greatest asset. The driver of an express

20

Slip coaches were a feature of the Great Western, in fact it operated more slips than any other company and was the only one to reintroduce them after the 1939–45 war. Usually one coach was sufficient but on Mondays the Didcot slip off the 7.00 am Weston-super-Mare–Paddington ran to two vehicles. They are seen here dropping back from the main train on the up main line at Foxhall junction c1959.

After the 1914–18 War hundreds of Great Central design 2-8-0 locomotives became available at reasonable prices. The Great Western purchased 100 after having a batch on loan. Eventually the best 50 were retained and given GWR fittings, e.g. chimney, top feed and safety valve bonnet – the last examples being withdrawn during 1958. No 3047 leaves Stratford upon Avon with a freight train in the early 1950s.

reaching Paddington in style expected to be thanked by passengers. Exploits (or sinning) were quickly common knowledge around a depot or whole district. Just as the children of GWR parents were expected to do better by many school teachers, so it was assumed the company's employees would be prominent in politics, local government, on the bench, in social work. Then, who ever heard of a staff shortage on the Great Western?

Much of the Great Westernry of course continued (and so does our tale) well beyond nationalisation. When depots like the LNER's Neasden were reduced to near impotency by staff and material shortages, Old Oak Common and the rest carried on as normal, regretting only the disappearance of best Welsh steaming coal for fuel. Predictably Paddington was the last London terminus to employ coloured people in an age less sensitive about race relations. And, as is well known, after the first shock of nationalisation the Western restored much of its sovereignty, uniquely still installing lower quadrant signals, bringing back chocolate-and-cream coaches for the (many new) named expresses, and adopting a totally different (hydraulic) dieselisation policy.

A typical GWR country branch line terminus, Helston on 19 June 1938. The branch locomotive, 45XX class 2-6-2T No 4517 is busy shunting the yard leaving the passenger coaches and two or three ventilated vans in the platform. There is the usual mix of traffic in the yard including open wagons, some with sheet supports, covered vans and cattle wagons which may have been for the broccoli traffic. There is also one container being transferred by the fixed crane.

Evening departure. A dramatic picture of No 6945 Glasfryn Hall with a Bristol–Swindon stopping train leaving Bristol Temple Meads station in the late 1950s. The scene has hardly changed since nationalisation.

The ultimate dominance of BR standardisation was inevitably harder for Great Western than other railwaymen. Not only was the familiar swept away often for an import commanding little respect, but the waste caused by so frequent changes of plan in BR days was unbearable to those who had lived with and respected cautious evolution. Even the gentlest of employees became bitter, and when huge job cutbacks were combined with a large inflow of strangers from other regions (BR staff could apply for jobs anywhere and the grass was greener on the Western) the misery for many was complete.

Why the Great Western was so successful while its rivals were less happy and its successors had their problems is something experts in man management could well ponder. What is for sure is that the Great Western's achievements cannot be rationalised off the slate. The enjoyment those achievements, especially the generations of closely-related locomotive classes, still give is very real – and well beyond the GWR's own territory. When the taxi driver in Melbourne, Victoria, Australia, said he had so good a start to the day that after this fare he was retreating to his hobby, it came as no real surprise that that turned out to be 'modelling the Great Western Railway of England, the world's best'.

Rural South Wales. The Brecon & Merthyr section pick-up goods at Pontsticill Junction on 19 August 1950 headed by two 57XX class 0-6-0PT Nos 5793 and 4635. Two locomotives would be necessary because of the climb from Talyllyn Junction to the summit of the line at Torpantau. A number of the wagons are sheeted (not very well in some cases!) to protect the contents from the elements.

A typical holiday train in the 1950s. Hall class 4-6-0 No 5941 Campion Hall *leaves Torquay with the 9.05 am Paignton to Manchester (London Road) on 4 August 1956. The locomotive carries the large train reporting numbers on the smokebox, an invaluable aid to signalmen in identifying trains at busy week-ends especially when they were running out of course. The visible coaching stock is two LNER corridors and an LMS brake third corridor.*

The heart of Great Western territory. A Manchester and Liverpool to Plymouth express passes Dr Day's Bridge Junction on the approaches to Bristol Temple Meads in the mid 1950s. The locomotive is a County class 4-6-0 and the coaches are all Great Western including a handsome 12 wheel composite restaurant car No W9674W built in 1938 and refurbished post war.

County class 4-4-0 No 3816 County of Leicester *at Swindon about 1927 showing the eight wheel bogie tender which was built for the GWR's solitary 4-6-2, No 111* The Great Bear *in 1908. It was allocated No 1755 when built and carried 7 tons of coal and 3,500 gallons of water. Following the rebuilding of it's intended partner in 1924, it was paired with 8 different locomotives before being cut up at Swindon during October 1936. The tenders unique shape was thus seen behind 1 Pacific, 2 Stars, 3 Saints and 3 County class 4-4-0s during its 28 years.*

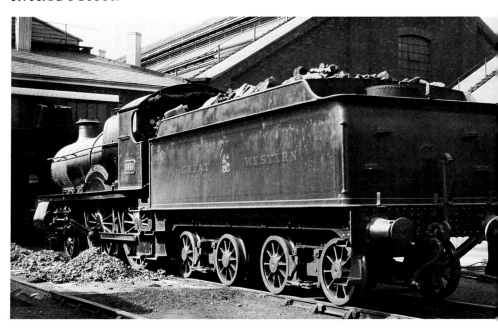

Broad Gauge Footplate Trip

It is often said the Great Western had two 'great days', early in its history when the *Flying Dutchman* was the world's fastest train and after the abolition of the broad gauge in 1892. Much fossilised during the broad gauge's last years but not everything was bad and until the end the seven foot way stirred much enthusiasm especially among those who admired its earlier achievements and pondered what might have been.

Some of the excitement is captured in an article called 'Broad Gauge Engines' that appeared in *The English Illustrated Magazine* in 1892. The author was the Rev A. H. Malan. It serves as our centenary tribute to the broad gauge.

It was remarked by a recent writer that 'no engines in the world have so long and so famous a history as the old engines of Sir Daniel Gooch'. This is high praise, but not overdrawn. It is indeed a surprising thing that a type decided upon so early as 1846 should be found capable of performing the duties of express engines in 1891, when the weight of the trains is at least double that which they were designed to draw. If with no material alteration in their structure they are still capable of the results we see, the question naturally arises: What would prevent new broad gauge engines – with ten feet driving wheels, larger cylinders and ports, and with boilers in proportion working up to say one hundred and eighty pounds – from covering the distance between London and Newton (only a few miles from Torquay) comfortably in three hours? True, Mr Brunel once built an engine, the *Hurricane* (nicknamed 'Grasshopper'), with ten-feet drivers, which was a failure, but then that was a monstrosity, with, it is said, the boiler beneath the crank-shaft.

The father of these express engines was the *North Star*, a six-wheeled engine, built in 1837 at Newcastle, by Messrs R. Stephenson & Co, from a working drawing bearing the signature of Mr Daniel Gooch. Then followed after an interval the *Great Western*, an eight-wheeled engine with eight feet driving wheels, built at Swindon in 1846, on precisely the same model as those now at work – barring the cab; while the *Lord of the Isles*, which attracted considerable notice in the exhibition of 1851, and was exhibited again at Edinburgh last year, gave an admirable account of its merits by running close upon eight hundred thousand miles, before resting from its labours in 1881. The very names of these engines, *Tornado, Lightning, Timour, Amazon, Swallow, Dragon*, indicate the great or swift things of nature, and to see

Cambrian line goods in the mid 1950s when a much higher percentage of freight was conveyed by rail. 2251 class 0-6-0 No 3200 is leaving Llanbrynmair with the down pick-up freight consisting of about 35 wagons and a brake van. Apart from higher capacity wagons the pick-up freight had changed very little from Victorian times; loose coupled vehicles controlled only by the brake van and steam brake on the locomotive.

that expense has not been spared to make them appear worthy of the names they bear one has only to look at their polished brass domes, splashers, and name letters; their bright dark-green boilers picked out with bands of black and gold; their warm Venetian red wheels and framings and their bright steel nameplates and axle-covers. Carping critics have affected to observe elements of weakness in the rise of the framing to clear the centre of the driving wheel, and at the break in the boiler at the firebox. To them it is a sufficient answer to point to the length of time many of these engines have been running, without any such weakness having ever made itself apparent. The secret of that steadiness of motion for which the broad gauge 'eight feet singles' have long been so famous, lies primarily in the *framing*, and secondarily in the *length*. The gentle curves on the main line down to Newton permit the great rail-base of nineteen feet (ie the distance between the points where the tires of leading and trailing wheels touch the rail), without the necessity of employing bogie-wheels; while the double sandwich frame, composed of two skins of iron with wood between, and the indiarubber cushions in connection with the several laminated springs, conduce to an elasticity of movement which has never been approached by any other class. Years ago the directors were able to report that the 'expense of locomotive repairs, especially on that heavy class of repairs which arises from lateral strains on the wheels and framing of the engines, have been materially less than on other lines,' and further experience has probably in no way given them any reason to alter the statement then expressed. These remarks do not of course apply to the saddle-tank engines with low coupled wheels, nor to the Bristol & Exeter single-wheel engines, with eight- (formerly nine-) feet drivers. The latter had bogie-wheels in front, and single frames, and while not running so smoothly, required more repairs than the *Lord of the Isles* class; while the former though good for steep banks and sharp curves, are certainly not beautiful.

Having photographed broad gauge engines at odd times, in every possible attitude, and having seen how they looked from the line, the wish was natural to see how the line looked from the engines, and to gain some practical acquaintance with the routine of engine-driving. Accordingly, permission being granted from Swindon, I boarded the *Iron Duke* one morning last autumn, in Newton yard, as I awaited the up Dutchman's arrival from Plymouth. When we hooked on, there happened to be another engine behind us, and so there was no need for the display of much enginemanship on the journey to Bristol. The first problem that presented itself was where it would be advisable to take up one's position with the likelihood of being least in the men's way: and a seat on the front of the tender seemed about as good a place as any. But as we bowled along by the estuary of the Teign, with Shaldon nestling away under the Ness on the right, and the pretty ivied tower of

Bishopsteignton peeping out of its trees on the left, the discovery was quickly made that such a position was a particularly unpleasant one. Hold as one might, by tender-rail and tender seat, and with feet wide apart, the oscillation between engine and tender was so great that the first stop at Teignmouth was thankfully welcomed as an opportunity of abandoning once and for all any notion of sitting down. The driver suggested gripping the head end of the regulator with one hand, and the cab-edge with the other; and the remainder of the trip was comfortably performed in that attitude. In this position there was the advantage of an uninterrupted view through the right hand glass – the driver standing close behind, and watching the signals through such portions of the glass as were not obscured by the cap and head of his visitor. The men, in fact, are bound to *stand* during the whole of their run on quick trains, because they could not sit down much without being shaken to pieces; and if they did sit down, the signals would be invisible unless they looked out over the cab, which would be unbearable for any length of time. But, as might be conjectured, such protracted standing makes them subject to various complaints of the leg, whereby they are not infrequently placed temporarily on the sick list.

It was in passing the oaken glades of Powderham when it became apparent that the footplate of an express is by no means so good a place from which to study the scenery, as might be supposed. A novice has enough to do to keep his balance, when holding tight with both hands far apart; he cannot venture to let go one hand and turn around his body, or he would be infallibly precipitated head-first among the coal; the vibration is far too severe to permit of his facing backwards; to keep leaning over the shelter of the cab would make his eyes run, to say nothing of smuts and grit; and the view inside the cab, through the glass, is very much circumscribed, like that of a horse with his blinkers on: save for a pretty peep here and there, he does not see half so much of the view on either side, as from a carriage window.

Such being the case, the scenery had to be given up, and the attention concentrated upon the signals, the work of the shovel, the index of the pressure-gauge, the manipulation of the regulator and lever, and the system of firing. And there was so much to interest in these ways, and the endeavour to see everything all at once proved so absorbing, that the run came to an end far too soon. The signals soon became a fascinating study. Everything – our very lives – depended on their being seen, and their being right; it was surprising how far off one was able to detect them; and, caring only for those on the left side of the posts, to tell at a glance whether the arm was up or down; it was wonderful too how close one distant signal seemed to the next as we flew along after passing Exeter at a mile a minute. 'Enginemen are at all times to exercise the greatest watchfulness; they are to be ever on the alert, and while on duty, to keep their minds entirely fixed on that which is required to be done.' This instruction was carried out to the very letter; never for an instant, from Newton to Bristol, were the eyes of the driver (and those of the fireman also, except when firing or working the injector), otherwise occupied than in keenly and penetratingly scanning the road ahead; while the same was the case on the journey back. Their ears were also constantly on the alert, to catch the beat of the engine which indicates that all is right with the 'motion'; though how they could tell, amid the multitude of noises, was altogether beyond my comprehension.

Hele and Silverton flashed by, and Cullompton quickly came in view. Here the whistle was sounded long and loud, to warn some rash person on the platform to retire before being demolished. Then a whiz, rattle and bang through Tiverton Junction, and so on towards Burlescombe and the Whiteball Tunnel. With two engines there was no difficulty in mounting the bank; in fact the lever was pretty well in the seventh notch (one next the centre of the sector plate) all through the run.

There is the distinct advantage in being on the engine in going through this tunnel, that the other end shows as a small speck of light from the first, and therefore one can be sure the line is clear. The broken lumps of rock in the top make it look like a great black cave; the roar, shaking, and bumping are of course echoed and intensified. There comes to mind the remark of one of the witnesses in the House of Commons when the Box Tunnel was contemplated: 'The noise of two trains passing in a tunnel would shake the nerves of this assembly.' But had the witness ever been through a tunnel on an engine, he would have modified his opinion about the other train, as his own locomotive would effectively drown any noises but those made by itself.

As a matter of fact, being in almost total darkness, going through a tunnel was not half such a risky sensation as dashing past platforms, or through a network of points. This trip served indeed to correct several wrong impressions. Someone has written somewhere, that in going round sharp curves the feeling is frightful, as though the engine were actually off the line. But nothing of the sort was experienced; the engine then, on the contrary, seemed unusually steady; in consequence, no doubt, of the flanges all pressing against that rail which bore the centrifugal force; and moreover the lines are hidden for some distance ahead, on account of the length of the boiler. A long stretch of straight line was infinitely worse; for a bad length of rail here and there would cause the wheel to bang against the metals, first one side then the other, with a series of jerks, and deafening crashes, like the united blows of many hammers breaking up iron plates in a foundry yard (it is right to add that when any of the drivers report a bad piece of line the platelayers are at once set to work to rectify matters.) It seemed, on these occasions, as if the tyres of the wheels, especially the big driving wheels, were bound to snap, or the spokes to break off at the axles. Let the metal be of the very best, it is well known that constant vibration quite alters its character, rendering it crystalline instead of fibrous, and surely such tremendous strains must influence its nature, if anything in the world can. The sensation at these times was indescribable – 'terrific' being the only word suggesting itself. If this be 'steadiness of motion', one thinks, is it possible for anyone to conceive the state of unstable equilibrium in which a narrow gauge engine must find itself under the circumstances? What may be the length of life of the driving-wheels is unknown, but at least their tires would need regrinding about every fifteen months.

The down Dutchman was timed to leave Bristol at 2.2pm, but came in a few minutes late. The *Rover*, bright and clean as a new pin, backed down to the platform, and Sansom, the driver, looked along the platform, counted the carriages and chafed at delay.

'Heavy load?' I remarked.

'Seven eight-wheeled coaches, sir, each weighing twenty-one tons; third class compartments choke full. This train used to have no third class, fewer carriages, and was allowed the same time.'

'Shall you save any coal to-day?'

'No coal to be saved by this train,' he replied.

And so it appeared. From start to finish the fire door was perpetually opened, and dripping coal shovelled in. Cook, the fireman, did his work well, never missed shooting the coal (chiefly placed in the centre of the fire) without dropping any of it outside; and when a speck of dust got on the footplate, promptly sweeping it up with his brush. He was a model fireman, always at work, and silent, and never in the way; which is a good deal more than he might have said of his passenger. Of course though coal may be placed in the centre it is obvious that the jolting of the engine will soon shake the several lumps into any hollow in the fire where there may be a lodging place for them, so that the molten mass quickly appears as a level homogeneous layer. We started with the needle at 140, and ended at Teignmouth with the same pressure, as the *Rover* was to work its way back, with a stopping train, shortly after reaching Newton.

The injector, a more modern one than that of the *Iron Duke*, was immediately below the pin of the regulator; it was kept gently 'on' the whole way, replenishing the boiler by the amount of exhaustion, and keeping the water in the glass tubes wonderfully steady.

It was a fine, sunny afternoon. The ground rises the first six miles to Bourton, and this has to be done in nine minutes to keep time. The regulator was full open, and the lever in four-and-a-half notch to the top of the bank. Posted at the left hand glass, it was the fireman's turn this time to have his observations interfered with. The most dangerous part seemed, as before, crashing past the platforms; there was just time in many cases, but not in all, to spell out the names of the stations; one's whole attention was concentrated once more on the signals. And here an unforeseen difficulty presented itself. The

The footplate of broad gauge 4-2-2 Iron Duke *c1890. The controls were very basic, regulator, brake valve and lever reverse. The communication cord can be seen on the tender but it is not connected to the whistle. Note the individual type of headgear – grease-top caps were not yet issued.*

sun was getting low (3pm November) and shone full in our faces right up to sunset; the farther we proceeded the worse the dazzle; it was utterly impossible for one unused to the work to see whether many of the signals were on or off, right in the glare and against the sun, and this must be a great strain on the men's eyes. When questioned about it, the driver confessed that it was 'bad enough', but remarked that after all it was not half so trying as snowstorms, when the snow would darken the glass so that scarcely anything at all could be seen.

At Taunton the tug of war was to begin, it being a steep pull from here right up to the Whiteball.

'You generally take a bank engine here, don't you?' I observed to Sansom.

'Yes, generally, but I shall try and get through to-day,' he answered.

This was good news indeed, seeing that an engine in front would smother us with its smoke, and prevent one seeing how the *Rover* would mount the long bank single-handed. On this point Sansom was evidently of the same opinion as one of his former comrades, an ex-driver of the *Lightning*, who told me: 'You must start at Taunton if you are going to get up the bank in time, and not put the lever back in the seventh notch, but after getting away let it stop in the sixth, until after passing Wellington, then give another notch or two, and not wait until the speed has got too slow. With a big wheel you must keep them going, if you don't, and your engine should start slipping, you would be very soon brought to a stand. I have had many a hard struggle up the banks

The second portion of the down Dutchman passing Worle Junction hauled by 8ft single Inkerman. *The driver, G. Eggar, is acknowledging either the signalman or the photographer. It would appear that it was a regular practice for signalmen to exhibit a white flag when the road was clear in addition to pulling off the signals.*

with heavy trains, though I always go through with them both up through Box Tunnel and Wellington bank; but I always started *at the bottom* for them.'

After Norton, the pace soon began to be less violent and the panting of the engine showed that the resistance on the pistons was increasing. As Wellington was neared another notch was given the lever, and still another. Then began an anxious time. Having read in a certain work that 'to climb a long bank, instead of the engine blowing off, it should rather be inclined to be short of steam, so that the steam can be allowed to push the pistons nearly to the end of the stroke, following it up with an even pressure,' I thought that with a boiler full of steam, as ours was, some steps would be taken to partially close the regulator, or notch up the lever. But here, again, doctors obviously differ. The regulator was

wide open, the lever in the second or third notch, and the intention evidently was to mount the bank as quickly as possible by the sheer force of high-pressure steam.

The driver and fireman 'stood by' eagerly listening, and at the least suspicion of slipping, worked the sand-gear quickly. A little rain was falling, the rails were moist, and the sand-lever had to be worked more than once.

'Then you don't put down the damper, or check your steam in any way, up the bank?' I remarked.

'No, let her have it: the *Iron Duke* stuck in the tunnel last week,' answered Sansom.

I noticed as we laboured on how the fireman kept tending his fire with extreme care, selecting nothing but clean lumps without any small stuff and constantly feeding the furnace, keeping the needle well up to 140. There must be a tremendous blast in the furnace when the lever is well over. A great lump of coal does not get dull red first round the edges, as in a grate, but disintegrates uniformly and at once; fiery smoke comes from between the strata of the block; it seems all in a simmer and grows white hot almost in a moment.

And now the pace was at last really slow, but then here

we were entering the tunnel, and our troubles were over. The lever was put back in the seventh notch, and away we started for Tiverton, Cullompton, and Silverton – here the speed is always great on down trains – and so on, in the waning light, through Stoke Canon, right into St David's, without a single check from Bristol, and only one adverse distant signal, which, being observed far ahead, was 'blown down' by the whistle without altering the speed.

Many trains had been passed, some broad, some narrow gauge; these did not look at all as if they would run into us, as one saw a long way off that the coming train was on its own line; and in every case the din and turmoil of our own engine entirely drowned all noise from the other; even as an express rushed past, no increase of sound whatever was perceived: it might have been a phantom train; or standing still.

At Exeter we went down under the engine but there was no need to oil anything as the *Rover* proved to be in tip-top trim; cranks of driving-wheels quite cool, bands of eccentrics just luke-warm. Between St Thomas's and Exminster attention was drawn to the 'new road', which

was pronounced much better than the old, being 'more springy'; this, like many other things, had to be taken on trust by one who could not detect the slightest difference in the vibration; anyway I am sorry to see the old longitudinals thus disappearing, which have always proved so safe, when an engine has gone off the rails. We flashed through Starcross at great speed; a nasty, risky piece of line, where it looked as if the engine would bump against the wall of the hotel, and *ricochet* on to the pier; and so on in the gloaming, through the warm red cuttings and tunnels of Dawlish, by the sea-wall of Holcombe, and on into Teignmouth, where the trip ended. And yet scarcely ended, for a brand new kind of nightmare was evolved from the run, and it soon transpired, from the vivid pictures of one's slumber, that the racket of the footplate could be well rehearsed in dreams.

The basic broad gauge express locomotives were the 8ft singles. The design dated back to Great Western *of 1846.* Amazon. *built in September 1878 and withdrawn in May 1892, is seen at Newton Abbot on 25 July 1883. The leading coach is a composite third class and TPO.*

A portmanteau photograph depicting many Great Western features. The train on the up main line between Reading and Didcot is a Bristol–Paddington express hauled by Saint class 4-6-0 No 2924 Saint Helena. Note the wide 'six foot' between the up and down lines – a relic of the broad gauge. The ATC shoe can be seen between the leading bogie wheels of the Saint and the ramp is visible on the up relief line. The down relief distant is at caution and the driver, on the right hand side of the cab is applying the brake in response to the ATCs warning hooter.

2
AN ALIEN VIEW

THE character of God's Wonderful Railway, the isolationism and the superiority complex that were its trademarks, was pre-ordained when its *Great* Western title was adopted in 1833. No other major railway was Great until the Great Northern adopted this adjective in 1846. Contemporary companies were satisfied to be defined by the cities or towns between which they ran, or by the area in which they operated; the Grand Junction came nearest to the self-styled majesty of the GWR. And inevitably this greatness must have preyed on the minds of its directors and officers. How else could I. K. Brunel have persuaded them to build the railway, in this tiny island of Britain, to a gauge almost half as wide again than anyone else? It was as though he was building a nineteenth century TGV route, unsullied by close contact with *ordinary* railways.

This aura of superiority which pervaded the GWR lived on until, and even beyond, nationalisation in 1948. It was fed by the most remarkable record of inbreeding which can have been the lot of any railway in Britain. It might export some of its bright sparks now and again – usually because, like William Stanier in 1932, they tired of waiting for dead men's shoes – but one almost needed a visa from the Almighty Himself to get in (other than at the bottom). Taking the four principal officer posts of superintendent of the line, chief engineer, chief mechanical engineer and signal and telegraph engineer, held by a total of thirty two individuals up to 1947, only one was not GWR-bred. Ironically this was Louis Trench, brought in as chief engineer from the LNWR in 1891, whose lot it was to carry through the final massive slaughter of the Broad Gauge. He retired shortly after, his tenure lasting only eighteen months, probably for ever branded as the arch-vandal.

For many years the company operated in a sort of cocoon, a religionist worshipping inwardly but making no serious attempt at proselytising. Once the gauge nonsense was out of the way it could afford to do so, secure in a wedge of country with no serious competitors. But with nationalisation, and the prospect of being swamped under weight of numbers, that changed. The ex-GWR people fought tooth and nail to persuade the heathen that enlightenment from Paddington or Wiltshire was now available to them, and that they would be most unwise to spurn it. To a degree they were successful – though a surprising number of these proffered jewels proved to be less than precious stones. Shades of Stanier's first three years on the LMS!

One piece of GWR technology which could speak for itself, however, well before BR days was the system of Automatic Train Control (ATC).

Loyalty
The loyalty of Great Western staff was legendary . . . and sometimes ridiculous. It was during the company's final year that a Dawlish woman asked what time she could travel to Birmingham. '2.22,' came the instant reply, referring to the single daily service via the North Warwick line. Was there not an earlier train, asked the woman. 'Do you want to go by London or the LMS?' retorted the booking clerk, implying that taking the obvious route was not quite proper.
But then a Birmingham business man, in giving a word portrait of another who clearly he looked down on, included the statement 'He goes to London by LMS'.
When a Plymouth business man said he would have to drive to Exeter Central to take an earlier train up to Waterloo than anything running to Paddington, his friend employed in the district office warned: Go at a decent hour or take the sleeper, or you'll be the richest man in the churchyard'.

Part of the GWR cab layout showing vacuum gauge, roof rack for notices etc, brake handle, ATC warning bell, regulator handle, sight glasses of the hydrostatic lubricator and top of reverser below the drivers cuff. The locomotive, Castle class No 5054 Earl of Ducie *is (as were all Great Western engines) right hand drive – the only member of the Big Four to retain this practice on newly built engines.*

From small beginnings in 1906, it was progressively developed and linked to the vacuum brake until in 1929 a start was made on equipping all main lines and more important secondary routes, a task which took a decade to complete. By that time it was no longer state-of-the-art, but it was effective, it saved fogmen, and it was *there*. It was, of course, no more foolproof than the later BR inductive AWS, and in a high speed era had to yield place to it. But it matched the current system of discreet semaphore signalling to a tee.

For the traveller, his first contact with the railway might well be the presence of the stationmaster, with his French general's cap, pillboxy and encircled by vine or creeper or whatever; his minions had to manage without the vegetation. The station would be well-kept, in some cases quite modern, but oh! that all-pervading drab chocolate and cream paint. And the platform barrows, wonderful wooden creations that might have come straight from an out-of-date DIY catalogue (if such things had then existed). You looked at the standardised signal box (very neat) and its nameboard pronounced it to be 'Leamington Spa North *Signal Box*' or wherever. Was there some risk that it might be confused with the engine shed, the lamp room or the shunters' cabin? And when it reached the stage of the palindromic 'Box Signal Box' – words fail.

The Express train of the 1930s and 1940s might well be of flush-panelled stock, but with the near-certainty that it would be side corridor

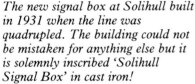

The new signal box at Solihull built in 1931 when the line was quadrupled. The building could not be mistaken for anything else but it is solemnly inscribed 'Solihull Signal Box' in cast iron!

SOLIHULL SIGNAL BOX

coaches with doors into each compartment. No automatic slam locks to those doors, either; when you had shut the door, you lowered the droplight by the strap to turn the handle to the horizontal – or left it for some harassed porter to deal with, along with a high proportion of the other handles on the train. The two northern companies might pander to their third class passengers with three-a-side seating and reading lights, but not the mighty Great Western. Even as late as the early BR Mark 1 stock the Western Region demanded, and got, third class compartments with no armrests so that holiday traffic might be best catered for four aside.

Unless you were travelling on the Cheltenham Flyer or the Bristolian, speed seemed of rather secondary importance. The Paddington-Birmingham route put on a show with its business trains, being in competition with the 1hr 55min services out of Euston, and the Bristol traffic was considered important enough to warrant a few fast trains. But away from these the running was usually pedestrian in the extreme. A typical Saturday train from Torbay, described in the timetable as a 'Paignton, Torquay and Exeter to Bristol Express' was allowed no less than 183 minutes for its 104 mile journey to Temple Meads with eight intermediate stops, while on the London route 255 minutes for the 202 miles from Paignton with four stops was one of the better services.

But everything went to pot on the West of England line on summer Saturdays; it was privately admitted that there were just too many trains to be realistically pathed west of Taunton, even if the services were not disrupted by late running or engine failures. So it was a case of feeding trains into the bottleneck and hoping for the best. There were plans for a new relieving route, but they came to nought. In 1938 an investigation was launched into electrification west of Taunton, but a year later it had to be admitted that the pandemonium of a dozen summer Saturdays would not sustain electrification for the rest of the year. It was perhaps as well, because inevitably the GWR would have chosen a system which was different from everyone else.

Then there were the rural branch lines, scenes of corrugated iron pagodas and milk churns. So wedded was the GWR to the 0-6-0 pannier tank – they were still ordering the wretched things by the hundred after World War II – that on one or two coaches 45mph was regarded as quite sufficient adventure for any day. And what a thirst they seemed to work up; like camels at oases, they could scarcely pass a water column or parachute tank (why did the latter have conical covers, by the way?) without stopping to replenish. Perhaps that was the secret of their adhesion for those sure-footed starts.

What an unvarying, standardised railway it was, and how reluctant to depart from those standards even when they were obsolete. One can accept some of the standard signalling idiosyncrasies – backing signals with a pair of holes in the arms, goods line signals with rings on them (retained long after their demise on other railways), 'shunt ahead' signals with an 'S' on the arm – even the slavish adherence to lower quadrant semaphores when all others had fled. But actually to take out upper quadrant signals on ex-LMS routes, ostensibly worn out, and *replace*

Smooth, Polite
I left Paddington at 10.30 Friday 13, 13 coaches on the train. The Great Western is *the* line. So smooth. So polite. West country politeness. So fast. 186 miles to Exeter and done in exactly 180 minutes. As fast as the *rapide* from Paris to Boulogne, and yet no liquid spills out of the glasses. The country gets richer and richer, and the villages and towns neater and neater. The whole line is brushed and oiled and painted. The stations look as if they might be model stations exhibited at Wembley. At the end of the 186 miles the train seems to be as clean as at starting. I went into the lavatory; spotless. The weather gradually improved, and warmed, and the sun shone on the richly treed hills.' – From a letter by the late Arnold Bennett written from *Yacht Marie Marguerite*, Salcombe, June 13, 1924, published in *Arnold Bennett – a Portrait done at home together with 170 letters from A.B.*, by Dorothy Cheston Bennett.

The GWR stuck resolutely to lower quadrant signals even when electrically lit and worked by electric motors. An example is this bracket at Newton Abbot which lasted from 1927 until the resignalling in May 1987 – almost forty years into BR.

Opposite *The up main line platform at Cardiff General in the late 1950s showing the single aspect colour light signals installed by the GWR in 1934. The upper signal was the stop aspect and showed red or green and the lower the distant showing orange or green. The train taking water is the 2.20pm Milford Haven–Paddington hauled by Castle class 4-6-0 No 5077* Fairey Battle *one of the class renamed during World War II to commemorate RAF and Fleet Air Arm planes then in action.*

them with Western Region lower quadrants – that was unforgivable. And then, when they dallied with the upper quadrant semaphore, was it really impossible to accept everyone else's configuration? Did they *have* to invent a misshapen version of their own, *vide* the home and distant signals that now greet visitors outside the National Railway Museum at York?

One symbol of the Great Western's individuality in the field of modern signalling lasted for nearly forty years. When Paddington, Bristol and Cardiff were resignalled in the early 1930s, two-aspect searchlight signals were installed in a *direct copy* of semaphore practice; yellow/green distants were placed below red/green stop signals. At a time when a consensus on the other three railways had established a common system of three- and four-aspect colourlight signals to get the maximum benefit in line capacity, whatever possessed the GWR to sacrifice it, ostensibly to avoid drivers having to learn new signal aspects? In practice they had some learning to do anyway due to station rebuilding and layout changes.

Of the Great Western's singular practices which affected their liaisons with other companies on a day-to-day basis, probably the most infuriating was the use of the vacuum brake working at 25in instead of 21in. Only the use of crosshead-driven vacuum pumps made it even *practicable*. It meant that every vacuum braked train handed over to other companies required that the release strings be pulled on every vehicle to get rid of the high reservoir side vacuum before the oncoming engine could release the brakes. In the opposite direction, of course, the GW staff were laughing; all *they* had to do was create another four inches of vacuum all round. But was there not a strong whiff of hypocrisy involved on Swindon's part? When BR was formed the air was full of dire warnings of under-braked trains failing to stop at signals if 21in vacuum was imposed on the Western Region; curious, therefore, that when GWR coaches were used on through services little thought was given to the braking distance problems which *other* railways might experience when running at 21in with stock with brake power designed for 25in.

Even the vacuum brake cylinders had to be different in design, using a sliding rubber band to seal the piston instead of the rolling ring that was universal elsewhere. So eloquently did Swindon extol the virtues of the sliding band that it was adopted as the first BR standard. Only when thousands were in use was it found to be the cause of so many brake failures; it was promptly ousted in favour of the rolling ring. Swindon knew best? Not this time.

Another fiendish invention, the responsibility for which must be laid squarely at Swindon's door, is the Instanter coupling, used on many wagons to the present day. It was a very laudable objective to reduce the coupling slack by the shunter using his coupling pole rather than by going between wagons to tighten a screw coupling. In practice it proved a cheap and nasty non-solution to the problem, because it could not bring buffers into contact and thus did very little to change the handling technique when braking freight trains. Some of the snatches during

AN ALIEN VIEW

The Great Western had signals for every conceivable movement and type of line. Goods line signal arms carried a ring and in September 1952 four arms guard up goods loops at Abergavenny Junction. 43XX class 2-6-0 No 5335 of Llanelly (87F) is passing on an up through freight.

braking had to be seen – and felt – to be believed; during the brake trials on fast coal trains on the London Midland Region in the early 1950s there were trains broken into several sections and Instanter links pulled all shapes.

Talking of wagons, how ever did Paddington get into the silly business of identifying wagon types by names? Minks, Macaws and Toads? It seemed to strike a receptive chord with railway officers and lives on with the civil engineer in piscine profusion – the whole range from Salmon and Turbot to Herring and Mackerel. What passengers made of it can only be guessed.

The GWR and Western Region engine sheds were a very mixed bunch, ranging from splendid square roundhouses (if you will forgive the contradiction) to abysmal wooden erections often in terminal decline. But one thing was common to them all; there was no mechanical provision for getting coal on to tenders. '*We* use Welsh coal, which is too friable to be dropped from great heights in conventional coaling plants.' It apparently did not matter that in railway-owned South Wales ports Welsh coal for export was dropped from considerable heights into the holds of ships. But had Western officers never travelled the six miles (with the crow) to Stratford shed to see a low bunker at work, or a lesser distance to Kings Cross or Marylebone to look at miniature coalers? No great height involved in any of them. What else could it be but complacency again, with an army of coalmen employed in unpleasant conditions shovelling coal from wagons into skips to be tipped into tenders?

A 'modern' steam locomotive depot on the GWR, Aberystwyth opened in 1939. The brand new brick building is of the usual GWR design with substantial swing doors to each road. On the left is the coaling stage which, when other railways were installing mechanical coaling plants, is still the traditional hand type where coal was shovelled into small tubs and tipped into the engine tenders. On the left is a 'new' engine – one of the 'Dukedogs' completed from 1937 using old Duke class boilers on Bulldog frames perpetuating double framed engines long since abandoned for construction by other companies but ideal for the Cambrian lines.

In the realm of the civil engineer, the GWR's most apparent individuality lay in its use of two through bolts to fasten chairs to the sleepers rather than the three chair screws used by other railways. Advantages were claimed for both systems, so it is probable that the choice was finely balanced. In which case, why differ?

Undoubtedly it was in the locomotive field that controversy was strongest. Few would argue seriously that by the start of World War I the GWR steam locomotive fleet was way ahead of its competitors in terms of thermal efficiency and freedom from serious maintenance shortcomings such as heated bearings. In train handling there were serious rivals, but the Churchward products had the virtue of making a hard duty look and sound easy. By 1914 the basic two- and four-cylinder designs, and their principal components, were highly standardised. Nor was there any upheaval in design practice arising from the 1923 amalgamation, as happened on the other three railways; for the GWR it was not an amalgamation but a takeover. The Swindon locomotive impressed the observer with its green livery, lots of polished brass, impressive nameplates and copper capped chimney. The safety valves sizzled instead of going off with a roar. Even the running sounds were unique – the loud burps of the vacuum brake ejector, the 'phut-phut' of the vacuum pump and above all the sharp explosive bark at the chimney. Some of the tenders looked ill-matched to the locomotive. And was not *two* whistles rather extravagant?

But as someone once said, standardisation is an excellent servant but a fearful master. It is a dead straight road for easy driving from which it is essential to recognise the turning-off points if a moving destination is to be reached. Progress is easily stultified. At a time when the other three railways first caught up with the Swindon product and then surpassed it, there was not the slightest crack in the facade while Collett reigned as chief mechanical engineer (1922–41). While he continued to turn out Castles, Halls, Granges, Manors and 2-8-0s from common moulds for a quarter of a century, these had been dislodged from their pedestal by A4s, Duchesses, Stanier Class Fives and Class 8Fs. The Great Western sailed on an unchanged course.

It was ironical that an ex-Swindon man should be at the root of the eventual change of tack. In 1943 Swindon (on government direction) started to build Stanier 2-8-0s; the new CME, Hawksworth, had to admit that some features were an improvement on previous practice and worthy of adoption. 1944 saw the first modified Hall with throughout plate frames, separate cylinders and smokebox saddle and larger three-row superheater – sixteen years after the first production Hall. (Compare the developments on the original Stanier Class Five which took place over a similar period.) In the following year came the County class with what was in effect the Stanier 2-8-0 sloping throatplate boiler (the same flanging blocks were used) though with a slightly longer barrel. Then in rapid succession came further increases in superheat on Kings and Castles, with mechanical cylinder lubrication – one feature which had originally deterred Churchward from using higher superheat. Double chimneys (still with copper caps but oval in shape to retain individuality)

Safety

Much has been said about the contribution of ATC (automatic train control, in fact automatic warning) to the Great Western's incredible safety record – unmatched by any other form of transport, anywhere, anytime. But there were, of course, many other ingredients. The high morale and the fact that most signalmen and train crews knew they would be with the railway until they retired, and often hoped their sons would follow in their footsteps, obviously helped.

A major contribution was the amount the railway invested in its signalling. Often there were more signals, catch or safety points and even down to hand point locks for wrong-way working, generally better equipment than on the three others; and while the others might well criticise the GWR for its fixed ways (sticking to lower quadrant, for example), signals and points were readily renewed if it were thought desirable and maintenance kept to a high level. Signals were generally well-sighted with none of those complex gantries that grew piecemeal on some other systems.

Throughout Britain you could find signalboxes kept spotlessly clean; the difference on the GWR was that pride and good housekeeping were displayed uniformly. Uniformity helped in many ways, since in 1923 the GWR took over a number of other railways, especially in Wales, but did not have to create new standards by being made up of former rival routes as happened elsewhere. Everybody knew the GWR way, and that left time for refinements. For example, if engine drivers complained they were distracted by bright lights off the railway, enormous efforts were made to have them removed or shaded. People living in Great Westernland, proud of their railway's safety record, were only too pleased to assist.

When an assistant engine was required to be attached to the front of a train (as opposed to banking in the rear) the pilot was usually (but not invariably) attached inside the train engine as seen here. The train engine Castle class 4-6-0 No 4000 North Star *and the pilot 2251 class 0-6-0 No 2203 are starting the climb out of Stratford upon Avon towards Birmingham with the* Cornishman, *the 10.45am Penzance to Wolverhampton on 3 September 1952. The Castle was working home to Stafford Road (84A) and the Collett Goods was a Tyseley (84E) based engine, sub shedded at Stratford.*

followed. Swindon had finally been dragged into the latter half of the century – if only partly.

The retention of various design features amazed the informed outside observer. Take piston valves as an example. By 1930 the other three railways had adopted valve heads with multiple narrow rings, and were finding that they would run up to 35,000 miles between examinations with minimal wear and leakage. But did Swindon see the light from its Wiltshire fastness? It did not. The Churchward version of the American semi-plug piston valve did duty to the end, and was solemnly opened up at mileages a fraction of those elsewhere. What did that cost in labour and locomotive availability?

Then there was the cab layout. Long before ergonomics was a household word, three railways had gone to considerable lengths to place all immediate controls – reverser, regulator, brake, etc – within ready reach of a seated driver. And the fourth railway? The brake valve, ejector steam valve, even the whistle, could only be reached if the driver stood up! Not that he could sit down in any comfort because the sanding controls came just where his shins should have been. Many classes which did little shunting retained lever reverse, which left little room for a seat anyway. There was never more than a single water gauge; if the glass burst, you were expected to judge whether the boiler was safe by using a pair of try-cocks which were supposed to allow you to distinguish between steam and boiling water which flashed off into steam when released. It was archaic. Did Swindon get no effective feedback on all this from running inspectors, from enginemen, from the trade unions? Or did they take the line that father knows best and please just get on with it in silence?

Did you ever watch a Great Western fireman at work? To start with he was given a shovel with a blade substantially bigger than those on other railways (which he was conditioned to pronounce as useless). Yet was not this the railway that boasted of its fuel economy? In action our fireman was the very antithesis of a smoothly working machine. Was the teaching never questioned whereby the poor man loaded his shovel, turned round to drop the firehole flap, turned back to grab the shovel, swung it to fire the coal, turn again to put it down on the shovelling plate, and then back again to lift the flap again? All that for *every* shovelful; his rhythm was totally destroyed. Nor could the driver help him – the flap chain was on the far side of the firehole door. And how ever did the footplate inspectors manage to indoctrinate all and sundry to keeping up this farce? Would the boilers not steam if they let down the flap, fired eight or ten shovelsful and then lifted the flap again, as they did on other railways?

With the formation of BR the Western Region, the only one in which locomotive running came directly under the chief mechanical engineer, argued passionately that this organisation should be retained. But by the retention of these nonsenses into the middle of the twentieth century, by the utter lack of critical appraisal of design, they were their own weakest advocates.

So when the outside observer looked critically at God's Wonderful Railway, it was in a strongly cynical tone. To use its initials GWR was an adequate means of identification. But 'Great'? Let us just say that, by comparison with its fellows, it once had been.

The GWR ran a large number of auto trains on branch lines and on stopping trains on main lines usually one auto-trailer hauled/ pushed by a class 14XX 0-4-2T or a 54/64XX 0-6-0PT. One such branch was that from Chippenham to Calne in Wiltshire. Class 14XX 0-4-2T No 1446 is seen at Chippenham in 1950 with one car for the Calne service. It was allocated to Swindon (82C) but resided at the sub shed at Chippenham. A second car is standing on the middle road together with a travelling gas tank wagon. Many of the auto trailers were gas lit and the tank wagons were filled at various gas works around the system and sent to stratigic locations for recharging gas lit carriages and restaurant cars which used gas for cooking. The gas which had a very distinctive smell and was produced from oil could be stored under higher pressure than ordinary coal gas. (No Hornby 'O' gauge train set was complete without a model of one of these distinctive wagons!).

Topdog, Underdog

Almost wherever it went, the GWR was either *the* railway or (such as at Birmingham and Exeter) a powerful competitor for the prestige traffic as well as having its own monopoly services. It is indeed difficult to think of it as underdog, yet there were of course places where it slipped in quietly very much as the minority railway and where its services must have been looked down upon by the local population.

Winchester was a good example. The GWR maintained its own inconveniently-sited station for the sparse Didcot, Newbury & Southampton all-stations cross-

The Great Western was in the minority at Salisbury being at the end of a subsidiary main line from Westbury. It had its own terminus off to the left of the photograph but this was closed on 12 September 1932 and thereafter all GWR trains used the Southern station. Saint class 4-6-0 No 2950 Taplow Court *is departing with a Portsmouth to Bristol train on 27 July 1951. The leading coach adds to the Great Western atmosphere – it is a 'Dreadnought' introduced between 1904 and 1907 and the first examples of GWR main line stock without a clerestory roof.*

country service just before the route joined the South Western main line for the rest of the run into Southampton. Yet even at Winchester Cheesehill, a mile from the Southern, the atmosphere was more that of a prospering village station than that of an almost-ran city affair that belonged to the underdog railway in so many other places.

The GWR's role at Salisbury was greater, though until 1932 its trains terminated at an undistinguished though historic terminus beside the Southern's – rather like the LMS's at Oxford and of course the Southern's at Reading, though the latter was always much busier. Reading to Basingstoke was a GWR branch, but also busy and nearly always with through trains.

Down in the West, GWR enthusiasts would never have admitted their railway played the lesser role at places like Dorchester, Yeovil or Chard, and even Barnstaple GW, though with a much worse and usually only stopper service, provided the shorter route to London as well as being the obvious line for places via Bristol. GWR trains may not have been allowed to serve intermediate halts between Bodmin and Wadebridge, but again the railway held its head high, and at Bodmin

itself the GWR was altogether more of this world than the Southern's ex-Bodmin & Wadebridge terminus even though that once enjoyed the only through coach from London.

Tavistock had to be conceded as more Southern territory, while at Lydford the single GWR branch (by which Waterloo trains had first reached Plymouth) was from 1876 definitely inferior to the double South Western/Southern main line sweeping round Dartmoor, and Launceston's single platform terminus closed in 1952 was well below the Southern's through station served by its daily fraction of the Atlantic Coast Express.

In South Wales the GWR played second fiddle to the pre-Grouping railways at a number of places, but that is going back a bit, and anyway the 1923 Grouping was here generally regarded as an excellent thing, especially as more powerful Swindon locomotives were steadily drafted in. The same was true at Aberystwyth where the GWR ran only four or five times a day into the platform now allocated to Devil's Bridge trains and the Cambrian was much more powerful.

We forget, perhaps, that in mid-Wales the GWR reached Llandovery where however its stopping train services from Llanelly were always sparser than the LMS's from Shrewsbury to Swansea sharing the route down to Pontardulais. But even here the laugh was really on the LMS for the GWR never, nowhere, did anything as far fetched as the LMS running a through service from London to South Wales this way.

At Hay on Wye, however, the Golden Valley branch, its passenger trains withdrawn by the GWR itself, was undoubtedly a minor participant in a minor overall scene. South of Birmingham, the story was the same

Crewe was served by a branch from Wellington with running powers over the LMS from Nantwich. Although it was an important route for freight, passenger trains were nearly all locals worked by a variety of superannuated classes. Barnum class 2-4-0 No 3216 stands in one of the south bays used by GWR trains on a local to Wellington c1928.

LMS 'domination' at Alcester, the GWR's branch (closed to passengers) running into an LMS branch. Elsewhere there were many reverse examples of 'branches off branches' meeting the GWR such as at Corwen in North Wales and Wells in Somerset.

At places like Birkenhead and Crewe the surprise was perhaps more that the GWR was there in force at all; some Liverpool people always preferred to cross the Mersey for the Paddington day or night expresses from Birkenhead. These of course called at Chester where GWR trains may have been in the minority but were distinctly not underdog.

The remarkable thing was that south of Wellington this Birkenhead-Paddington main line marked the GWR boundary all the way to London with only one exception: the branch to Aylesbury. At various places en route the LMS and LNER were definitely underdog: Warwick, for example. Only at Aylesbury were GWR trains by the branch from Princes Risborough obviously inferior. So much so that the last map the GWR published lied!

The former Great Central is shown as a thick black line ('Railways with which the GWR runs in connection') down to Woodford & Hinton and then into Banbury, but the continuing route to Marylebone is not included even as a thin line ('other railways'). Thus Aylesbury appears

A 1947 view of Chester shows GWR 43XX class 2-6-0 No 7319 passing under Chester No 6 signal box with an up express, probably a relief to Paddington. There are at least two LMS coaches in the formation. The mogul will run through to Wolverhampton Low Level from where a 4-6-0 would normally take the train forward.

to be GWR only. Out of Marylebone the former GC is shown only as a thin line joining the thick red GWR at Northolt.

There is no doubt that the GWR's belief in its superiority was encouraged by the fact that so rarely did it play second fiddle. Other lines might share its territory, but almost throughout the wealthy wedge of England between the West of England and the Birken- head lines out of London it ruled the roost, and at places like Plymouth, Highbridge, Bristol, Hereford, Shrewsbury, Leamington Spa, Banbury displayed varying degrees of condescension to its rivals.

It was undoubtedly the other railways penetrating into the GWR's rightful territory that seemed inferior, the only real exception being the former Midland main line down to Bristol.

You thus lived on Great Western territory or right off it. And that made it all the harder for staff and customers to cope with the upheaval that came not with the immediate post-nationalisation adjustment but with the more sweeping later boundary changes. Ultimately the Western was the loser. Weymouth, Birmingham, mid-Wales, Birkenhead were entirely removed from Paddington's orbit.

Worcester was one of the centres where the GWR was the major partner, the Midland Railway only gained access by running powers, although they did have their own loco shed (closed 1932) and jointly owned Shrub Hill station. Even in

March 1961 the scene was very much GW/LMS. Castle class No 7004 Eastnor Castle of 85A (Worcester), waits on the middle road with the restaurant car portion of the 12.55pm to Paddington. Modified Hall class No 6975

Capesthorne Hall is in the up main platform with the 12.55pm to Leamington Spa and LMS Jubilee No 45629 Straits Settlements stands in the bay with the 12.20pm local train to Gloucester Eastgate.

At Chester the honours were more even. The GWR came in from Saltney Junction at the end of the main line from Paddington while the company jointly owned the routes to Birkenhead and Warrington. The LMS presence was represented by the important Chester & Crewe and Chester & Holyhead lines. In the last year of the Great Western (1947) Castle class 4-6-0 No 4076 Carmarthen Castle waits in the dock line for a Paddington express whilst LMS compound No 1158 is in the down bay with a local for the North Wales coast.

Hop Pickers arriving at Ledbury Station.

Tilley & Son,
Ledbury.

3
THE SEASONAL GREAT WESTERN

THE broccoli are going to be early and good. The forecast would be greeted with enthusiasm well beyond Cornwall. It meant traffic, heavy traffic, prosperity for the Company, security for everyone, overtime for train crews. In the days that railwaymen expected their tasks to vary as much as landworkers' with the seasons, there was keen awareness about the state of crops, interest in the weather. The Great Western served the community and the community used its services; good and bad times were mutual. Thus engine drivers would mourn the damage caused by a late frost almost as strongly as the growers themselves.

Altogether the Great Western was a very seasonal railway. It would never have thrived had it not made the most of often short, peak seasonal demands. Daffodils from the Scillies, broccoli from Cornwall, strawberries from the Cheddar Valley, early potatoes from the Channel Islands and Pembrokeshire, plums from the Vale of Evesham, were just a few of the seasonal headlines. Cattle came across the Irish Sea into Fishguard. Milk from various parts of the system into the big cities varied tremendously according to the season and the weather in the particular season: the greener the grass, the better cows were yielding, the shorter the average transits, since seasonally the creameries furthest from the centres of population turned the surplus into cheese and butter. Volumes of fish were of course totally dependent on the elements. We should remember that it was the railways who helped make life and foodstuffs more sophisticated, brought fresh fish into inland areas for the first time, and exchanged locally caught fish with that from the deep-sea fleets landed in Eastern ports; you could thus see fish trucks pass each other on the main line into London. In the South West, for example, 'rail' fish stabilised prices when 'local' was scarce because of storms, though generally rail was a copper or so cheaper per portion for the ultimate consumer.

Fertilisers were big railway business, scarcely a country station not being enlivened with a truck or two in spring, when many branch lines with normally two or three freights a day might suddenly have an extra one or two to clear the junction yard. The amount of fertiliser carried to some extent depended on how well farmers had done the previous season; and that applied more strongly to farm equipment most of which (tractors and even the first combines) went by train until well after World War II. You could tell how prosperous or not local farms were by the quality of the farm machinery arriving at country stations whose staff would assemble to examine the latest model yet to be unloaded. The number of farmers (and particularly the size of their family parties)

Bananas were not truly seasonal traffic but one of irregular peaks throughout the year. The Great Western's port for discharging this fruit was Barry and the 'hands' were conveyed between ship and railway vans by conveyer belt, the whole affair being extremely labour intensive. The bananas were still green on arrival and to assist ripening all banana vans were fitted for steam heating.

Hop picker's specials are traditionally linked with Kent but Worcestershire and Herefordshire also grew large quantities which required harvesting in August and September. The local card published by Tilley & Son of Ledbury shows a late Edwardian scene at Ledbury, the train made up of non corridor clerestory stock.

Station Images

Of much more crowded scenes at Paddington as passengers and porters met as fifteen coach expresses arrived but of more genteel departure arrangements, the stock of outbound expresses having been brought in by the Pannier tanks lined up at the buffers well before most passengers were ready.

Of those very Great Western wayside stations with platforms four tracks apart since they were served by loops which stopping trains entered gently, and of long sojourns in the loop while 'flyers' overtook.

Of flyers dashing through the great junctions, homes and distants all off, whistles shrieking, but of periods of an hour or more when all traffic was local and there were no expresses, calling or non stop. And of the frantic to-ing and fro-ing when up and down expresses called together to be fed by and feed half a dozen connecting branch and stopper trains.

Of the perpetual to-ing and fro-ing of the shunter serving the steep approach to Bristol goods station, said to be the world's largest, clearly seen from Temple Meads platforms and the squealing of wheels of the frequent freights on the middle roads.

Of the gentlemanly orderliness of Birmingham Snow Hill, approached by expresses at surprising speed, compared to the noisy, dirty chaos at New Street.

Of the constant topping, tacking, dividing, joining of trains keeping station pilots busy at numerous stations and of the brisk business by refreshment and newspaper sellers who sold their wares through compartment windows.

Of so very many more railwaymen from wheel tappers to seat reservation official, lines of porters with and without barrows, station inspectors et al who used to ensure our journeys went smoothly.

able to afford a trip to Smithfield also depended on how the season had gone. Many restaurant car crews did better with tips at Smithfield than any other time of year, though passengers on the first class specials to the major racing events such as Newbury and Cheltenham also had a generous habit. The numbers passing through the special race course stations at those two places and many others were also affected by the state of the national economy and of course the weather outlook on race days themselves. In the era when race horses went around the country by train, the Lambourn branch's fortunes were especially affected by the current state of the racing business.

Hardly a station did not have some special seasonal characteristic. In the Somerset levels it was willows for baskets; in the surrounding countryside teasels which were such an important traffic that a few stations remained open specially for it once freight facilities had generally been centralised in later years. South Molton was starting point for the nation's only rabbit special, very seasonal, strongest in late autumn, when mangelwurzels kept many other freight yards busy. Weymouth handled prodigious quantities of Channel Islands tomatoes once the potatoes had finished. Hops came from the Bromyard district and all kinds of vegetables and especially plums from Evesham and Pershore.

Everyone knew what would come next and be alert if timing and volume were different from previous seasons. District offices of course had carefully-kept records of the average, planned carefully, and were seldom taken by surprise. Rolling stock and other resources were deployed with military precision; only after nationalisation were there first reports of an inadequate number of trucks for the Cornish broccoli. Much of this traffic was carried in especially cleaned cattle trucks, the cattle business which had reached a crescendo just before Christmas being slack in the New Year.

It was not, of course, just the freight side that was affected. For a start, much seasonal business (calves, cattle, fish, rabbits, flowers, fruit) was carried 'tail end' in vans and trucks attached to passenger trains and often shunted en route. Whatever the cost and the complications, the Great Western wanted the business. It was the Common Carrier par excellence, never questioning the economics of peak traffic as did parts of the LMS even between the wars. But complications there indeed were, affecting how many locomotives had to be shedded at certain depots and covering the redeployment of clerical staff to help at peak times such as at Pershore for the plums, where the normally sedate life of the local staff station was overtaken by the pressure and the arrival of much-needed extra pairs of hands was always welcome.

Agricultural events were a major source of revenue: the big regional and county shows, which in Great Western days nearly all went on tour, especially taxing the cattle-loading facilities of different stations each year ('why did they make that shunting spur so you can only get two in at a time?'), and the regular local cattle, horse, sheep and other fairs, which often generated huge volumes of passengers as well as trainloads of four-legged beasts. 'Please send 42 cattle wagons for the 25th,' the

stationmaster would proudly order district office from the signal box since at most country stations the GW only invested in one telephone. West Exe just outside Tiverton on the Exe Valley was among Halts provided with a mini hut occupied by a roving booking clerk on peak days. Here the peak days were the Saturday after the Heathcoats textile factory closed for its summer holiday and the two Sundays it was closed ('If you live in Devon there's no point in going away except on day trips') and the third Thursday of October when at least a hundred joined the morning down train – five coaches instead of an autocar – for Bampton horse fair. Seasonal pressures also used to include moving whole farms by train – especially at Michaelmas.

In fact very few traffics were not affected by the seasons. Much more coal went up from South Wales through the Severn Tunnel during the cold months than in summer, when locomotives and line capacity were coping with other traffics. Mail of course peaked at Christmas, delaying passenger trains in a manner that now seems disgraceful. Yes, the dear old GWR thought nothing of allowing station overtime (especially on full-length cross-country services) to add up to hours. Cement and other building material business was especially busy in the spring, slack in winter especially if severe weather brought construction work to a halt. Apart from coal, sharp spells were generally bad news, especially in Cornwall, for the thirty or forty trains at the peak of the broccoli season

Between the wars the introduction of paid holidays created huge traffic peaks in the summer, especially on Saturdays as all boarding houses were geared to Saturday change overs. This is a typical Saturday scene at Birmingham Snow Hill in the late 1920s/early 30s, with literally hundreds of passengers waiting for holiday trains to the west and south. The train running in is headed by an early member of the Hall class and is possibly bound for Weymouth. No luggage is in evidence as it would have been sent by 'Passenger's Luggage in Advance' special trains over the previous two days at a cost of two shillings (10p) per package collected and delivered!

49

After World War II more workers received holidays with pay and before the increase in private motoring c1960 the railways carried even greater numbers of passengers on Saturdays than in pre-war days reaching an all-time peak in 1958. To work all this extra traffic many unusual locomotive classes were utilised including the nine 47XX 2-8-0s. These were eminently suitable for such trains with their 5ft 8in driving wheels and 30,460lbs tractive effort. No 4706 is seen just west of Exeter St. Davids with a down express reporting number 149, on 7 August 1955.

were a godsend when the system was generally at its quietest. (If the broccoli ran seriously late, in a compressed sprint it clashed with other business.) Christmas was a peak for many traffics: cattle, turkeys, all foodstuffs, prodigious quantities of individual parcels by goods and passengers. Remember the days when you had to decide whether to spend more on sending the family presents by the latter? Many thought it was safe by goods GWR but paid the extra for passengers elsewhere. And one of the six great to and from school migrations, trunks as PLA and thousands of kids, was of course in the middle of the Christmas rush.

The Great Western never closed as does BR for Christmas. Indeed, throughout its existence, special Get You Home early Christmas morning connections off overnight trains were a well marketed feature. Many who would never have questioned going two or three hundred miles to have Christmas dinner with their family began the return on Boxing Day, when most branch lines (including those normally closed on Sundays) ran a limited special service.

But when we think of the Great Western as a seasonal railway it is the holiday traffic that most comes to mind. Paddington was indeed remodelled in the thirties especially for the summer Saturday business; again, absolutely no question of the GWR turning any business away, peak or trough. The way in which hundreds of thousands were carried, mainly in comfort and indeed style, to West Country resorts has been often told. It was indeed one of the highlights of the Great Western's success, and many were the details associated with it ranging from the large numbers (three figures) placed on the front of locomotives to help train identification to the provision of small signalboxes that opened seasonally to break up busy sections. Planning was undertaken with great care. Every Friday night, for example, a whole train of restaurant cars left Old Oak Common for Newton Abbot, each car to work back a different holiday train the next day. But hardly any of those or other summer Saturday only cars were *only* used for this weekly holiday change over traffic. A few ran on business trains except summer Saturdays. Some would normally be at overhaul, but such work stopped for a dozen weeks. Some were usually used on special and excursion trains such as race and works outings.

But holiday trains were not confined to the South West. All parts of the system were rejuvenated on summer Saturdays, when for example many more passengers crossed the Irish Sea from Fishguard and the Pembrokeshire resorts welcomed most of their visitors, while the two single-line routes to the Cambrian Coast were often worked to capacity, occasionally beyond.

Even on summer Saturdays the GW could still manage a few Sunday school and works outings, but generally the demand for these was mercifully midweek. Many stations actually welcomed a greater number of passengers by special than service trains. Windsor was an example. For many years it was terminus for dozens of tightly-packed excursions from all over the system. Many of these were school excursions, advertised in advance and patronised by a dozen or even more different schools until they were full. Such trains took the direct chord avoiding Slough if coming from the Midlands or the West Country.

Even at Paddington the specials up from the Welsh Valleys, West Midlands or Weymouth frequently changed the atmosphere. Regular passengers made a point of visiting the platform departure boards where under the printed details of the service trains were pasted those of that day's specials, telling you much about the Great Western and sporting, trading and social life out there on its territory. They were of course the days when you could also read as a kind of regional *Who's Who?* the names of passengers by the sleepers, including on summer Friday nights a whole train of sleepers solely for passengers bound for the Scilly Isles. And the days when there was another great seasonal change: one more coach on many trains in summer when there was no need for heating. Most enginemen agreed that steam heating was the equivalent of an extra vehicle.

Alongside all this there was a quite different seasonal calendar: the railway looking after its own staff and infrastructure. The company

Collecting Curves

From South Greenford you could turn east or west on the Paddington-Princes Risborough line; in Cornwall you could go from Perranporth to Redruth avoiding Chacewater; and every day expresses bypassed the main stations at Reading and Bristol.

Curves completing triangular junctions abounded. Excursion trains from the West and Wales to Windsor took one at Slough, for example. Up from the West you could turn directly onto the Portishead branch.

Only the most scrupulous covered all such curves when claiming that they had 'done' that part of the system. And being scrupulous for the sake of a few yards you could anyway clearly see from the other two sides of the triangle meant unsocial hours, or in many cases taking an excursion or other special. Not all the curves marked on the timetable map ever had a regular service: in some cases it was seasonal or otherwise spasdmodic.

A curve with a specially interesting if sparse service was that enabling trains from Gloucester to cut right to the route through Cheltenham South & Leckhampton and so on to either Kingham or the Midland & South Western Junction. The 'Ports Express' from Cardiff to Newcastle was the sole train using the curve for the first of these, while for the latter there was once an early morning Mondays only to Foss Cross where it spent half an hour before returning.

Broccoli special. Fast fitted freight trains conveying perishable goods were regular features of a Great Western landscape and continued to be so in the Western Region of BR for well into a decade of nationalisation. No 5998 Trevor Hall *raises the echoes as it pounds up Hemerdon bank with a train of suitably cleaned cattle trucks containing Cornish broccoli in the late summer of 1954. The down road has already been laid with the new flat bottom track.*

doctor, the rat catcher, and many more went their annual rounds, the company doctor for example having his own private medical coach parked in a bay for weeks on end at the largest stations. Station painting was at its peak in the spring. Most young men aspiring to Great Westernhood joined instantly after leaving school because the company needed them for the summer, while many due to retire from Easter onward were encouraged to stay on until September. Camp coaches had to be delivered to their sites in spring. Laundry followed shortly afterwards. And so it went on, each month of the year having a distinct character, indeed often individual days being unique in their demand on the traffic department. The major similarity was between one year and another, for with the GWR there were ever variations upon a familiar theme. Thus on the same Tuesday in June for peacetimes decades on end (for this purpose the GWR not really ending until the late 1950s) a train with the same number of vehicles running –given a minute or two – at precisely the same times took people from the same towns and villages of somewhere in Great Westernland to go round the same organised tour – including generous free samples – of Cadbury's Bournville chocolate works. That of course included the same extra-territorial arrangements

with the LMS. In GWR days tours *to* factories were if not as common at least as desirable as tours of the workforce from their factories.

In the GWR calendar, of course, it was the annual closure of Swindon works (let it be emphasised this began long before lesser employees were given holidays with pay) that really started the season off. Swindon Junction despatched half a dozen specials or reliefs as well as filling many regular services – mainly with passengers intent on travelling to the ends of the system such as St Ives and Pwllehli so as to maximise the value of their free travel. They naturally chose their accommodation from the GWR *Holiday Haunts*. The collection of advertisements for that and the distribution of the ever fatter finished product was just one more seasonal task for stationmasters, like supervising the display of the latest posters and timetables and circulating excursion details to hotels and boarding houses.

Activity at Wolverhampton Low Level in 1963. Pause for a chat during the station master's rounds whilst pre-Christmas traffic is loaded aboard a London bound parcels train. Note that the GWR station master's pill box hat has been abandoned and the cardboard box of 'Triang Toys' – perhaps some 00 gauge trains and/or Minic road vehicles. The platform trolley is very Great Western. The platform awning support is the stopping point for 8 car DMUs recently introduced.

The Railcars

By the early 1930s the GWR was well aware of the threat of bus competition and the need to cut the cost of running lightly-patronised trains. It was therefore quick to snap up the Associated Equipment Co's (AEC) offer of their prototype diesel mechanical railcar weighing a lightweight 20 tons with a standard AEC London bus engine. The eyecatching streamlined bodywork was designed by the Park Royal Coach Works of Willesden although (as the vehicle had a maximum speed of 60mph) this can have been of little practical use.

Railcar No 1 as it became was put into public service from Southall depot on 4 December 1933 and immedi-

Railcar W14W in the bay of the Great Western half of Dudley station ready to work the 7.00pm to Birmingham Snow Hill on 28 May 1956. The train is unusual as it sets off backwards into the tunnel then reverses and runs non-stop through both the ex LNWR platforms and Dudley Port Low Level, before making the first stop at Great Bridge South. No 14 was built in March 1936 and was withdrawn in August 1960. It is shown here in B.R. crimson and cream livery.

ately appeared on local workings in the Reading area including turns on the Windsor and Henley branches. The interior was furnished in similar style to that of contemporary buses, even down to the notice requesting smokers to occupy the rear seats. As the vehicle was double-ended this must have caused confusion at times! The external body fairings, which swept down to within a foot of the rail surface, also acted as access panels to the underfloor engine and transmission. At the end of its first full month in service No 1 had carried over 10,300 passengers, many making a journey simply for the novelty value.

The success of No 1 led to the construction of a series of more ambitious vehicles incoporating improvements such as the provision of two engines. That made possible a maximum speed of between 75 and 80mph. Numbered 2–4 their seating capacity was only 44, as room was made for a four-seater buffet and two lavatories in addition to the general more spacious layout. The first of these buffet railcars entered service in July 1934 on a Cardiff to Birmingham Snow Hill working, 34 minutes quicker than the previous steam hauled service. The GWR thought this attractive enough to charge a supplement of

Twin unit railcar No W35 (with presumably No W36 at the rear) enters Reading West station with a train probably for Newbury, their usual Reading duty. The intermediate coach is a corridor third adapted with through control cables to work with these diesel railcars.

2s 6d (12½p), the same as the LNER 1st class Silver Jubilee surcharge. The additional railcar fare was dropped after 12 months after causing bad publicity.

Built by the Gloucester Railway Carriage & Wagon Co, Nos 5–16 retained the pair of 121hp engines but reverted to the higher capacity, short-haul service seating layout of No 1. Sliding doors were provided this time together with deeper windows in a successful attempt to improve the view for passengers. These alterations were accompanied by a less obvious change to the curves around the ends which resulted in a more pleasing streamlined shape allowing the disparaging soubriquet of Flying Bananas applied to the earlier railcars to be forgotten.

At first these new cars saw use in the Oxford, Worcester and Hereford areas, but as more became available their sphere of operation expanded and took in the cross-country route between Bristol and Weymouth, three cars equipped with lavatory accommodation (Nos 10–12) being rostered to this duty. Many cars appeared in Wales, areas served included Pontypool, Monmouth, Swansea and Carmarthen, while at weekends they were also used on excursion and private hire work. By the time the 1936 summer timetable was introduced, the cars were running a total of almost 3,600 miles per day and the footnote 'Streamlined Rail Car – Limited Accommodation' appeared in many pages of the timetable.

The seventeenth railcar was adapted for carrying parcels, the object being to free certain passenger trains of long station stops loading and unloading. Its design was identical to the other cars except that there was no passenger accommodation and three sets of sliding doors on each side replaced the normal arrangement. Initially used in the London area, one of its early diagrams took it out to Reading and Oxford with cake and confectionery products from Messrs Lyons factory for distribution to their depots. The return journey to the capital saw it picking up parcels and other general traffic at all stations on the way back to Paddington and was seen by passengers of many overtaking expresses over the years.

Car No 18 was something of an experiment for although outwardly resembling its predecessors it was designed to haul a tail load of up to 60 tons. It was the first to be fitted with standard buffing and drawgear as well as the necessary control lines so that it could work with an auto-trailer if required. Extensive trials were carried out with the chassis on the Southall to Brentford branch before the bodywork was fitted. On one test it managed to haul 124 tons. When the vehicle eventually entered service it was allocated to Reading for use on the Newbury to Lambourn branch and immediately changed the fortunes of what had been a loss-making line, its light axle loading causing less wear and tear to a poor permanent way than the traditional steam hauled passenger train.

Following No 18's commissioning in 1937 the GWR reviewed the whole railcar policy. Their raison d'être had been to augment existing services where the traffic was insufficient to justify the provision of an additional steam train. This was so successful that often the cars were unable to cope with the extra traffic generated. However experience with No 18 had shown that by altering the design to allow a trailing load to be carried, railcars could transform previously uneconomic services and retain the ability to work fast stopping trains on the main line when required. So in 1938 the GWR placed an order with AEC for the construction of a further 20 railcars. Probably due to the worsening political situation, progress was very slow and Nos 19–38 were not delivered until after the start of war, between July 1940 and February 1942. With new angular cab design, the first fifteen were intended for branch and secondary services while car No 34 was another express parcels unit for use in the London area. The final four, Nos 35–38, represented a total departure from normal practice being turned out as single-ended cars, vestibuled at the non-cab end, to work as twin sets. These were meant to replace the earlier streamlined buffet cars on the Birmingham to Cardiff service which were proving too small for the business. Being geared for a top speed of 70mph they were also fitted with the wiring to allow them to run with a standard GW third class coach sandwiched in the middle, the whole ensemble thus being quickly converted to a higher capacity three-car unit.

One car of each of the twin sets was equipped with a 12-seat buffet section but by the time they entered service all catering facilities had been withdrawn because of wartime restrictions. And when peace returned there was such an increase in people wanting to travel that the GWR was forced to use conventional trains on the Cardiff to Birmingham workings. The twin sets were relegated to the Bristol to Weymouth and Reading to Newbury services where no buffet was needed.

Apart from two casualties the entire railcar fleet became British Railways property in 1948. Within a very short time the BR crimson and cream livery was adopted (except for the two parcels cars which were painted in all crimson) followed by the all green livery that was standard for diesel multiple units introduced from the mid-1950s.

The older railcars were generally withdrawn first, though the wartime-built examples did not last much longer and by October 1962 all had gone. Unfortunately many withdrawals were occasioned by fire. No 9 burnt out at Heyford in July 1945 followed by No 37 two years later. On March 9 1956 No W10W was damaged by fire at Bridgnorth while on April 10 the same year twin set cars W35W and W36W were destroyed while working the 9.5pm Bath to Bristol.

Car No	Built	Withdrawn	Last shed
1	2/34	8/55	Oxford
2	7/34	2/54	Newport Ebbw Junction
3	7/34	3/55	Oxford
4	9/34	7/58	Newport Ebbw Junction
5	7/35	12/57	Worcester
6	8/35	4/58	Worcester
7	7/35	1/59	Stourbridge
8	3/36	1/59	Stourbridge
9	2/36	5/46	Oxford
10	2/36	4/56	Reading
11	2/36	11/56	Landore
12	2/36	6/57	Oxford
13	3/36	8/60	Newport Ebbw Junction
14	3/36	8/60	Stourbridge
15	4/36	1/59	Stourbridge
16	4/36	10/57	Reading
17	4/36	1/59	Leamington
18	4/37	5/57	Reading
19	7/40	2/60	Cheltenham
20	6/40	10/62	Worcester
21	7/40	8/62	Southall
22	9/40	10/62	Worcester
23	9/40	10/62	Worcester
24	9/40	10/62	Worcester
25	9/40	8/62	Bristol
26	9/40	10/62	Worcester
27	11/40	9/60	Southall
28	12/40	9/60	Bristol
29	1/41	8/62	Reading
30	1/41	8/62	Southall
31	2/41	8/62	Southall
32	2/41	10/62	Worcester
33	3/41	8/62	Reading
34	9/41	9/60	Southall
35	11/41	4/57	Bristol
36	11/41	4/57	Bristol
37	2/42	9/49	Bristol
38	2/42	8/62	Reading

4
A DAY IN THE LIFE
OF 'A' SHOP

IT is 7.30 am on a cold crisp morning and the Swindon Works hooter sends its melancholy note across the air waves of the town. This is the first official indication that a new working day will shortly begin. The roads soon start to fill with the men making their way towards the various factory entrances. Already a large number in the outlying districts have caught their trains or buses, while many from closer to town are cycling or walking. Today is pay day so there is a little more spring in the gait of the walkers.

The West Gate entrance to the 'A' Shop is in Rodbourne Road which, by the time the hooter sounds its second blast, is now thronged with people. Passing through the factory gates, past the watchmen's office, they make their way to the factory turntable and on to the entrance to the AE Shop. Some have taken another route, over the outside traverser table road to the AM (Machine) Shop entrance which leads to the machining area or to the AV (Boiler) Shop. Others have gone through the Dean Street tunnel entrance which runs under the main London to Bristol line to enter the shop at the West End. At each of the entrances there are the check boxes hung on the wall, which operate like sash windows, having timber backing covered with hooks. On each of these hooks hangs a numbered brass check. Every man is allocated his own number, and his first action on entering is to take and pocket his allocated check which will ensure that he is officially on duty. By each check box is the 'Checky' who is responsible for its operation, especially the pulling down of the sash when the fourth hooter sounds at 8 am, this being the official starting time. Anyone arriving after this time can remove his check but will have a 'Time Reduction' check replaced on his hook by the 'Checky'. This will show whether he loses a quarter or a half hour. They then make their way through the engine and table roads to their various gang areas.

Changing into overalls, preparing the hand tools, probably rubbing 'Rosalex' into the hands to keep out some of the oil, grease and soot, a quick natter to their mates, or a look at the paper, the men then wait for work allocation.

Next to appear are the 'staff' who have a time allowance after the official commencing time. These include the foremen, inspectors, piecework checkers and clerks, who make their way to their various offices. They have booked on at the West Gate Time Office and are not subject to the 'check-in' procedure.

There is the noise of an anvil being banged with a hammer, the drivers of the overhead cranes start to move down their respective crane roads.

Double Telegraph
These days we go to the station to catch a train. The time was when we also went there to buy our newspapers, the *Great Western Magazine* and *Holiday Haunts*, and to enjoy the general scene (even if we were not enthusiasts). The time was, indeed, when many people called on the stationmaster much as they paid their weekly respects to the parson or minister, and when the station was as likely a place to hear the latest news of the locality as anywhere else.

Ticket collectors were seldom without someone to talk to, and were a particularly useful source of information about who had gone where to do what . . . as the police frequently discovered. Booking clerk, stationmaster, porter, ticket collector might all recognise you and be genuinely interested in your reason for patronising the company and be proud there was an appropriate service.

If you were up to no good that presented a great difficulty, for if you somehow got yourself to another station and were seen perhaps by a friendly guard trying to get on incognito, the staff at the station you *should* have started from would quickly learn about it and be outraged. The GWR developed its own excellent telegraph and telephone systems backed by one of the world's most fearsome bush telegraphs.

The GWR post war mixed traffic 4-6-0s took the form of thirty 2 cylinder locomotives with 6ft 3in driving wheels. They were named after English and Welsh counties. The first of the class No 1000 County of Middlesex was fitted with a double chimney when built and is seen here on the stationary testing plant at Swindon, The staff from right to left are R. Lucas (Technical Assistant), M. Casey (Technical Assistant – he eventually became Managing Director BREL), W. Waterhouse (Chemist), A. N. Other, M. Herd (Technical Assistant), H. Titchener (Chief Assistant – Loco experimental section), S.O.Ell (Engineer in charge, Loco experimental section), J. R. Smith and S. Davis (Technical Assistants), D. Stagg (Senior Technical Assistant), P. Perry (Technical Assistant), E. J. Nutty (Senior Technical Assistant).

The chargemen move from their 'boxes' with work allocations for the day to the men, who are now on their allocated pits and locos. Down the main road of the shop, the familiar bowler hat of the chief erecting shop foreman is seen as he makes his way to his office situated on the landing of the office block overlooking the shop. The day's work has begun, and with it a deafening noise of much activity.

The bay foremen make their way to the various chargemen under their control to check the up-to-date position on the construction or repair of the locomotives in their section. Problems, shortages of materials, availability of men and so on, have to be assessed as by 9.30 am they will be required to meet the 'Chief' for a general appraisal and to bring the 'Progress Board' up-to-date. This board is on the wall behind his desk, and contains all the locomotive numbers that are in the shop. It is columned out in the various main items of a repair, such as 'stripped', 'framework', 'erection', 'boilerwork', 'cabwork', 'motion', 'plating', 'wheels & bogie', with anticipated completion dates to be inserted against a final 'output date' which is set by the Works Manager's Office on instructions from the CME's department office. The chief erecting shop foreman is responsible to the works manager with assistance from the chief machine shop foreman and the chief boiler shop foreman, for all work carried out in the 'A' Shop.

On this particular day it is noted that 1023 *County of Oxford* (a new build) and 5949 *Trematon Hall* (general repair) also 4555 and 5683 (both generals) must be trialed if they are to keep to tomorrow's scheduled output date. It's reported that the first two and 5683 are at present being steamed and will be ready for trial by 11 am so they should be cleared by the end of the day. 4555 has however some trouble on the pony truck and will not leave the shop until later this afternoon which will mean an early trial on Friday. Instructions are given for a priority on this loco in order that she may be released early during the night from the shop and lit up by the night boilerman. Meanwhile outside the shop on the turntable roads, the outdoor foreman is in conversation with the trials inspector and the two 'trials' footplate crews have reported in from the running shed awaiting their instructions.

On the 'New Work' bay at the west end of the shop, the last pair of frames for No 30 of the County 'lot' have arrived on the road trailer from the frame shop and are being manoeuvred into position under the 100 ton overhead crane. These will be transferred to the 'marking off' trestles under the guidance of the crane groundsman to the requirement of Bill, the new work chargeman, who incidentally, was the fitter that went to the USA with *King George V* in 1927. All marking-off and drilling of frame details including stiffeners, gussets, cross plates, will be done here for rivetting or bolting when set upright on the frame stands ready for commencement of the locomotive's erection. After this, the crane will be used to hang the cylinders ready for setting, using the Ziess Optical Equipment on No 28. The night shift will then be given the job of broaching out and bolting up with 'fitted' bolts which are driven in by

Churchward designed small wheeled 2-6-2T No 4555 built in 1924 was withdrawn from service in December 1963 and purchased privately. It is seen here in Swindon roundhouse prior to running in from Swindon to Kemble and back after an intermediate repair. On the right is R. F. Hanks, late Chairman of the Western Region board. Middle left, carrying raincoat is Sidney Ridgeway, Works Manager. Jack Hancock, with Homburg hat, H.Q. Loco Inspector, Wolverhampton stands below the cab steps.

Finding Out

Snow Hill station boasted what the Great Western Railway once called First and Second Class Refreshment Rooms on each of the great island platforms. They were presided over by ladies of indeterminate age dressed in black who dispensed ales, stouts, wines, spirits, cakes and sandwiches from under glass covers and, if requested in advance, luncheon baskets (NOT supplied on Sundays); Bovril with bread, cold meat with salad and pickles, sardines on toast, sausages and hard boiled eggs – so on it went in the pre-microwave oven day.

One thing the ladies did not like was small boys. They got very short shrift. That was good for the automatic machines – and anyway refreshment rooms reduced train-watching time and getting to know drivers. And thus it was that we were encouraged to discover such things as why No 2916 *Saint Benedict* had a strange looking tender, carried on two four wheeled bogies with the wheels outside and not behind any tender frame. One day a kindly knowledgeable driver explained that it once belonged to *The Great Bear*, perhaps Churchward's only folly, much of it going for scrap in 1924, but with parts rebuilt into the new No 111 *Viscount Churchill*, for all practical purposes a Castle. As a matter of interest other locos which at various times carried the *Bear*'s tender included Saints Nos 2912 and 2914, Stars Nos 4022 and 4045 and, seemingly strangely, 2-8-0s Nos 3802, 3804 and 3816. – PBW

a compressed air gun hammer. A number of pits in this bay have flat level plates with fixed height movable jacks to ensure that erection of the locomotive, up to wheeling will have a positive datum. 1025 is ready for valve setting so at the moment the second overhead crane is stationed over with its twin hooks and chains dangling ready to place in the lifting positions on the rear dragbox and the front buffer beam.

It is nearly 10 o'clock and time for the morning ten minute break. The men are breaking off from their work, cleaning off some of the grime from their hands and making their way to the lockers to make a cup of Oxo or tea. Around the shop the urns containing water have been boiling merrily away over a gas ring, and queues soon form there to mix the brew, and also at the little snack bar manned by the canteen staff, selling sandwiches and biscuits – all waiting for the sound of the shop klaxon horn. The break gives a short time for a chat, smoke or read of the paper, and a chance to make up a 'head of steam'. It also gives 'Jock' one of the fitters, who runs the tool club, including Oxo's and washing liquid sales, to expound to some of the apprentices the intricacies of model locomotive construction, of which he is well versed. Most of his spare time at home is used on this hobby and the models he turns out are indeed a work of art. Needless to say, most of his subjects are scaled down versions of GWR stock. Another topic that always seems to arise during these intervals, are the prospects of the 'Town' at the next football match with plenty of arguments about who should be playing.

The 'klaxon' sounds for the end of the break and the relative quiet is again disturbed by the movement of cranes and traversing tables. Over in the AV Boiler Bay the noise of rivetting starts as the front end of a smokebox is rivetted into position on the shell. This bay also carries out repairs to boilers from light repairs up to a general repair, including new boiler shells and fireboxes. The shop employs about 350 men which includes those scattered around the shop on various boilermaking work on the locomotives on the pits under repair. At the present moment the bay's overhead crane is lifting a firebox into position, over the vertical rivetting machine, to connect in with a boiler shell which will then be rivetted. Alongside, the rivet boy is preparing the rivet forge fire which is connected up to the compressed air supply. Many a young apprentice has been sent either to this shop or to the main V (boiler) Shop by his mates for 'A bucket of blast'. The main locomotive repair circuit is situated on the eastern side of the main traversing table and it is here that the bulk of main line locomotives have a general repair. At present the bay is nearly full of locos in various stages of stripping and repair. The worst part of this area are the stripping pits with grease, oil and soot in abundance. The stripping gang are usually attired in the oldest overalls available with bits of towelling around their necks, and using any sort of headgear available.

Some of the lads revel in this type of work; to others it is a chore to be undertaken quickly in order to get on the 'cleaner' work further up the bay. Woe betide anyone who upsets his mates at any time. Sooner or later he will be in the smokebox removing steampipes, blastpipe, superheater tubes or saddle bolts, and it is amazing the amount of soot

that can be dislodged by a couple of flogging hammers descending on the outside of the smokebox. At the end of the pit there are two boshing trucks which are being loaded with all the greasy and oily items, and these will eventually be taken by the traverser table and rope propelled by the table capstan up to the 'Boshing Plant'. The main boshing tanks contain a heated caustic solution and all items are immersed for a period and then removed in their trays or trucks, cleaned off with hot water jets and passed over to the resident inspectors. Inspection comprises of checking items against a standard and being marked with a 'blob' of paint; red for scrap, yellow for repair, and green for use again (no attention necessary). Also in this area is the nut and bolt reclamation, and about half a dozen 'light duty' men are employed using a hammer and plate running nuts onto appropriate bolts and sorting into marked bins.

'A' Shop was the main erecting shop in Swindon Works where all new construction and heavy overhauls to the larger classes of locomotive were carried out. 47XX Class 2-8-0 No 4703 is under repair in September 1952. The replica broad gauge North Star *can be seen on its stand in the background.*

1025 has been settled onto the valve setting machine and the resident fitters are fitting the valve marking plates that will be used for trammelling piston valve movement. This area is noted for its extreme secrecy and the operations involved in setting are jealously guarded by the occupants. Any adjustments necessary will be calculated and the eccentric rods marked accordingly for finalisation by the resident shop smithy.

Meanwhile outside the shop, 1023 has gone trial to Dauntsey Bank and back. As well as the footplate crew and inspector, two fitters and an apprentice from the new work gang are also in attendance. The chance of a 'trial' run is much sought after by the apprentices and is looked upon as quite an experience. 5949 is scheduled for its trial at 1.15 so the fitters and apprentice will 'work the lunch hour' and book off from work at 4.30. Trial of 5683 is scheduled for 2.25, again to Dauntsey and back.

On the 'circuit' the frame of 2912 has been zeissed and is being lifted by the overhead crane onto the horn grinding machine, as it has been found that all horns require squaring. The work pace begins to slacken, the overhead cranes and traversers are run to their parking areas, rivetting ceases and there is a general lessening of the noise in the shop.

In the AM (Machine), machines are switched off and the overhead

Castle class 4-6-0 No 7033 Hartlebury Castle *in A shop on 23 March 1952. This was probably the engine's first general repair as it was only built in July 1950.* Behind Hartlebury Castle *is a brand new, contractor built, 94XX pannier tank.*

drive shafting becomes still. Except for one or two wheel lathes, which will be working through the lunch hour, the noise abates in the AW (Wheel) Shop. The staff prepare for the lunch hour from 12.30 to 1.30. The hooter sounds. Some of the men go home for their midday meal if they live within walking distance, others take sandwiches and tea in various parts of the shop, and some make use of the canteen, which is situated in the basement of the building housing the pattern stores. All those taking the lunch break have put their time checks into the check boxes. When they return for the afternoon shift they will take off the oval copper pay checks which are at present being arranged on the respective hooks. Also during this period, the pay tables are being taken from storage and placed adjacent to the pay points.

During the lunch hour, two sets of footplatemen, one set working the down 2.10 Weymouth, and the other set working back home 'on the cushions' have been into the 'Shop' for a general look around. Both the drivers are interested in what is being repaired and how, as they are both instructors for their local mutual improvement class. They have made the acquaintance of one of the erecting shop foremen discussing some of their problems, including oscillation on the 1000s at short 'cut off'. Swindon 'A' shop is the mecca so far as depot crews and staff are concerned, and there is a very noticeable comradeship by all those in GWR steam. No 6022 *King Edward III*, having rear driving wheel attention was released from the light repair gang, adjacent to the main line wall of the shop, removed outside by the traverser and shunted into the engine weighbridge for general weighing and spring adjustment. Arrangements are being made for lighting up by the night staff, with release to traffic tomorrow.

The final 1.30 hooter announced the beginning of the afternoon shift. At 1.45 the assistant chief erecting shop foreman meets the elected shop committee representatives to discuss some of the problems that will always occur when some 1,500 staff are employed in one production area. There is an amicable working atmosphere and wherever possible a viable solution is usually obtained, on such things as staff welfare, working conditions, and safety. Any item not obtaining mutual agreement is usually referred to senior management and the works committee.

At this time of the week the various 'Financial' chargemen start submitting the gang piecework sheets for scrutiny by the piecework inspectors. All work carried out under standard conditions has what is known as a registered price and the various classes of locomotives have 'price sheets' allocated accordingly. Each locomotive in for repair is allocated a set of piecework documentation which is 'called-up' against work on the inspection schedule, showing work requirement for its classification of repair. Any deviation from the work content call-up must have covering authority from the relevant inspector. The piecework inspectors visually ascertain that the work has actually been done. In some cases, especially on light repair schedules, work content can be non-repetitive. These are one off prices agreed between the foreman and financial chargeman. Bill, the light repair gang's financial chargeman,

End of Walk Reverie
Walking tickets may not be the railway's best seller but they attract an appreciative kind of customer. And in starting his walk from one place and ending at another (probably on a different line) the enthusiast has the opportunity to use and get to know new stations.

Today's walk started from a little used Platform on the main line and took us over high ground (from which we could follow the progress of trains on both main line and branch from the locomotives' steam and smoke). After tea in a village cafe we still have over a mile to the station that bears its name on a typical GWR branch and aim to arrive in time to see the down train that crosses ours at the next loop.

We arrive by the footpath built to emphasise the station's importance in the 1910s though by the late 1940s the bus has captured the chief passenger traffic and we are into the era of a high proportion of those going by train having privilege tickets, taking prams or starting long-distance journeys. Probably not many of the latter from this station despite its typical display of GWR posters, but there are two mothers with prams in the shelter on the opposite platform.

But, it being near the end of the summer holidays, most enquirers of the sole functionary on duty want to know about Passenger Luggage in Advance; the kid goes by car, the trunk by train, more evidence that the station is being left with odds and sods. Hauled by a purring Mogul, a down freight of a dozen trucks (none off here) goes gently through the loop and is waved back by the signalman from his cabin near the platform end into the up platform, the beaming guard benevolently acknowledging our interest.

Immediately the road is set for a down passenger and the signals

continued overleaf

continued

pulled off. A Prairie tank pants in with a GWR non-corridor two-coach branch set. Of the fifteen passengers, one gets off, only the two mothers on.

The freight now backs down in the up direction, and a couple of minutes later comes to a stand in the up road, the guard still smiling at all he surveys. Even on branch lines, freights are ever being shunted out of the way, and goods loops and refuge sidings are by no means universal.

A few minutes later the road is set for the up passenger. The signalman waddles along the platform with a package of wallflowers as well as the token, and briefly discusses his plants with the guard before the porter joins them as another Prairie tank comes in, this time with a composite corridor as well as a branch line set. Only we get on, but half a dozen school children get off: the State school is back ahead of the public ones. And another thirty or so boys and girls along with a score of adults including shoppers returning home (more get out at the next Halt close by a hamlet without a bus that at this inconveniently situated station serving a larger village) make this a well used train.

Before we start, there are half a dozen parcels to load including the daily empty Lyons ice cream container. The postman cuts it fine jumping out of his van with two slender mail sacks as the train stops. Half a minute is allowed for platform work; it takes five times as long, but the driver welcomes the challenge of recovering the two minutes.

must have a 'liver' today as he cannot agree with his foreman on one particular price he requires, so it is held in abeyance for payment. The foreman returns to his office and makes arrangements for a member of the manager's cost office to be present tomorrow morning to act as an adjudicator.

1023 has returned from trial with no serious defects, other than one or two items requiring a final tightening up, and will be released to shed this evening. *Trematon Hall* has also returned but requires changing of its exhaust injector and the right hand front cylinder cock together with the provision of a new armoured hose on the water feed delivery between engine and tender. Arrangements will be made for the night men to do this, so allowing for release to traffic tomorrow. Due to a hiccup by the trial crew 5683 missed her 2.25 path and is now back on the table road. with a banked down fire and on the attention list for the night boilerman, she will have first priority tomorrow morning. Not a very successful day for the BSE foreman!

In the middle table road of the shop, a trailer load of timbers, rail and platelaying gear has arrived. This will be used for construction, by PL (platelayers) shop, of a temporary 1ft 11½in narrow gauge track, on one of the empty pits at the main line end of the bay, to accommodate a Vale of Rheidol locomotive, due in a fortnight for a general repair. The trailer is parked near the allocated pit and the motor vehicle released.

The foreman and chargemen of the various sections have been working on the work schedule requirements for the night men. Lists have been made out by the chargemen and will be left on the relevant locomotives. It is usual practice to overstate requirements to allow for alternative work should there be any unexpected delays due to craneage or traverser moves. The materials required have already been stacked near to the appropriate locomotives. Night stores availability is arranged. The boiler, machine and wheel shops will also be working; any utilisation of their facilities will be arranged by the night foreman using authority under the 'Foreman's Sub-Order' (FSO) procedure.

It is now 5.10 and the general noise and clatter in the shop begins to die down, as the men clear up tools and wash off their grime. The pay tables have been set up in the traversing table roads and await occupation.

During the day the money for the factory wages has been collected from the bank in a steel safe trailer, drawn by a tractor, under escort. Taken to the central cash office in the general office block, it has gone through a pay make-up procedure and finally ends up in little round tins having stamped numbers on their lids. These are the individual pay tins for each man and hold the reward for a week's work. The tins are then allocated to their appropriate tray boxes which are locked and stacked awaiting transportation to the various shops.

A number of these tray boxes are now arriving at the shop, by road transport and are carried by labourers, accompanied by wages clerks, to the respective pay tables. Payment will commence when each table is also staffed by a shop foreman.

The men begin to form a queue in numerical order, each with his little

An interesting scene taken in 'A' Shop in April 1962. On the left is No 4003 Lode Star *being carefully restored ready for presentation to the Museum at Swindon. The burnished back head fittings clearly show the love put into this particular job. The King is No 6012* King Edward VI *on her last visit for repair as withdrawal was September of that year.*

pay check. The foreman arrives and payment begins. The pay clerk starts calling the numbers of each tin he bangs onto the metal plate of the table and sweeps the correspondingly numbered check received into a round lockable container. Each man takes his tin, removes the money and payslip, checking that it is correct, and deposits the empty tin into a receptacle adjacent to the pay table. About a hundred men are paid per minute. At the end of the payout the container, with the numbered checks is locked and together with any unissued tins returned to the cash office. The receptacle with the empty pay tins will be returned tomorrow morning. The salaried staff have already left on their way home.

As the men disgorge back into Rodbourne Road, Dean Street and so on, the hooter sounds its last strident note announcing day's end for those who work 'inside'.

Great Western London

For many, the dominant feature of GWR London was the main line passenger traffic into a magnificent terminus. Handsome motive power and dignified arrivals and departures brought devoted admirers, from infants in the charge of nursemaids to elderly men, to congregate day after day at the outer ends of the platforms of that stately train shed, Paddington, inspired creation of engineer Brunel and architect Wyatt, redolent of royal journeys, and in constant use by the most influential and wealthy in the land, exemplified the almost imperial character of the GWR.

Main line traffic is one thing, but London means commuters, and it has to be said the GWR never took these very seriously, banished as most were to the dingy recesses of 'Bishop's Road' in the far north corner at the entrance to the Metropolitan's tunnels. For although it did operate suburban services of a sort, some of them

most conveniently running through to the City over the tracks of the Metropolitan, the GWR disdained this traffic, content to leave the hard grind of much of it to the Metropolitan, the District, and later, the Central London Tube. All three of these were able to distribute commuters efficiently through the central parts of the City and the West End, providing an answer to the constant grumble that Paddington was not London, or at any rate the London most wanted to reach. Of course the GWR *did* serve 'The Queen of Suburbs', but Ealing's population grew only slowly until the 1870s and it was the arrival of the District, alongside the GWR station, rather than the GWR itself, which had much to do with Ealing's expansion from just over 18,000 in 1871 to 47,510 in 1901. In truth it was the places at the outermost fringes of metropolitan influence that got the best of GWR residential service. By the early 1910s (with some help from the Great Central), fast trains to and from

Paddington departure platforms c1912. Very much a picture of its time, the platforms are crowded with well dressed upper class passengers possibly bound for a Royal Garden Party at Windsor or Henley Royal Regatta.

London were beginning to place a suburban stamp on places as far out as Beaconsfield and Gerrards Cross, whilst Burnham, Taplow, Maidenhead and the Thames Valley branches were also seeing the beginnings of commuter traffic. Closer in, many stations got little more than an infrequent service of steam rail cars and later, autos, not generally admitted to Paddington. Nor was there much improvement after World War I: apart from the opening of three or four new halts, the huge suburban growth of west Middlesex between the wars provoked little or no reaction from the GWR, and not surprisingly its services made only a marginal contribution to the dramatic outward expansion of the capital. A London office worker purchasing a new semi on the Hangar Hill Estate could hardly be expected to be interested in an infrequent and dusty auto train which never got to Paddington when he had the slick Piccadilly tube and its smart new station as an alternative.

In contrast, freight into and out of London was big business for the GWR, vigorously pursued. Few travellers using Paddington could fail to be impressed by the huge goods shed just outside, always bustling with activity; and a little further out, the large yard at Acton. Almost every station in the London area had its own goods yard. The Brentford branch, with its GWR-owned dock serving Thames lighters, gained its livelihood from freight. But perhaps more intriguing were the little-known GWR depots accessible only over joint or other company's lines: distant Poplar, Royal Albert Dock and Victoria Dock, Smithfield meat market, providing the piquant spectacle of a pannier tank fussily shifting meat vans amidst the Metropolitan and Inner Circle electrics, a coal depot at the end of the Hammersmith line, again injecting some steam activity into the preserves of electrics, this time the famous GW & Metropolitan joint stock; Shepherds Bush and Warwick Road on the West London, competitively tucked in alongside L&NWR/LM&SR establishments; and finally the mis-named South Lambeth Goods, built as late as 1910–13 and latterly overshadowed by the huge bulk of Battersea Power Station.

Mention of South Lambeth recalls the one-time sharing of the eastern side of Victoria with the LC&DR and later SE&CR, reached by running powers from Longhedge Junction. This produced curious passenger services between Victoria and Southall and beyond, not to mention five years of Sunday steam railcars from Victoria or Clapham Junction to the Denham and High Wycombe line via Greenford and, in 1910–12, a flash of main line splendour in the form of a service between Wolverhampton and Victoria via Bicester. But after 1915, GWR trains were no longer seen at Victoria, although a workmen's service between Greenford and what is now Kensington (Olympia) was started in 1922 and extended to Clapham Junction twelve years later.

GWR London was full of variety and unexpected little oddities like that.

GWR London: A Chronology

4.6.1838	First Paddington terminus on the site of the later goods depot, west of Bishops Road. Line from Paddington to Maidenhead & Taplow (renamed Taplow, 1869), with intermediate station at West Drayton.
1.12.1838	Ealing and Hanwell stations opened.
1.5.1839	Southall station. Trains begin to stop at Slough (no permanent station until 1 June 1840).
13.6.1842	Queen Victoria makes her first rail journey, from Slough to Paddington.
3.6.1844	GWR trains stop to provide interchange with West London Railway (until WLR passenger service ceased on 30.11.44).
1.5.1846	Langley (Bucks) station opened as 'Langley Marsh'.
16.1.1854	Departure side of the present Paddington station opened.
28.5.1854	First Paddington terminus closed, site used for goods station.
29.5.1854	Arrival side of new Paddington station opened.
9.6.1854	Opening of Great Western Hotel, Paddington, designed by Philip Hardwick.
8.9.1856	Uxbridge (Vine Street) branch opened.
18.7.1859	Southall-Brentford Docks opened for freight.
1.5.1860	Infrequent passenger service on Brentford branch.
10.1.1863	GWR passenger trains over Metropolitan Railway to Farringdon Street with separate station at Bishop's Road, Paddington.
1.4.1863	Passenger services over West London Extension Railway, Southall-Kensington-Victoria, using new west curve, West London Junction-North Pole Junction. Other GWR London area destinations were subsequently served from Victoria.
1.10.1863	Through service Farringdon Street-Windsor (until 31.12.1863).
1.5.1864	Hayes station opened.
13.6.1864	Hammersmith & City Railway; stations at Notting Hill (now Ladbroke Grove) and Shepherds Bush; service Hammersmith-Bishop's Road-Farringdon Street, worked by GWR with broad gauge trains.

Transept of Paddington Cathedral. View from one of the oriel windows of the office block on platform 1 showing Matthew Digby Wyatt's ornamentation on Brunel's wrought iron roof. There are two openings across the station which were originally intended to accommodate large traversers to be used for moving carriages from one track to another; these were never brought into use.

1.7.1864	New line Latimer Road (Hammersmith & City) to Uxbridge Road Junction, West London Railway, served by through carriages between Kensington (now Kensington (Olympia)) and Farringdon Street, added to and detached from Hammersmith trains at Latimer Road Junction or Notting Hill (now Ladbroke Grove). Also local service Notting Hill-Kensington.
1865	GWR and Metropolitan Railway lease Hammersmith & City Railway. Joint Management Committee.
1.4.1865	Metropolitan Railway standard gauge trains to and from Hammersmith taking over the service entirely. GWR through train service Kensington (Addison Road)-Farringdon Street.
1.2.1866	Westbourne Park (platforms on Hammersmith & City Line only) opened.
1.3.1866	GWR services over Metropolitan Railway extended to Aldersgate Street.

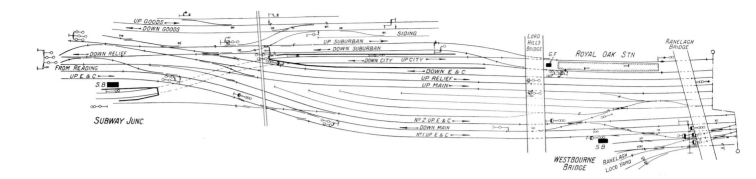

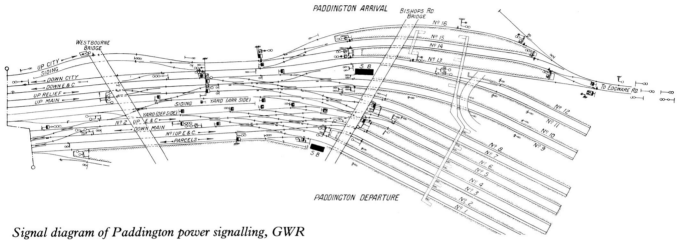

Signal diagram of Paddington power signalling, GWR installed 1933.

1.7.1866	GWR services over Metropolitan Railway extended to Moorgate Street.
1.7.1867	Hammersmith & City Railway becomes joint property of GWR and Metropolitan Railway.
1.2.1868	Acton station opened.
16.12.1868	Latimer Road station opened.
14.3.1869	Last broad gauge working over Metropolitan Railway from GWR.
1.5.1869	Smithfield Goods depot opened under Market.
1.6.1869	GWR standard gauge services over Metropolitan Railway.
1.6.1870	Service from Bishop's Road to Richmond via Hammersmith & City (withdrawn on 31 October 1870).
1.3.1871	Castle Hill (now West Ealing) station opened.
30.10.1871	Separate suburban lines provided for Hammersmith & City trains between Bishop's Road and Westbourne Park. Stations opened at Royal Oak and Westbourne Park (main line).
1.11.1871	Most main line trains begin to call at Westbourne Park.
1.8.1872	New service Moorgate Street-Bishop's Road-Kensington (Addison Road) Mansion House (so-called 'Middle Circle'), worked by GWR. Started and terminated at Bishopsgate (now Liverpool Street) 12.7.1875, Aldgate 4.12.1876.
1.9.1872	Second Taplow station, on new site.

12.7.1875	GWR services over Metropolitan Railway extended to Bishopsgate (now Liverpool Street) on opening of station.
4.12.1876	All GWR trains over Metropolitan (except Middle Circle) terminate at Moorgate.
1.1.1877	Junction at Acton, providing access to North London Railway and Docks.
1.10.1877	Metropolitan service between Aldgate and Richmond via Bishops Road and Hammersmith & City. (Jointly worked by GWR and Metropolitan from 1.1.1894).
1.4.1878	Poplar Goods Depot completed.
12.5.1878	Flat junction with Hammersmith & City line at Westbourne Park eliminated.
1.4.1883	District service Mansion House to Windsor via new junction at Ealing (service ceased 30.9.1885).
8.9.1884	Two additional lines from Portobello Junction-west of Taplow. Second station at Slough.
1.1.1894	Some GWR trains from Hammersmith to Aldgate.
1.7.1894	All GWR trains over Metropolitan Railway extended to Aldgate.
1.7.1899	Burnham Beeches station opened.
30.6.1900	Last GWR Middle Circle trains to and from Mansion House.
1.7.1900	Middle Circle shortened to Aldgate-Bishops Road-Kensington-Earls Court.

5.1902	Long distance trains cease to call at Westbourne Park.
9.1902	Rebuilding of Notting Hill & Ladbroke Grove (now Ladbroke Grove) completed.
15.6.1903	Park Royal station opened for temporary services for Royal Agricultural Society Show (ceased 4.7.1903).
1904	Island platform at Royal Oak.
1.5.1904	New lines Old Oak-Greenford-West Ealing opened for regular traffic. Park Royal station opened for regular traffic; steam rail motors★ Westbourne Park-Park Royal-Southall via Greenford East loop. Halts opened at Castle Bar Park, North Acton, Perivale and Twyford Abbey.
2.5.1904	Steam rail motors★ on Brentford branch.
1.7.1904	Steam rail motors★ service Park Royal-West Ealing-Acton. Trumper's Crossing Halte opened.
1.10.1904	Cowley station opened. Greenford station opened. Most steam rail motor★ services call.
1905	New carriage sheds at Old Oak Common.
1.2.1905	Middle Circle replaced by Aldgate-Bishops Road-Kensington service (electrified and operated by Metropolitan November/December 1906).
1.3.1905	Drayton Green Halt opened.
1.10.1905	(from) Westbourne Park-Park Royal-Southall service ceases.
2.11.1905	Steam rail motor★ service Westbourne Park-Park Royal-Greenford-Acton-Willesden Junction.
2.4.1906	First services on new line, Greenford-High Wycombe. Beaconsfield, Gerrards Cross, Denham (for Harefield) and Ruislip & Ickenham (now West Ruislip) stations opened.
17.3.1906	New locomotive depot at Old Oak Common, replacing Westbourne Park.
1.10.1906	Old Oak Lane Halt opened.

5.11.1906	Electrification of Hammersmith & City service using joint GWR/Metropolitan stock. Full service 3.12.1906.
31.12.1906	GWR/Metropolitan joint service Aldgate-Richmond ceases.
1.1.1907	GWR steam locos replaced by Metropolitan Railway electric locomotives at Bishops Road for haulage of GWR services over Metropolitan Railway (partial; all trains from 2.9.1907). GWR steam rail motor★ shuttle service Richmond-Notting Hill (now Ladbroke Grove) in connection with Hammersmith & City electric services.
1.5.1907	New branch to Uxbridge (High Street). Steam rail motor★ service Denham-Uxbridge (High Street)-West Ealing. Northolt Halt opened.
1908	Rebuilding of Hammersmith station completed.
13.4.1908	Crimea Mileage Yard (Westbourne Park) opened.
1.5.1908	Northolt Junction station (now South Ruislip) opened. Wood Lane (Exhibition) station (later White City) opened.
1910–16	Extension of Paddington Arrival Side (east side), three new platforms.
1.7.1910	GWR services over Metropolitan Railway terminate at Liverpool Street instead of Aldgate.
1.10.1910	Victoria to Birmingham and Wolverhampton via Bicester service, calling at Kensington.

Nearly all stations in the London area had their own depot and coal yard. A 2361 class double framed 0-6-0 enters Ruislip and Ickenham with a local goods c1934. The train is conveying a typical mixture of covered vans, coal wagons and tanks. The station is now named West Ruislip and the Station Master's garden has been submerged under the post-war London Transport Central Line extension.

The GWR worked some trains, both passengers and freight, over the Metropolitan from Bishops Road. After electrification of the Met these were confined to freights to Smithfield which ran until the 1960s. These trains were latterly worked by eleven 0-6-0Ts, Nos 9700–10, specially fitted with condensing gear and altered tanks. The pioneer No 9700, originally No 8700 (rebuilt with condensors in March 1932 and altered to conform with the ten built as such, and renumbered in January 1934) is seen in Old Oak Common shed, where all the class were allocated, in 1935.

31.12.1910	GWR steam shuttle service Notting Hill (Ladbroke Grove) Richmond ceases.
1911–16	Work begins on improving Paddington approach lines, segregating all ecs and light engine traffic from running lines (completed 1926–7).
30.4.1911	Twyford Abbey Halt closed (replaced by Brentham).
1.5.1911	Brentham & North Ealing for Greystoke Park Halt opened.
1.2.1912	(from) Long distance GWR train to and from Victoria cease.
3.1912	Westbourne Park-Park Royal-Acton-Willesden Junction service curtailed at Acton.
22.7.1912	Denham Golf Club Platform opened.
1.1.1913	South Lambeth Goods Depot completed.
1914	Auto trains on Uxbridge branch, with some fast through trains to Paddington. Westbourne Park-Greenford-Acton service withdrawn.
1.4.1914	Shepherds Bush station resited; new station at Goldhawk Road.
11.5.1914	Freight service over Uxbridge (High Street) branch.
23.12.1914	Beaconsfield Golf Links Halt opened to public (now Seer Green & Jordans). Previously open to golfers only from 2.4.1906.
21.3.1915	Last GWR services in and out of Victoria.
16.4.1917	Ealing & Shepherds Bush Railway (Ealing-North Acton-Viaduct Junction with West London Railway). Freight only.
3.8.1920	Central London tube services extended over Ealing & Shepherds Bush Railway to new platforms at Ealing GWR station. East Acton station opened.

Seventy 2-6-2Ts, the 61XX class were built between 1931 and 1935 to replace earlier four coupled tanks on the London suburban services; until the mid 1950s all 70 were allocated to the London Division. They carried boilers pressed to 225lb/sq in but were otherwise similar to the 41XX and 51XX series with boilers at 200lb/sq in. No 6126 is seen heading a Paddington–High Wycombe train entering Gerards Cross in 1950 on the GW and GC joint line. Note, British Railways, in full in GWR style lettering on the tank side and temporary W suffix under the number plate.

Cathedral of Steam. Old Oak Common shed 20th July 1958 with Castle class 4-6-0 No 5032 Usk Castle, *two Hall class 4-6-0s and another Castle. Note the covered turntable – a GWR safety precaution applicable to all roundhouse type sheds and the smoke extraction vents on each stabling road.*

71

The 0-6-0PTs were very versatile and could be found on many different classes of trains. No 9659 of Old Oak Common is working a parcels train from Wood Lane milk depot approaching North Acton Junction. The London Transport Central Line to Ealing Broadway is on the right and the new GWR Birmingham line is on the left.

1922	Workmen's service Kensington-Greenford via Ealing & Shepherds Bush Railway. Provided for J. Lyons & Co.
5.11.1923	West Acton station opened. Ealing & Shepherds Bush platforms at North Acton opened.
1.12.1924	Iver station opened.
30.1.1926	Trumper's Crossing Halt closed after traffic.
20.9.1926	South Greenford Halt opened.
24.9.1928	Harefield Halt opened (renamed South Harefield, 5.1929, closed 30.9.1931.
1929–32	Semaphores replaced by electric light signals between Paddington and Southall.
1930–34	New passenger concourse (on 'The Lawn') at Paddington and new office blocks, both north of the hotel. Enlargement of Bishops Road station, now fully integrated with the main line station.
20.6.1932	Augmented auto train service Old Oak Lane-Northolt. Denham-Greenford-West Ealing auto trains extended to Ealing Broadway.
20.6.1932	Park Royal West Halt opened.
1933	Kensington-Greenford workmen's service extended to Clapham Junction.
11.9.1933	Bishop's Road station renamed Paddington (Suburban).
9.7.1934	Ruislip Gardens Halt opened.
26.9.1937	(from) Park Royal station closed to passengers.
10.1937	Ealing & Shepherds Bush line quadrupled in preparation for extension of Central Line tube trains alongside main line to West Ruislip.
16.9.1939	(from) GWR services to the City over Metropolitan Railway cease.
1940	Poplar Goods depot closed.
2.5.1942	Passenger service on Brentford branch withdrawn.
14.6.1947	Old Oak Lane, North Acton (main line), Park Royal West, Brentham and Perivale Halts closed. Replaced by LT Central Line tube service North Acton-Greenford and new stations at Hanger Lane, Perivale and Greenford, from 30.6.1947.

*The steam rail motor services introduced from 1904 were replaced by auto-trains from c 1908 onwards.

5
A TALE OF
FOUR CASTLES

IT is early April 1964 and the office 'phone rings. 'Good morning – how are you fixed next week and the week after?' It is Jack Hancock, headquarters locomotive inspector Wolverhampton, a long time friend. 'If you're in London how about coming back with us on the 17.15 Worcester?' That is the down Cathedrals Express. 'We are trying out some Castles for that high speed special next month. Bill Andress is riding the Old Oak engines and me the Worcester ones.'

Three Castles, Nos 5091, 5096 and 7022, are moved to Worcester specially, but home based Nos 5054, 7023 and 7025 are on the list too. They are checked over by shedmaster Harry Cureton and works manager Don Green. Two other regular performers, this time from Old Oak, Nos 7029 and 7032, are also put through their paces, as are Nos 4079 and 7008. Three are going to be needed for the special, one from Paddington to Plymouth, another Plymouth to Bristol and the third, the engine deemed able to reach the magic 100mph, from Bristol to Paddington. Reserve engines to be held at Old Oak, Taunton. Plymouth, Bristol and Swindon. Someone has given this a great deal of thought so the organisation must have blessing from On High. The hand of general manager Gerard Fiennes is writ large.

Past the barrier at Paddington's long No 2 platform, blue overall coat in briefcase, to find Jack Hancock, buttoned up to his neck, Homburg hat on his head standing alongside double chimneyed No 7023 *Penrice Castle* ready to introduce the crew already well briefed by Harry Cureton. By now these Worcesters are the only regular express turns for Castles and one feels wistful. The Beyer Peacock Hymeks are already on their way. But today is today and the thrill of riding with this friendly crew is for real. No 2 platform is on the driver's side so as 17.15 approaches he keeps his eyes towards the Lawn.

Prompt to time platform whistles shrill and the guard's green flag shows; a poop on the engine whistle and the regulator is opened to first then second valve. The fire is already banked up to the door and burning bright so the fireman takes a quick look round, has a final sweep up and wipes his hands on his cloth ready for a daunting evening's work. The load is ten for 350 tons and the horse is about to head for home. No 7023 barks out past Ranelagh Bridge, Old Oak sidings and shed and makes for Reading, the ATC bell sounding loud and clear as the green distant signals present themselves in a steady procession. This is one of the Western's scenic runs, a water level route out along the Thames Valley, through Sonning cutting, the Reading stop, past the steam shed on the left then down the winding main line again as far as the avoiding

Odd Days, Even Days
It was at the northern extremity – Birkenhead – that I entered railway service. This was at the parcels office at Woodside terminus (now a car park) and immediately there was confusion to sort out. A special calendar over my counter had the days printed in alternations of black and red. On a black day outgoing parcels for a destination served by both companies – Birmingham, for instance – were stamped from a roll of non-adhesive 'Western' tags involving the use of a messy gum brush, while on red days I extracted a neat perforated stamp from a post office style folder and licked the quite tasty gum of Euston.

Outside the parcels office were horse-drawn vans, one in the purple and white carriage livery of Wolverton and the other in a warm chocolate shade with gilt 'GWR' lettering. Later there was to arrive a new van in the 'Premier Line' colours but with the initials of both railways and 'Jt.' in small lettering. Not a hundred yards outside the station was the LNWR 'Town Office' whose double-fronted windows extolled the advantages of travelling to Scotland by the 'West Coast Joint Service' (LNWR and Caledonian) while a mile away was the Great Western 'Town Office' well postered with 'Cornish Riviera' and 'Welsh Coast Resorts' placards.

When my father (the Woodside stationmaster) came into the parcels office on his rounds he was arrayed in the silvered buttons of Euston, whereas I recalled that
continued overleaf

73

continued

my grandfather (retired from the same position at Shrewsbury) had sported the gold braid and 'porkpie' hat of the GWR.

When the joint superintendent visited what was called the 'Birkenhead end' he had to show his watch-chain medallion either to the ticket collectors on the interposed Great Western section to Chester or on the other partner's route to Chester via Crewe.

Printed notepaper read respectively 'Great Western & London & North Western Joint Railways', 'London & North Western & Great Western Joint Railways', also 'London Midland & Scottish & Great Western Joint Rlys.' Printing alternated yearly with the parent companies and it was a nice little courtesy for A to put B's name first. One memory in this connection is of my father spotting two separate gentlemen going round his station with a tape measure looking at the advertising space and writing down details. They turned out to be from the publicity depts at Euston and Paddington respectively, one object being to see that 'my' company was getting a fair deal in advertising space. The stationmaster tactfully invited both to lunch and in the first class refreshment room. – R. S. McNaught.

curve at Didcot, another shed on the left and right to the end of the platform at Oxford with its branch line bays. Until a couple of years ago a 54XX tank for Fairford would be blowing wisps of steam eager to leave for the junction at Yarnton and the great water meadows of Windrush and Evenlode but now all is quiet.

Away at 18.35 for Kingham running well into the 60s on comparatively easy grades but climbing steadily up the Cotswold hills to Moreton in Marsh from where, until 2 June 1960, the old branch to Shipston on Stour wound its way over part of the old Stratford and Moreton Tramroad using venerable Dean Goods 0-6-0s. There is a very short level stretch out of Moreton so *Penrice Castle* gets away hard with the needle on the red line; much to Hancock's disgust – he is an old firing instructor – the engine has been blowing off in the station. They accelerate well making 35mph by the time the Cathedrals gets to the summit. Down through Aston Magna and Blockley to rush the 1:165 and 1:154 up to Campden then down again through Campden tunnel when the exhaust starts knocking the soot from the roof – this usually only happens going the other way! It is 1 in 100 down now and No 7023 begins to vibrate as the speed increases and the needle of the speedometer inches over the 90mph mark; by Honeybourne South junction it is 96, Honeybourne 98, but try as they may it goes no further. Littleton & Badsey and then it is braking for the Evesham stop. Perhaps one of the others will make it. As the train rolls into the station No 5054 *Earl of Ducie* is heading for the stiff climb back up to Campden, a fine sight in the late evening light.

There is a brisk sprint out along the Vale, past Fladbury with its old water mill, and through Pershore where the speed is 77 over little easier than level track. Worcester Shrub Hill comes three minutes early, very good going indeed. Here No 7023 hooks off to go on shed and is replaced by an 85A engine No 6950 *Kingsthorpe Hall* and the observer wends his way home via the Lickey dirty but delighted.

A proposed high speed special to Plymouth can scarcely be kept quiet and the BBC get hold of the Railway Roundabout team to see if a programme can be made; it is decided to concentrate on the final dash to Paddington. Hancock and Andress have conferred and the engine for the Bristol-Paddington run has been chosen, No 5054 *Earl of Ducie* from Worcester shed. This is brought up to Honeybourne for some initial filming: footplate shots and views of the wheels and motion at speed. The special effects are achieved by using Collett 0-6-0 No 2222 and a flat truck on one of the four parallel roads the 22XX pushing; the camera crew aim at the wheels and slide bars as the Castle and the 0-6-0 run sedately side by side. The illusion of speed is given by running the camera slowly giving less frames per second.

Simultaneously things are moving apace at Plymouth. The engine chosen for the run to Bristol (and which unofficially is to make a showing against *City of Truro*'s exploits of sixty years back) is 1950 built double chimneyed No 7029 *Clun Castle*, sent down from Old Oak Common in plenty of time for preparation. It is now up to chief running inspector Harold Cooke of the Newton Abbot and Plymouth Divisions. Hancock

TV star. The 9 May high speed run from Paddington to Plymouth and back attracted the attention of BBC TV and the Railway Roundabout team who filmed the last leg from Bristol to London. To obtain details from the footplate and shots of 5054's motion in action a special filming sequence took place at Honeybourne during the week (the special was on a Saturday). These two pictures show Earl of Ducie *with the producer and his assistant plus the locomotive inspector at the station and the film crew on board a flat truck attached to Collett 0-6-0 No 2222. The 0-6-0 ran parallel to the Castle on the four track section enabling the camera to get a sideways view of the engine running.*

and Andress are not going to have all the glory. Cooke's dictum has always been a Great Western one. Good maintenance and servicing are the secrets of good running. No 7029 is thoroughly cleaned and Cooke spends the whole day preparing her personally, paying special attention to lubrication and, as he says afterwards, 'using every trick of the trade'. It proves to be time well spent.

On the day excitement is extreme; this is to be the very last time – ever – that Great Western 4-6-0s will be able to make a high speed run from Paddington to Plymouth and back. The fact that it is happening at all in 1964 is almost unbelievable. So 9 May goes down into history. The august Cecil J. Allen makes the point strongly: 'On a day like this it would be almost like brawling in church to mention the word 'diesel.'' The weekly notice contains special instructions; the 'Great Western' is to be signalled 4-1-4 – 'must run strictly to time'. Even the 08.30 Royal Duchy is to be held at Newton Abbot for the special to get ahead.

The train is made up of seven second opens, 243 tons tare (twice the weight of *City of Truro*'s train) and the crew is three – driver and two firemen. Bill Andress is travelling with them to Plymouth then back to Bristol, Jack Hancock Bristol to Paddington. Hancock has rated the locomotive as follows; 5054, 4079, 7029, 7023, 7008, 7032, 7022, 7025.

Historic Castle No 4079 Pendennis Castle *returning to the turntable in Old Oak Common shed (part of which has already been demolished), her tender piled high with best Ogilvie coal which is later to cause problems. The date is 9 May 1964 and* Pendennis Castle *will shortly be taking the very last high speed steam hauled train out of Paddington en route to Plymouth. Sadly the engine's fire bars melted near Lavington and No 4079 became a failure.*

So today No 4079 *Pendennis Castle* is at the head end and looking in mint condition, her paintwork shining and the brasswork polished like gold. The driver is aptly named Perfect. His view of No 4079 is that 'it's a rough old thing for riding but still a very good engine'. Dead on time with every whistle and diesel horn sounding the 'Great Western' leaves Paddington in high hopes of getting down to Plymouth in three and a half hours.

The 34½ minute timing to pass Reading is not very demanding and is bettered by a minute without anything more than 77mph on the almost level road. Up the twisting Kennet valley, against the collar, speed does not exceed 75, and the final climb from Bedwyn to the hilltops of Savernake Forest takes its toll from 72 to 60. But the next eighteen miles, on generally falling grades are Castle racing grounds, and No 4079 takes full advantage, reaching 96mph at Lavington. Now nemesis strikes.

A watchful traffic inspector riding in the van spots red-hot pieces of metal strewing the track to the rear. *Pendennis Castle* has melted her firebars and the grate and fire are dropping into the ashpan! It is a crawl to Westbury where No 4079 is taken off. A bitter blow. Planning has not allowed for a Westbury standby and the only engine available is No 6999 *Capel Dewi Hall* so the four footplate occupants now transfer themselves. The will is still there and the modified Hall is fortunately in good order; from 65 at Blatchbridge Junction they are over Brewham summit at 54 rising to 72 at Bruton and after slacking to 60 through Castle Cary are up to 74–82 at Charlton Mackrell. Taunton 47.20 miles is reached start to stop in forty three minutes eleven seconds. Without question a wonderful achievement. No 7025 *Sudeley Castle* comes on and makes a spirited run to Plymouth 82.80 miles in 97.85 minutes – three quarters of a minute over schedule thanks to two checks.

There are three hours at Plymouth buoyed up by a beautiful afternoon and a launch trip from Sutton Harbour across the bay and up the River Tamar to the two great bridges. By now a stiff breeze is beginning to blow up which could perhaps affect the train running on the way to Bristol.

Just after 16.00 No 7029 backs down and is coupled on; like *Pendennis Castle* she is spotless. The 'Great Western' is due out at 16.30 and driver Roach is ready to go. Bill Andress looks down the platform for the flag and to the minute the green comes with a flourish. *Clun Castle* barks her approval and accelerates firmly up the stiff grade to Mutley Tunnel before racing down to the foot of Hemerdon bank at 55mph. Speed falls away as they attack the almost unbroken 1 in 41–42 for the next two and a half miles, the sound of the exhaust slamming back from the trees bordering the line. Roach has the lever at 20 per cent at the bottom of the hill but by half way up he has slowly moved it to 45 per cent maintaining this to the summit. The exhaust beats are like gun shots and the white feathers from the gleaming safety valve cover show that the steaming is superb. Cecil J. Allen averages the climb at 32.7mph. They pass Newton Abbot 3¾ minutes early and Exeter to time. There is some bad language on the footplate, as control has allowed a parcels train to

---

Superiority

The GWR had many admirers who preached its virtues and seemed convinced of its superiority in almost everything. But nobody perhaps did more to enhance its Olympian character than the indefatigable W. G. Chapman, whose Paddington-published books for Boys of All Ages ran through numerous editions and earned the railway a small fortune while extolling its virtues.

Even the title *The King of Railway Locomotives* deftly implied GW supremacy in readers' minds, as perhaps did *The Royal Road*. But Chapman is at his most persuasive in the final paragraphs of the bestselling *The 10.30 Limited*. As the train approaches Penzance, he rounds off the dissertation that with only a break for 'excellent though low priced luncheons' has continued since Paddington:

'From the knowledge you have gained, you will, I think, be able to realise what a wonderful thing a modern railway is, and particularly (note this, please) what a wonderful railway the Great Western is. If I have enabled you to realise that, I have not altogether failed in my undertaking.

'You will now be able to appreciate why so many thousands of travellers "Go Great Western" when on business or pleasure bent – They "Go Great Western" because the going's good.'

get in front of the special in spite of the 4-1-4 instructions and there has been a slack at Hackney for signals – down to 15mph. It is not until Exminster that this offender is passed in the loop.

Once past Cowley Bridge Junction the fireworks begin again and to the passengers riding in the second coach it is the experience of a lifetime. The acceleration is so great that the back of the seat gives a distinct push! Speed rises rapidly and the howling exhaust from the engine's chimney stings the eardrums. Roach has to ease No 7029 from 75 on the 1 in 200 between Hele & Bradninch and Cullompton for the 65mph restriction on the curves, which they take at 62.

As the train nears the summit at Whiteball the sensation is almost overpowering. The dining car attendants are serving tea but even the gourmands are finding it difficult to continue eating. Every seat is occupied with stop-watches, calculators and speed tables on every hand as the scenery flashes by. Just before entering the portal the shadow of the engine cast by the western sun shows two plumes of steam still maintained after twenty three long miles of climbing culminating in two miles at 1 in 115. The drop in speed is no more than from 75 to 67mph and they go over the summit with the lever at 25 per cent. As *Clun Castle* roars in to the tunnel the light dims and the thunderous pandemonium of sounds makes it seem that this simply cannot last.

In the three miles before Wellington (where the chief engineer has a limit of 80mph) Roach brings the cut off slowly back to 18 per cent and No 7029 is doing 90 quickening to 94mph before the slack. The easy five miles to Norton Fitzwarren allows another tremendous acceleration with a maximum of 96 – some recorders make it 97mph and O. S. Nock is in his element: 'The speed at the summit would have made a three figure descent easily possible.'

There is another slack, to 35mph at Cogload Junction to cross over to the Bristol line but with the cut off at 18 per cent they tear down towards Bristol, 78mph at Bridgwater, 82 at Dunball, 86 at Highbridge, 88 at Brent Knoll then 90 through to Yatton where they touch 91. There is a slow approach into Temple Meads arriving 9¾ minutes early on a schedule of 72 minutes from Exeter. Cecil J. Allen sums it up: 'The entire run of 127.4 miles from Plymouth has taken 133 minutes 9 second or 128 minutes net – a clear gain of 15 minutes on the booked time – a triumph for both engine and crew.' He adds: 'it would be interesting to know if ever a faster time has been made from Exeter to Bristol.' Certainly *Clun Castle* is now a record breaker.

At Bristol there are scenes of tremendous excitement. People swarm all round the engine to offer congratulations to the crew and are met with broad grins. Roach tells the locomotive inspector that he would like to go on to London. He is loud in his praise of No 7029 and one of the two firemen remarks that he has had a job to hold her back. What a day it has been, much of it due to Harold Cooke's care in preparation, a fact too easily forgotten in the triumph.

Whilst all this is happening Jack Hancock's team gets down to the

Taking City of Truro *down a peg. No 7029* Clun Castle *at Langford's Bridge near Aller Junction on 9 May 1964. A permanent way slack before Wellington prevented any real high speed running but the climb up to Whiteball and the descent were to remain in the minds of the passengers for well over two decades.*

Opposite HQ *locomotive inspector Jack Hancock's log of the last leg of the high speed run – Bristol to Paddington with No 5054* Earl of Ducie *on Saturday 9 May 1964. Note that two firemen were used.*

The last leg of the high speed run was into the hours of poor light, well into dusk and darkness hence a lack of available pictures. No 5054 Earl of Ducie, *the engine specially selected for this section and the possibility of the 100mph achievement was moved to Worcester for trials in April 1964; it is seen here leaving Shrub Hill station during July 1964. Apart from the maroon Mark I coach the scene is almost one hundred per cent Great Western, the Castle with its Hawksworth tender, the signals truly GWR semaphores and the chaired track.*

final oiling up and checking over No 5054 which is sitting over a pit outside Bath Road diesel depot. News that *Clun Castle* is doing well has filtered through and spirits are high. Driver Higby has his name on a small plaque on the cabside just below the window – a personal decoration still actively encouraged but soon to be discontinued. He is adamant that he can get the 'ton' out of 5054. On an adjacent pit is the standby engine No 7032 *Denbigh Castle* a double chimneyed engine from Old Oak Common shed. Its crew are hoping against hope that they might get the job but even if the engine gets changed it is Higby and his two firemen who are rostered. Jack Hancock, too, is in high spirits. *Earl of Ducie* has been *his* choice and he is looking forward to seeing just how hard it can run. At 18.30 they move off to be ready, in good time, for the away at 18.53.

The scene at Temple Meads is charged with excitement and the crowded platform is reminiscent of the days of the GWR/LNER trials. *Earl of Ducie* leaves no doubt of its Swindon origin as the sharp exhausts echo over and beyond Brunel's great roof as the special heads out towards Dr Day's Bridge Junction where there is a 15mph speed restriction. It is two miles at 1 in 75 up from Stapleton Road to Horfield, on which speed only falls from 45 to 37mph, and then the eleven miles of 1 in 300 from Stoke Gifford East to Badminton. Jack Hancock's log shows that the Bristol crew are unable to sustain full boiler pressure (it

DRIVER **F. HIGBY**   FIREMAN **R. GITSHAM** **C. RICHARDS** OF BRISTOL - BATH Rᵈ.

Report on the performance of engine **5054** on **SATURDAY, 9ᵗʰ MAY, 1964.**
working the **6/53 p.m. SPL** from **BRISTOL T. MEADS** to **PADDINGTON.**

M.CH.	Mins. Secs.	Stations	Speed	Position of Reg.	% cut off	Water in boiler	Steam pressure.	No. of Galls. of water consumed.
00.00	00.00	Bristol T.M.	00	CLOSED	F. GEAR	FULL	225	
1.50	4.05	Stap. Rd.	40	1/2	40	FULL	220	
2.42	5.25	Ashley H.	36	3/4	40	FULL	220	
—	7.05	Horfield	36	3/4	42	FULL	225	
4.64	8.32	Filton Jcn.	44	1/4	30	7/8	210	
7.63	12.02	Winterbrne	58	3/4	35	7/8	220	
10.40	14.45	Westerleigh	61	3/4	35	7/8	215	
13.05	17.10	C. Sodbury	64	3/4	35	7/8	225	500
17.50	21.02	Badminton	64	3/4	35	7/8	205	
23.31	25.25	Hullavington	86	3/4	30	7/8	210	
27.70	28.25	L. Somerford	90	FULL	30	7/8	220	
30.50	30.07	Brinkworth	84	1/2	35	7/8	210	
34.70	32.57	W. Bassett	61	1/8	35	FULL	215	
40.36	37.45	Swindon	78	3/4	25	7/8	220	
46.14	41.50	Shrivenham	82	FULL	30	7/8	220	
51.17	45.22	Uffington	86	3/4	32	7/8	215	
53.74	47.06	Challow	84	2/3	25	7/8	210	
57.26	49.30	Wantage Rd.	86	2/3	25	7/8	215	
61.18	52.00	Steventon	84	2/3	30	7/8	210	
64.50	54.30	Didcot	82	3/4	30	~~7/8~~	210	
69.23	57.43	Cholsey	80	FULL	30	FULL	220	
73.00	60.25	Goring	78	3/4	30	FULL	225	2000
76.17	62.50	Pangbourne	78	FULL	30	7/8	220	
79.07	65.00	Tilehurst	80	FULL	30	1/2	220	
81.62	66.45	Reading	76	2/3	25	1/2	220	
86.59	70.43	Twyford	72	1/3	25	2/3	220	
93.41	75.40	Maid'head	82	1/2	25	1/2	225	
99.24	79.50	Slough	80	3/4	30	2/3	210	
104.42	83.35	W. Drayton	80	FULL	30	7/8	215	
108.54	86.26	Southall	82	FULL	30	7/8	225	
112.04	88.47	E. Broadway	80	FULL	30	2/3	200	
114.38	90.32	O.O.C. West	82	FULL	30	2/3	190	
116.40	92.10	Westbne Pk.	34	1/8	45	1/3	200	
117.60	95.18	Paddington	00	CLOSED	45	1/3	200	1000

State of Weather **FINE - BUT HEAVY SIDE WIND**   Total **3500**
Class of coal **OGILVIE - 1A**
Condition of engine **VERY GOOD**
Load **7/250 TONS**

Average speed
Swindon to Padd
80.59 M.P.H.

J. F. Hancock

BOILER WASHED - 7/5/64
TUBES CLEANED - 7/5/64
AVERAGE SPEED - 74.1343. M.P.H.

drops to 205lb) on this hard effort, and speed gradually falls off from 70 to 66 on the bank. Sadly this kills any hope of reaching the magic 100 on the downhill miles to Little Somerford, and No 5054 can only make 94mph just those few seconds too long. By now the wind has got up, so maybe this and the loss of pressure requires a slightly longer cut-off than some might think desirable. Just a thin layer of icing has come off the top of an excellent cake. There is disappointment but to most *Clun Castle*'s epic run still rings through the ears. The running from Swindon onwards constantly in the high eighties, and touching 90 at Challow, is reminiscent of the Cheltenham Flyer or, to those who are younger, the betters runs of the Bristolian. Paddington comes 4½ minutes early; it has been an epic day. One never, never, to be repeated.

And what of the engines? *Pendennis Castle* and *Clun Castle* were saved from the scrapman by dedicated preservationists and lived to run into the 1990s; they hauled the last through expresses into Birmingham's old Snow Hill station and on to Chester and Birkenhead on 4 and 5 March 1967 making yet another entry into the GWR history book. *Clun Castle* took HRH The Prince of Wales on her footplate out of the new (and undreamed of in 1967) Snow Hill station on 14 September 1988, *Pendennis Castle* was unfortunately sold out of the UK to Australia where she is cared for in the far north-west. Perhaps both were rescued as a result of the 1964 run. *Clun Castle* most certainly was, but No 4079 also had the glory of the 1925 Exchange Trials behind her, making her departure 'Down Under' an even sadder loss to the 'Old Country'. *Earl of Ducie* was cut up at Swindon in November 1964, a sad reflection that even to lovers of steam failure sometimes results in death.

Opposite A sad weekend (1) Birmingham's Snow Hill station, once one of the Great Western's showpieces closed to through traffic on 5 March 1967 trains being re-routed via the old Midland Railway curve south of Bordesley into the rebuilt New Street station and northwards over ex LMS metals. To mark the occasion two castles then in preservation Nos 4079 Pendennis Castle *and 7029* Clun Castle *were chalked up for special trains on Saturday 4 March; these ran from Paddington to Chester and back with steam from Banbury northwards, ironically over sections of the route in London Midland Region hands.* Clun Castle *(with the lettering wrongly applied to its tender but at the time of preservation at the request of British Rail as steam was not welcome in normal service and a BR emblem was considered to be misleading) waits at Chester for the return run with an admiring but sad crowd in attendance – not a policeman in sight.*

A sad weekend (2) On the very last day of all the SLS (Midland Area) ran two through trains from Snow Hill to Birkenhead using No 7029 Clun Castle *and a specially prepared Class 5 No 44680 as far as Chester. The Class 5 worked the second train northwards and the first train on its return journey leaving* Clun Castle *to head the very last train of all from Birkenhead to Birmingham. The Snow Hill ticket collector was actually in tears as the last passengers came up those well remembered steps. This dramatic photograph shows the train climbing Gresford bank on the way home.*

Great Western Cross Country

Perhaps the Great Western looked first to Paddington much as the French railway systems looked to Paris but there the similarity ended – just try working out a cross country railway journey in France even before the days of 'rationalisation'. In many ways one could say that the GWR was a cross country railway balanced neatly against a main line west, the Black Country of the Midlands and the coal mines of South Wales. Certainly the stonework of its stations, its cleanliness, its bustling market town stations, the accents of its staff lent credence to this state of affairs; Devon, Somerset, Gloucester and Worcester burrs, the lilts of South and Mid Wales allying themselves with the clipped Cockney of the metropolis or the almost incomprehensible patois of Birmingham and Wolverhampton.

The branch from Kingham to Kings Sutton saw one through train pre-war, the Newcastle–Swansea, Ports to Ports Express. All other trains were locals some of which terminated at Chipping Norton. 2-6-2T No 4101 has run round its stock, propelled into the tunnel and is drawing forward into the down platform to form the 4.53pm to Kingham on 2 July 1962.

If you went cross country Great Western, and in those car-few days up to the mid 1950s many did, then there were three principal ways of doing so, none of them, except perhaps for the Birmingham-Bristol route, particularly fast. But whichever way was expedient, the train seemed to traverse stone walled countryside much of which turned orange with the lowering rays of the sun, apple blossom in spring and apple strewn orchards in autumn. One of the choices available was the joy of riding the expresses (or the locals) over the Old Worse and Worse from Kingham to Hereford via Worcester, the North to West line from Shrewsbury to Hereford and Bristol or the newer 1907 link from Birmingham via Stratford upon Avon, that wonderfully sounding country junction at Honeybourne, Cheltenham (Malvern Road) and Gloucester to the South West. If it was a South Wales train, once over the Severn at Gloucester the tracks ran along the north bank of the estuary, the Severn bridge to the left, before passing through Lydney junction for almost endless lines in the Forest of Dean. The Wye was crossed at Chepstow then along the river's edge once again to Portskewett before sweeping right at Severn Tunnel Junction for Newport.

Next came travel in through coaches over foreign and

(usually) friendly competitors' systems often in single vehicles but sometimes in whole trains. Last there were the happy times of market town cross country links, frequently over single lines – the Great Western had many of these – some long, some short, some originally built by the company and some absorbed into it by the great amalgamation of 1923.

There was a second cross country route from Birmingham's Snow Hill station to South Wales, slower than the journey via the North Warwick and Cheltenham/ Gloucester line but in its own way even more fascinating. This ran north out of the bay platforms through Hockley but swinging westwards at Handsworth Junction to Smethwick Junction which was the first stop of the erstwhile Birmingham and South Wales Express. Once there was a through coach which made a connection with the LNWR linking Kidderminster with Euston but that has long been gone; though when the LMR took over the GWR route north of Banbury it closed Snow Hill in 1972 and the link became 'permanent', trains to Kidderminster, Worcester and Hereford running out of New Street. Today, at huge expense, the old route including a new Snow Hill is being reinstated.

Then came Stourbridge Junction with its branch to Stourbridge Town, one of the last haunts of the GWR steam railcars, and Kidderminster, change for the Severn Valley line to Shrewsbury via Bridgnorth or the connection to the North to West route via Tenbury Wells. At the latter was an end on connection with the LNWR/ GWR joint single line limb from Woofferton; trains never ran through as the GWR kept to its own with services terminating at Tenbury. The onward journey, when they bothered to make a connection, was in an auto train pushed or pulled by an 0-4-2 tank. Thus, if the passenger got out at Kidderminster, there were cross country lines, slow but sure, to the Welsh Marches or to Shrewsbury. On then to Droitwich (Spa), Worcester (Foregate Street), Malvern, change for the MR/LMS branch to Tewkesbury and Ashchurch behind a Midland 0-4-4 tank, and Ledbury (change for Gloucester) to Hereford. From here the train joined the North to West route running over Llanvihangel bank to Abergavenny, Pontypool Road with its leads into the Welsh Valleys, Newport and Cardiff. Alighting at Hereford one could go cross country again to Ross on Wye continuing in the train to Gloucester or changing for Monmouth. Over the branch at Lydbrook there was until 1929 an opportunity to journey on to the Forest of Dean network or proceed to Monmouth (Troy) then Pontypool Road or change for stations to Chepstow where the GWR crossed the Wye on a tubular bridge.

There were yet other possibilities if one went over the Severn Valley line and changed at Buildwas; south westwards a single line ran through Much Wenlock to Craven Arms on the North to West line whilst north the tracks went to Wellington; here there was a change for Cheshire via the Nantwich line where trains continued

A Cardiff–Brighton train hauled by a 43XX 2-6-0 approaches the level crossing at Llanwern in the early 1930's. The stock appears to be a 5 coach set with roof boards plus two strengthening vehicles next to the engine. Note the up line signal on the down side of the line for ease of sighting on right hand drive locos. The scene is completely different today, the line is quadrupled and the giant Spencer Steel Works occupies the land to the left.

One of the independent cross country railways which came into the Great Western fold was the Midland and South Western Junction railway. Swindon Town station was the headquarters of the line and MSWJ 4-4-0, GWR No 1122, is seen here with a Cheltenham (Lansdown) – Southampton (Terminus) train in 1930. The MSWJ head office is the building in the left background.

Talyllyn was the meeting point of the Brecon & Merthyr Railway from Dowlais and Newport (Mon) and the Cambrian Mid Wales line from Moat Lane Junction. (The Midland which joined the Cambrian at Three Cocks Junction also had running powers over the Cambrian, B&M and Neath & Brecon through to Ynisgeinon Junction, although from 1931 trains ran only to Brecon). In early BR days 2251 class 0-6-0 No 2280 enters the station with a Brecon–Newport train. On the right an ex Cambrian 0-6-0 awaits the tablet for the single line with a Moat Lane–Brecon train.

The GWR line from Ruabon through Llangollen and Bala Junction made an end-on junction with the Cambrian at Dolgelley giving access to Barmouth and the Cambrian coast. A view from the footplate of a 'Manor' class 4-6-0 on a Talyllyn Railway Special about to cross the River Dee between Llandrillo and Llandderfel.

on by means of running rights over the LNWR/LMS metals right to the heart of the enemy Holy of Holies, Crewe. This and other infiltrations were part of the great expansion days. They gave passengers through journeys often market town to market town with vital links into rural areas. Others facilitated travel to the ever more popular holiday resorts. For example the Great Western made an end on junction with the Cambrian at Dolgelley via a series of small industrial and market towns, Ruabon, Llangollen, Corwen and Bala Junction whilst serving the holidaymakers with through trains to the Cambrian coast at the same time.

Then there were the absorbed routes. The Cambrian's Mid Wales line ran into remote Moat Lane Junction on that company's main line to Aberystwyth or Pwllheli via Machynlleth and desolate Dovey Junction. It ran up from Brecon and the junction at Talyllyn (for Merthyr) and Three Cocks (for the MR line, latterly Western

Tylwych station on the Mid-Wales line from Moat Lane Junction to Brecon. A down train is about to enter the station hauled by a Cambrian 0-6-0. The signal box is switched out and all trains use the up platform.

Region to Hereford via Hay on Wye). En route passengers paused at Rhayader (where Birmingham Corporation had invested in giant artificial lakes under Joseph Chamberlain's benign but autocratic rule) and prior to that Builth Road where their train ran under the North Western's Central Wales line from Craven Arms to Swansea. Also brought into the Great Western's fold was the old, Midland & South Western Junction Railway, linking the GW's own Cheltenham to Kingham cross country railway at Andoversford with Swindon (Town) via the Cotswold hills and Cirencester before moving on to the South Western and Andover with that short but surely profitable branch from Ludgershall to the Army's Tidworth.

In Berkshire, Wiltshire and Somerset there were countless more: the Didcot, Newbury & Southampton (pure GWR to Winchester), Westbury to the LSWR/SR at Salisbury and the loop south of the main line from Castle Cary back to Langport via Yeovil. This last was frequently well used by passengers from the South West going to Weymouth and the Channel Islands. Indeed all the cross country links carried people on long as well as local journeys, some long journeys perhaps involving half a dozen changes from one stopping service to another.

Carmarthen to Aberystwyth, for example provided a long slow service for people going from all manner of places in South Wales to dozens of destinations (some served by its own two branch lines) up the Cambrian Coast. Only on summer Saturdays was there a through 'express' – probably because the GW faced no competition for the traffic. Enterprise was greater where traffic might be generated at another railway's expense. Hence the Ports to Ports Express, Newcastle-Swansea, which used GWR or LNER coaches on alternate days though crews were changed at Banbury; as at other places where the trains worked through to other railways, the strings on the coaches had to be pulled, as the GWR used a higher brake vacuum pressure than other lines and it is well known that at one time there was actually a through coach from Aberdeen to Penzance, a long slow jaunt including a spell attached to an all stations stopper.

The cross country routes were especially interesting in their motive power. For instance, until bridge strengthening in the late 1920s and early 1930s on that part of the old Midland line to Bristol they shared, the expresses on the North Warwickshire line from Birmingham via Stratford upon Avon and Cheltenham still relied on the old 4-4-0 Counties. After bridge strengthening Saints

Buildwas Junction change here for Severn Valley Lines proclaims the station sign. On 12 March 1960 the guard of the Much Wenlock to Wellington train hauled by 2-6-2T No 4120 waits to confirm there are no connecting passengers from railcar W29 on a southbound Severn Valley service between Shrewsbury and Hartlebury. The passenger service to Much Wenlock ceased on 23 July 1962 and the through Severn Valley services on 9 September 1963. The site is now part of the Buildwas power station complex.

began to appear, though they were soon replaced by Castles which ran trains like the Cornishman right up to the demise of steam. The North Warwick route was used for a successful experiment with new streamlined diesel railcars (with buffet facilities at a supplementary fare) on the Cardiff services from 1934. Tyseley shed staff scratched their heads over this new form of power. There were wags who said that the railcars should be painted *blue* and cream like the Corporation buses. The Saints lasted longer on the North to West route – indeed to the end of their time, just into nationalisation. In their later years even Kings used this route via Hereford, hauling some of the heaviest trains on the system. Generally cross country power was smaller but not necessarily old. The Barnum 2-4-0s ran into Crewe, the small wheeled 44XX 2-6-2 tanks hurried their two coaches from Wellington to Craven Arms, Churchward's Moguls ran day to day from Carmarthen to Aberystwyth and rolled down the Didcot, Newbury & Southampton as well as from Ruabon to Barmouth (on summer Saturdays sometimes from Birmingham to Barmouth and Pwllheli). Dean Goods and Cambrian 0-6-0s plodded over the Mid Wales line and Collett 0-6-0s, 2-6-2 tanks, panniers, 48XX or 14XX 0-4-2 tanks over much of the rest. The old 4-4-0s saw out their last days on many of these services, the Birmingham and South Wales trains were hauled regularly by Bulldogs well into the 1930s when the Halls became prolific, they also made day to day appearances on the Ruabon-Dolgelley-Barmouth road. One veteran on the Birmingham-Worcester-Hereford run, No 3353, was even renamed *Pershore Plum* to show respect for the Worcestershire fruit traffic. And the *very* last of the GWR 4-4-0 classes (albeit hybrid rebuilds) the Dukedogs whirled their coupling rods outside their frames as they sped their way uphill and down dale over the Cotswold hills from Kingham through Stow on the Wold and Bourton on the Water to Cheltenham's Malvern Road and the terminus at St James, again carrying a mixture of local passengers and some ending many hours of slow travel.

For those with friendly relations at Tyseley shed there was one last cross country thrill right up into the 1960s: the Swindon parcels, leaving Snow Hill at 21.45 always behind a well maintained Hall as this was a smartly timed working, the last on the North Warwick which had already lost its through expresses. A late summer footplate ride was something to be savoured. As the evening drew on the train ran through leafy Warwickshire with a stop at Stratford, then the Cotswold country of Broadway and Winchcombe with its castle at Sudeley, Cheltenham, round the curve avoiding Gloucester Great Western and down again through the stone walled country of Stonehouse and Stroud, Sapperton and Brimscombe to Kemble and then Brunel's masterpiece of siting the home of God's Wonderful Railway, Swindon. What memories of former cross country triumphs and how remote London seemed!

6
THE SEA WALL

NO few miles of track better epitomised the Great Western as the holiday railway than the Sea Wall at Dawlish and Teignmouth. Hundreds of thousands of people caught their first ever glimpse of the waves here, and many more discovered a fascination in the railway itself as they walked between it and the sea along the path the local authority of the time cleverly insisted be provided for ever as the price for allowing the trains through. Famous named expresses, generations of travellers from the New World disembarking at Plymouth, the seasonal produce of the South West and the harvest of its fishing ports, queues of summer long-distance expresses and excursions and always heavy local traffic competed for the passage along what until recent times was the chief bottleneck all the way from Paddington to Penzance. As we show here, the kaleidoscope of trains popping in and out of the five short tunnels and running under the crumbling red sandstone cliffs along the ledge built by Brunel only feet above the high-water line has been uniquely well recorded, and at sometime or other a large proportion of the travelling population have looked forward to the salt-water part of the journey, down the Exe estuary to Dawlish Warren, along the sea to Teignmouth and then up the Teign estuary.

The elements have obviously played a major role in the operation of these expensive miles. For once there is actual proof that the railway ran more reliably in GWR days than before and after! Great difficulties were experienced with the Sea Wall in its early South Devon Railway ownership, and all the severest problems since happened from 1974 on. That is not to say that disruptions were not also fairly routine in the seventy one years of GWR ownership. Strong easterly gales with spring tides have always resulted in the ballast being washed at least off parts of the down track, and once (immediately after World War II) the North Mail had only passed seconds before a major cliff fall near Teignmouth. Decade after decade the cliffs have been eroding and after wet winters (especially if sharp frosts have quickly followed heavy rain) new falls threatening if not actually burying the up line. Never for more than a few years at a time since opening in 1846 has there not been a gang tipping the sandstone over the wall into the sea. But in GWR days there were not the total closures for a week or more that happened several times in the first three decades and seem to be happening with alarming regularity in the second part of our century. The Great Western's problem was not so much how to keep the route open but how to get the expresses through when for long periods the freights, perishables and local passengers could comfortably have absorbed capacity.

Go Great Western
The GWR holiday-lands are the pick of Britain, matchless for scenery, health and holiday pleasure.

The trains are superb – finely equipped and first for speed and punctuality.

The GWR is foremost in enterprising improvements – the 'progressive line'. Every year some new facility for patrons' benefit.

The holiday-maker, the health-seeker, the business-maker, cannot do better than go Great Western. – Just one version of the company's expression of self confidence as it became truly great just before World War I.

The Sea Wall over sixty years.
(i) In broad gauge days Iron Duke
rebuild Timour *heads the 8.30 am*
departure from Teignmouth on 7
May (the Rev. Malan did not quote
the year for this photograph). The
line from Teignmouth to Parsons
Tunnel was doubled in 1884 and
the short tunnel which was just
behind the train was opened out at
the same time.

(ii) A winter scene on the sea wall.
2-6-2T No 4109 of Newton Abbot
(83A) leaves Teignmouth with the
10.45 am local from Newton Abbot
to Exeter on 23 February 1951.

For Radiant Health

Ours is such a small country that one might suppose every part would be subject to the same conditions. But it is not so. The long stretch of seaboard from Weymouth in Dorset to Pwllheli in Carnarvonshire is directly open to the influence of the Atlantic Ocean . . . This is the 'Ocean Coast', where the ozone-laden Atlantic breezes reach Britain across four thousand miles of open sea, bringing the purest, healthiest air it is possible to enjoy. The secret of radiant health enjoyed by dwellers on the Ocean Coast is that they reap all the benefits of an Ocean climate. – From an advertisement for a booklet *The Ocean Coast* printed on the page opposite the folding map in a 1920s timetable. The cynical might have wondered if the timetable itself was subject to the same stretch of the imagination.

To go back to the beginning, there is no doubt of the wisdom of Brunel's choice of route; inland alternatives would have meant both immense engineering works and missing important sources of traffic. Originally Falmouth the packet port was seen as the prize of the west, and fierce arguments took place about the merit of a Tory-based broad-gauge route through Newton Abbot and Plymouth and a Whig-backed narrow-gauge 'Central' line down the peninsula's backbone. Except that it missed Torquay by a few miles, the broad gauge route served an amazing percentage of the West Country's population and trade as it wound its way down to Penzance. Where Brunel was wrong, of course, was in placing so much faith in the success of the atmospheric system that the climbs up the Dartmoor foothills out of Newton Abbot and Plympton and on either side of Totnes were positively built steeper than they need have been, and by the standards of the day ridiculously steep for the locomotives that in practice had to be used. Ironically, the atmospheric system which was supposed to be so valuable for hill climbing was only ever used on the flat between Exeter and Newton Abbot before its abandonment, but the fact that clean, silent trains travelling at up to sixty miles an hour did come this way for a year or so undoubtedly adds a touch of romance to the Sea Wall's story.

Because of the steepness of the gradients beyond, Newton Abbot became the great divide. Throughout the GWR period and well beyond, most expresses shed their tails at Newton Abbot for the Torbay line and were thus lighter for the struggle ahead. Likewise the great freights of yesteryear (including a nightly non-stop from London) changed their character at Newton Abbot's Hackney marshalling yard. In thinking of the Sea Wall's traffic, one has to remember that it was to the East of the Newton Abbot divide and that at busy times most passenger trains were made up to fifteen more likely than a dozen carriages and that most freights carried the maximum load of 54 wagons. Also remember that trains from both Paddington via Castle Cary and everything down from Bristol for both the Plymouth and Cornwall route and that to Torbay had to use the common Taunton-Newton Abbot section, that many extra local trains ran west from Exeter, and that Dawlish and Teignmouth were by far the most important stations between Taunton and Newton Abbot other than Exeter. Exeter St David's of course saw regular overtaking; Dawlish and Teignmouth were always just through two-platform stations with no facing points, though local trains were often overtaken at Dawlish Warren. Teignmouth, including its docks served by Old Quay signalbox, and Dawlish had active goods yards, the pannier tank out of Newton Abbot having to spend hours daily waiting for opportunities to shunt.

The failure of the atmospheric system left the South Devon Railway with severe financial problems and the doubling of the track (Brunel had advocated single line for the atmospheric) was tackled piecemeal and slowly. It did not reach the Sea Wall before the GWR took over in 1876. By then it was clear that the broad gauge was doomed and there was little incentive to make bridges, viaducts and tunnels wider than they would ultimately need to be for two standard-gauge tracks. Pressure of

Looking west along the sea wall with Dawlish station centre. The down train is hauled by an unidentified 2-4-0. The date may be before the 1914–18 war.

G for Saturdays Excepted

It is amazing how the older reader immediately slips back into GWR parlance when picking up an old timetable, not needing to refer to the note to know that G was always for Saturdays Excepted.

Generally the GWR's timetable was much more user friendly (as we would say today) than *Bradshaw* and its reprints used by the other lines before nationalisation. The layout was particularly clear; reference numbers always referred to pages, not tables, so it was easier to turn to the right page. Nearly all branch lines had their separate tables, so it was easier to understand the anatomy of the system than for instance that of the Southern with its complicated combined tables, and the GWR always provided its handsome folding map with its own lines in red.

continued opposite

traffic did however force the GWR to double between Parson's Tunnel and Teignmouth (where a short tunnel, at the point the railway turns inland was opened up) in 1884. Only in 1905 was the section between Dawlish and Parson's Tunnel finally doubled, completing double track all the way from Paddington to the Royal Albert Bridge at Saltash. Taking advantage of the generous broad-gauge clearances, the five tunnels were slowly widened without interruption to business. Parson's Tunnel signalbox was then closed for some years, to reopen for summer only in the years both before and after World War II (and for preparations for D-day).

Let us now take a walk along the Sea Wall on a summer Saturday. It makes surprisingly little difference if it is the mid-1930s or early 1950s! Of course there will be more Saints and 4-4-0s at the earlier time and the new Counties will have appeared at the latter, but at both periods the Cornish Riviera will be headed by a King and the Torbay Express usually by a Castle. The first thing we notice is the array of lower-quadrant signals, enhancing the beauty of the sparkling scene, making the railway look as though it were designed to show off the cliffs and the sea. Already the walk is alive with pedestrians, some of whom have obviously come especially to enjoy the trains, and among those sitting in deck chairs at Sprey Point (the projecting bit half way along the Sea Wall) and having their backs to the sea there are bound to be one or two with the latest *GWR Engine Book*. A few people bathe from the narrow sandy beach under the wall between Sprey Point and Parson's Tunnel; even in the morning rabbits can be seen scurrying up and down the cliffs.

On the up, there is Teignmouth's advance starter quite a long way round the curve and on the wrong side of the track, followed by Parson's

Tunnel distant and then its home. On the down, there is Parson's Tunnel's single stop signal, combined home and starter, followed by Teignmouth's distant, outer home (near Sprey Point) and home with Old Quay's slotted distant under it just before the route turns inland. Because trains come bunched, even on summer Saturdays there are gaps between them. If the line is clear, Teignmouth pulls off its up advance starter when the train has entered the section between Newton Abbot Hackney and Bishopsteignton. Especially if the train is one that stops at Teignmouth, that gives long notice. Parson's Tunnel asks Dawlish if the line is clear and pulls off on being notified by Teignmouth that the train is passing Bishopsteignton. On the down there is less notice of a train's arrival since Parson's Tunnel only asks Teignmouth if the line is clear when Dawlish is left. On a Saturday Old Quay will be switched out and its distant will drop automatically provided Teignmouth can pull off its down starter.

While it is not unusual to see all signals at danger (or caution) and the track empty even on a summer Saturday, for much of the day in both directions most trains will be checked. It is indeed possible to see four trains, two each way, at a total standstill, and passengers who regularly travel from Exeter to Newton Abbot on busy days look out to see how many trains they can see ahead of them as they round the curve at Dawlish Warren and much of the Sea Wall comes into view. Down trains are relatively rarely stopped by Parson's Tunnel; indeed it is sometimes questioned whether its existence is really worthwhile since, though it helps trains move forward, in most cases that only means waiting longer for the ultimate clearance through Newton Abbot . . . or Exeter in the reverse direction.

Down trains are far more likely to be checked by Teignmouth's distant and only be allowed past the outer home once they have come almost to a standstill and are close enough to the signal to activate the track circuit telling Teignmouth's signalman of their presence. Sometimes a down train is halted at the outer home because the one in front has not left Teignmouth's long down platform; if there are thirteen or more carriages, the tail can be seen at the platform from the far end of the Sea Wall, and those in the know will have watched a porter (alerted by a bell signal from Teignmouth's signalman) come up to check that the tail lamp is in place and notify that it is safe to give train out of section. It is not normal for trains to stop at the inner home, for they cannot be allowed beyond the outer home if a train is still at the platform, but drivers peer anxiously to see if it has cleared (the distant arm dropping slowly underneath it) and they can accelerate into the section ahead.

The timetable is arranged so that up trains from Torbay stopping at Teignmouth and Dawlish generally immediately follow runners from Plymouth to Exeter. If all goes well, they move out of Newton Abbot while Hackney's slotted distant is still at caution, and often arrive at Teignmouth with its distant at caution. Teignmouth's home will be off to allow the locomotive to pull up well beyond the short up platform (an operational nightmare; heaven forbid that someone needs to unload a

continued

Attention to detail was always good, the style consistent including the ampersand '&' sign in station names combining two places such as Bradford Peverell & Stratton Halt (though that usually meant the station was near neither). The great through expresses were beautifully labelled and you could conveniently follow them from table to table, though through services such as from some of the suburban branches into Paddington were not always indicated. (You could sometimes guess from the inclusion of first class.) Mileages were however not shown.

Mind you, it comes as a shock to see how sparse some train services were, how many were indicated X ('Limited accommodation,' usually railcars though sometimes autocars), how long it took to get from Reading to Paddington (generally 45 minutes) and how when more of the then anyway much smaller number of expresses undertook long nonstop runs what gaps there were in the service. In the GWR's final service, the first restaurant car express from Reading to Paddington – in the days when there was ample time to take a full meal on that journey – was not until 2.25pm!

Another surprise is how few trains wandered off their self-contained branches, little effort being made to create demand by linking services. And yet another how slow things were to get started in the mornings. No wheel turned on up trains on many branches (including the Torbay line) before 7am, on many not until after 8. But the fascinating end pages of the timetable spelt out the conditions for Workmen's Tickets for selected early-morning trains as into Paddington: 'Holders of Workmen's tickets travelling to or from stations or by trains other than those for which

continued overleaf

continued

their tickets are available will be liable for payment of the full ordinary fare and the forfeiture of the Workmen's Tickets.'

But then any communication 'between the Passengers and the Servants of the Company in charge of a Train without reasonable and sufficient cause shall be liable for each offence to a penalty not exceeding Five Pounds'!

More friendly were the lists of alternative routes for your return journey and boasts such as 'Radiotelegrams can also be sent from one steamer to another while the ships are at sea'.

With its map, summary services and pages of fascinating appendices the timetable was undoubtedly worth its old sixpence, as the meals at the restaurants at seven stations surely justified their 'popular prices'.

Mobile Art Gallery

The Company have recently made arrangements for fine art engravings to be exhibited in their passenger carriages. The engravings are printed on India paper, mounted on plate paper, and will consist of pictures of the beautiful scenery through which the Great Western line passes, and, for the guidance of travellers, views of the principal hotels on the Company's system.

This new departure will, it is believed, be much appreciated by all lovers of fine art work, and, in order to meet a desire which will no doubt arise, the Company have arranged for copies of these views to be mounted on plate paper ready for framing, and to be offered for sale at the nominal charge of 1s. each. The engraved surface will be approximately eight inches by six inches, and the full size of the pictures will be sixteen inches by twelve inches. A list of the views now ready can be obtained on application to the General Manager's office.

bicycle from the rear guard's van well beyond the platform's other end!) and thus leave not knowing whether the section ahead to Parson's Tunnel is clear. The advance starter is quite hard to sight, and there is generally a holidaying railwayman or enthusiast giving the appropriate wave if it is off. But trains not scheduled to stop at Teignmouth also frequently run through it with the distant against them and have to come gently round the curve onto the Sea Wall watching for the signal. If they are brought to a standstill, the driver might enquire of the holidaying railwayman what is in front of him. All day long banter is exchanged between footplate men and passengers and those on the Sea Wall. Occasionally friends recognise each other and have ample time to talk about matters of mutual interest. Where the railway rounds the curve to come close to the sea for the first time at Dawlish Warren, a religious chap between sandwich boards proclaiming the end of the world is nigh finds a more enthusiastic audience among the passengers of a stopped train than those carrying their buckets and spades to the beach. In these days well before air conditioning, all windows are open and heads popped out of most of them, especially if there is a delay.

After a series of trains that have been checked, it is refreshing to see the signals cleared and very quickly after a King or Castle thunder past with a crowded train at full speed. The timetable of course pretends everything will have a clear path since everything will run punctually, and just occasionally (though it has to be said more likely at the season's beginning and end than on a peak-season Saturday in late July or early August) everything does indeed go like clockwork, the Cornish Riviera running non-stop from Paddington to Plymouth, the Torbay Express to Torquay. Inevitably the greater the number of passengers, the longer the delay. Most people complain they reached their chosen resort very late. 'We sailed all the way to just outside Taunton and seem to have stopped at every signal thereafter,' was an accurate as well as typical comment. Even today one's splendid journey from Paddington is often rudely interrupted at Cogload Junction, near Taunton, because something is running late from Bristol.

Even if the sun did not help you, it was easy to tell the time of day along the Sea Wall by the nature of the traffic. Numerous overnight trains from all kinds of places in the Midlands, North and Scotland (including one-offs for the start of the holidays in industrial towns whose names were hardly known in Southern England) were scheduled to pass along the Sea Wall in the period from around 3am to 9. Then there was meant to be a gap in which an occasional freight might even appear until the first of the down Londons came through in mid morning, trains via Castle Cary and Bristol alternating for much of the rest of the day from about lunch time. The problem was often the late running of the overnights, some of which indeed sometimes did not reach Paignton soon enough to start their return journeys punctually. Both in the early morning and again in the afternoon, trains might arrive far more quickly than they could be handled at Paignton's single down platform, and the queue could stretch back to Newton Abbot and beyond, occasionally onto the Sea Wall itself. Then a Paddington-Penzance express would be held up at every signal from say Dawlish Warren to Newton Abbot by congestion on the branch line. All day long it was usual for trains to be occupying both sides of Newton Abbot's down island platform and the through platformless relief.

The up rush was more concentrated, the majority of passengers wanting to leave Torbay between breakfast and lunch time, though many trains starting in Cornwall did not reach the Sea Wall until afternoon. On busy Saturdays there was no spare capacity on the up line between 9am and 2pm, and once trains were made up to their maximum loads all the railways could do was force passengers into obtaining a regulation ticket and when the popular services were sold out direct them to earlier or later services. That however was after nationalisation, the peak holiday loadings not being carried until 1958.

In GWR days individual seat reservations were available by nearly all trains, and most also ran with restaurant cars. They were the days when you took a full meal or nothing at all, but an abbreviated two-course set lunch was served on Saturdays, making four sittings possible on many services. Seeing tables laid out with the standard cold meat and salad before the next sitting moved in was part of what summer Saturday Sea Wall watching was about. If you were on the Sea Wall on Friday evening

An up express on the sea wall near Sprey Point hauled by class 43XX 2-6-0 No 5327. From the fashions the date would appear to be the late 1920s. The train must be of some importance as all coaches carry roof boards and there is a restaurant car third from rear.

During the summer of 1985 the 150th Anniversary of the Great Western Railway was celebrated in many ways. Among the most spectacular were the double headed specials run between Bristol and Plymouth – the 'Great Western Limited'. On 14 July the return working is seen alongside the famous sea wall at Dawlish behind Castle class No 5051 Drysllwyn Castle *and Hall class No 4930* Hagley Hall, *both locomotives now privately owned and maintained at Didcot and Bridgnorth respectively.*

you would have noted the full length train entirely composed of empty restaurant cars, one to work each of a dozen or more expresses back to Paddington the next day.

Another feature of the Saturday scene was destination boards displaying their blank side. The set used for the Bristolian on Mondays to Fridays went to Paignton on Saturdays with its destination boards turned around, for example. Because time could not be spared for attaching and detaching at Newton Abbot, most services from Penzance and Plymouth and from Kingswear and Paignton were made up to full length. Instead of the Torbay coaches, therefore, the Plymouth trains usually had several without destination boards, and some Torbay services only had the usual three or four coaches displaying destination boards. Likewise trains which normally served Manchester and Liverpool now ran independently to both. Destination boards were however

provided for some services, such as to Kingsbridge, Newquay and Falmouth, that only ran on summer Saturdays.

You could always see where trains were going to; for trains without destination boards had paper labels in their windows. Today's faster speeds along the Sea Wall make it impossible to decipher the paper labels on the doors. Likewise in GWR days you could clearly see into each compartment, while today it is virtually impossible to tell whether an HST is fully loaded or not. It was rare for corner seats not to be occupied on summer Saturdays in GWR days.

Many trains ran at roughly the same time for decades. The end of another summer Saturday was heralded by the arrival of a disreputable string of LNER coaches on a train which had spent the whole day struggling across England from Newcastle. Apart from the famous coach from Aberdeen to Penzance, that was the only through service from the North East, and its return shortly after breakfast characterised Sunday mornings for many regular Sea Wall walkers. Long after the last of the up expresses had gone, the line remained busy with a combination of local trains (three an hour much of the evening to places as far away as Bristol) and empty stock and light engine workings. The empty stocks and light engines invariably followed a local out of Newton Abbot and so crawled through Teignmouth and onto the Sea Wall where again a helpful bystander would call attention to the fact the advance starter was now off. In those days of trust the driver would immediately accelerate though not of course pass the signal without seeing it himself. When it was not, the engineman told of what kind of a day they had had and how far they were going to have to take the empty stock. Sometimes the pressure on sidings was so great that it had to be sent as far away as Severn Tunnel Junction.

Summer Saturdays were not the only time that the Sea Wall was fascinating; in fact it was hard to tire of its attractions wet or fine, summer or winter. Some of its busiest periods were during the Cornish broccoli season when several dozen (sometimes up to fifty) daily specials would have to be fitted in between the regular services. But apart from summer Saturdays, the passenger expresses were notable for their small number. For many years only five day-time trains took the Castle Cary route from Paddington to the West, including the Cornish Riviera at 10.30 which did not serve Torbay and the Torbay Express at noon which involved a change at Exeter if you were bound for Plymouth or Cornwall. Each train was a time-honoured individual institution, a friend whose acquaintance you were pleased to renew. Once the rush of up expresses had passed in mid morning, usually there were long lulls and the next train was as likely to be a freight as a passenger. Mention has already been made of the fact that speed along the Sea Wall was appreciably lower, and whenever there was engineering work or the cliff was crumbling the GWR exercised its standard caution and kept the distant on, meaning that drivers had to check out each stop signal individually. Local passenger trains sometimes ran to considerable length, both in terms of their number of coaches and how far they were travelling. All stations Truro to Exeter was the first train of the day up

The Anatomy of the GWR

For much of its life the GWR was split into the following sixteen districts. This list is taken from the working timetable of 28 September 1936:

1 London and Didcot, London and Banbury, via Bicester and via Oxford.
2 Hammersmith and City Line, Kensington (Addison Road), and Ealing (Broadway) and Liverpool Street via Wood Lane.
3 Reading, Newbury, Chippenham, Westbury and Weymouth and Cheltenham Spa and Andover Junction.
4 Didcot, Bristol, Highbridge, Standish Junction and Severn Tunnel Junction.
5 Highbridge, Castle Cary, Kingswear and Ashburton Junction.
6 Ashburton Junction and Penzance.
7 Swindon, Gloucester, Cardiff and Pyle.
8 Newport and Blaenavon, Brynmawr, Rhymney (Lower), and Talyllyn Junction.
9 Cardiff (Bute Road), Merthyr, Treherbert, Rhymney Bridge, Penarth, Barry, Rhydyfelin, Barry and Bridgend.
10 Pyle and Neyland and Fishguard Harbour.
11 Pontypool Road, Aberdare and Neath Junction.
12 Shrewsbury, Worcester, Hereford, Pontypool Road and Maindee.
13 Aynho Junction, Wolverhampton, Dudley and Stourbridge Junction and Birmingham, Stratford-on-Avon, Cheltenham Spa and Bristol.
14 Wolverhampton, Chester, Birkenhead and Manchester, also Central Wales.
15 Oxford, Worcester and Wolverhampton.
16 West London and West London Extension Joint Railways.

Castle and King. Two early colour photographs taken at Exeter St. Davids station in October 1935. The first shows No 5041 Tiverton Castle (then relatively new having emerged from Swindon works in 7/35) at the head of a down

Plymouth train; neither the locomotive nor stock are particularly clean. In contrast No 6018 King Henry VI (the last of the class to remain in service and subject of a biography in this book) stands in the down main platform with the

Torbay Express with polished paintwork and brass plus well washed coaches. Both engines carry the recently devised GWR roundel on the tender sides.

Renamed Star. No 4021 British Monarch *(named* King Edward *until the commissioning of No 6001* King Edward VII *in 1927) pauses at Oxford with an up local in April 1939. The engine is still attached to one of the 3500 gallon tenders originally allocated to the class and although this carries the more modern GWR roundel it is still fully lined out – an unusual combination.*

South Wales freight. Modified Hall class 4-6-0 No 6962 Soughton Hall *passes Hullavington station with a partly fitted freight bound for the Seven Tunnel and beyond sometime in the summer of 1957. The engine is spotlessly clean and has only just emerged from a heavy overhaul at Swindon works. It was then allocated to Old Oak Common (81A), from where it was withdrawn in January 1963.*

From New York

'The territory served by the GWR is the richest in sights and scenes typically British,' stated a booklet (sub-titled The Quickest Route New York to London via Plymouth) given to visitors to the GWR stand at the centenary exhibition and pageant of the Baltimore & Ohio Railroad in September and October 1927.

'The Great Western Railway of England as originally conceived was intended as one of the links in a chain of communication between England and America. Brunel, its engineer, not only laid out a line between Bristol and London intended to be suitable for higher speeds than previously considered safe or economic, but he also designed the first steamship for the transatlantic service . . . By its extension, in later years to Plymouth, the great port of call for the most famous Atlantic liners, the GWR retains its original importance as the shortest link between the commercial capitals of America and England.'

Opposite *Early days at Exeter shed. A photograph taken round the turn of the century – probably just into Edwardian days. Scattered about the shed yard are Dean engines including 4-2-2s, 4-4-0s, 0-6-0s an 0-6-0 saddle tank under repair and some early Churchward double framed 4-4-0s most likely Cities and Bulldogs. Shunting cattle trucks in the centre of the photograph is another 0-6-0 saddle tank whilst the roof of an early coach with a clear view of its oil lamps appears bottom centre. The water crane is typical GWR as are the gas lamps and wooden armed signals, some fitted with discs. The tracks running into the goods shed appear to be baulk roads. This was still the period of polished brass domes, spectacle plates and safety valve covers. The Bulldog leading the Dean single to the left of the picture carries an oval brass numberplate on its cabside.*

from the Royal Duchy, for example, and those taking an early morning stroll in summer might see the day's first up passenger, the 6.30am Newton Abbot all stations to Bristol Temple Meads, used not only by people going to work but early birds for London (who disloyally walked or took the bus or tram from GWR St David's to Southern's Central at Exeter for the train that arrived much sooner at Waterloo than anything from the West did at Paddington) and those for the Midlands and North who transferred at Bristol to the LMS's 10.30am Bristol-Newcastle. Except at weekends, only one train ran from the GWR to the LMS Midland Division, the Devonian from Paignton to Bradford, which followed the morning Plymouth to Manchester and Liverpool express. But a second through service to Birmingham was provided by the Wolverhampton via Stratford upon Avon and the North Warwick line, the train that BR later christened the Cornishman when permission was given to restore chocolate-and-cream livery to named services. On summer Saturdays the North Warwick services were almost as frequent as those ex the LMS, stations such as Dawlish and Teignmouth being expected to telephone district offices at Exeter on Sunday with the number of arrivals from each, plus of course those from Paddington and South Wales. The normal single daily through train from South Wales to the South West also blossomed into a comprehensive service on Saturdays.

The author has now been a Sea Wall walker for well over half a century, indeed taking many of life's more important decisions on his walking. The Sea Wall still beckons and one notes the passage of trains and (if you can identify them) how well they are running. But there is nothing like the fun in it there used to be, nothing like the variety of locomotives and coaching stock (the Bristolian set mentioned earlier was one of the very few that looked like a set, most GWR expresses being made up of very assorted vehicles), the individuality of the different expresses and even many of the locals, the volume of regular or exceptional freight. Above all the line is now seldom worked to capacity.

In the 1930s everyone believed that quadrupling had to come between Exeter and Newton Abbot, the section between roughly Starcross and Bishopsteignton of course being duplicated by an inland route for which the government provided money to help ease unemployment. The land was bought and fenced off, but the war came before building started. Had the alternative been made, one suspects that it would have survived, and that having been given branch-line status for a time Dawlish and Teignmouth would eventually have been axed off the railway map.

Whatever pleasure the Sea Wall gives today's travellers (and many still wax lyrical) there is no doubt that its Great Days were the Great Western ones when among other things the railway totally governed the local economy and you could tell how well Cornish boarding house proprietors and broccoli growers were doing by the evidence passing in front of you.

Locomotive Sheds and Allocation January 1938

Figures in brackets are included in the totals of the parent shed

(a) Old Oak Common maintained a locomotive at Park Royal Trading Estate.
(b) Two of these locomotives were supplied by Old Oak Common, one by Slough, and one by Banbury.
(c) No shed: locomotive stabled in the open.

London Division (1)

BR 1950	Depot (sub-sheds inset)	Numerical Code	Letter Code	Allocation
81A	Old Oak Common (a)	101	PDN	174
81B	Slough	141	SLO	36
	Aylesbury	11		(4)(b)
81C	Southall	131	SHL	65
	Staines	151		(1)
81D	Reading	121	RDG	81
	Basingstoke	31		(2)
	Henley	61		(1)
	Marlow	81		(1)
	Wallingford	161		(1)
81E	Didcot	41	DID	34
	Lambourn	71		(1)
	Newbury (c)	91		(1)
	Winchester	181		(1)
81F	Oxford	111	OXF	41
	Abingdon	21		(1)
	Fairford	51		(2)

Bristol Division (2)

BR 1950	Depot (sub-sheds inset)	Numerical Code	Letter Code	Allocation
82A	Bristol, Bath Road	22	BL	90
	Bath	42		(2)(a)
	Wells	152		(2)(a)
	Weston-super-Mare	142		(5)(a)
	Yatton	182		(3)(a)
82B	Bristol, St Philips Marsh	32	BL	118
82C	Swindon (b)	132	SDN	107
	Andover Junction (c)	12		(8)(e)
	Chippenham	62		(8)(d)(e)
	Malmesbury	92		(1)
82D	Westbury	172	WES	66
	Frome	72		(6)
	Salisbury	122		(7)
82E	Yeovil	192	YEO	12
82F	Weymouth	162	WEY	34
	Bridport	52		(2)

(a) Locomotives supplied by both Bath Road and St Philips Marsh.
(b) Swindon also maintained Cirencester and Tetbury which were sub-sheds of Gloucester.
(c) Southern Railway shed.
(d) Two auto locomotives supplied by Westbury.
(e) Approximate figure.

Brunel's Bridge. A Cuneo painting commissioned for a poster was this magnificent view of the Saltash bridge looking from the Cornish side with No 5021 Whittington Castle *rolling a train of WR chocolate and cream coaches through Saltash station. Note the fixed distant and the railwayman (without today's high visibility jacket) standing somewhat dangerously in the foreground. This figure in various poses can be seen with some regularity in Cuneo's railway paintings.*

BR 1950	Depot (sub-sheds inset)	Numerical Code	Letter Code	Alloca-tion
	Newton Abbot Division (3)			
83A	Newton Abbot	133	NA	63
	Ashburton	13		(1)
	Kingsbridge	73		(2)
	Moretonhampstead	103		(1)
83B	Taunton	203	TN	55
	Barnstaple	23		(3)
	Bridgwater	33		(1)
	Minehead	113		(1)
83C	Exeter	53	EXE	37
	Tiverton Junction	193		(2)
83D	Plymouth, Laira	83	LA	85
	Launceston	93		(1)
	Plymouth Docks	163		(2)
	Princetown	143		(1)
83E	St Blazey	173	SBLZ	37
	Bodmin	43		(2)
	Moorswater	123		(2)
83F	Truro	213	TR	24
83G	Penzance	153	PZ	31
	Helston	63		(2)
	St Ives	183		(1)
	Wolverhampton Division (4)			
84A	Wolverhampton, Stafford Road	194	WSR	80
84B	Wolverhampton, Oxley	114	OXY	77
84C	Banbury (a)	44	BAN	54
84D	Leamington	94	LMTN	28
	Alcester	14		(1)
84E	Tyseley	174	TYS	102
	Stratford-on-Avon	144		(9)(b)
84F	Stourbridge	154	STB	71
84G	Shrewsbury	134	SALOP	54
	Ludlow	84		(3)
84H	Wellington	184	WLN	20
	Crewe	74		(1)
	Much Wenlock	104		(2)
84J	Croes Newydd (Wrexham)	64	CNYD	44
	Bala	34		(4)
	Penmaenpool	124		(1)
	Trawsfynydd	164		(1)
84K	Chester	54	CHR	66
6C	Birkenhead	24	BHD	40

(a) Supplied one auto locomotive to Aylesbury.
(b) Approximate figure: some locomotives supplied by Leamington.

BR 1950	Depot (sub-sheds inset)	Numerical Code	Letter Code	Alloca-tion
	Worcester Division (5)			
85A	Worcester	215	WOS	81
	Evesham	75		(2)
	Honeybourne (a)	105		(1)
	Kington	145		(2)
	Leominster	155		(3)

BR 1950	Depot (sub-sheds inset)	Numerical Code	Letter Code	Alloca-tion
85B	Gloucester	85	GLO	93
	Brimscombe	15		(1)
	Chalford (a)	35		(1)
	Cheltenham, Malvern Road	45		(13)
	Kingham	135		(1)
	Lydney	175		(16)
	Cirencester (b)	25		(1)
	Tetbury (b)	205		(1)
85C	Hereford	95	HFD	33
	Ledbury	165		(1)
	Ross	195		(2)
85D	Kidderminster	125	KDR	16
	Cleobury Mortimer	65		(1)

(a) No shed, locomotive stabled in the open.
(b) Maintained by Swindon.

BR 1950	Depot (sub-sheds inset)	Numerical Code	Letter Code	Alloca-tion
	Newport Division (6)			
86A	Newport, Ebbw Junction	76	NPT	160
86H	Aberbeeg	16		35
86B	Newport, Pill	106	PILL	49
86C	Cardiff, Canton	66	CDF	122
86D	Llantrisant	86	LTS	23
86E	Severn Tunnel Junction	136	STJ	83
86F	Tondu	146	TDU	42
	Bridgend	56		(3)
86G	Pontypool Road	126	PPL	83
	Branches Fork	46		(3)
	Pontrilas	116		(1)
86J	Aberdare	26	ABDR	53

BR 1950	Depot (sub-sheds inset)	Numerical Code	Letter Code	Alloca-tion
	Neath Division (7)			
87A	Neath	137	NEA	64
	Glyn Neath	67		(5)
	Neath, N&B	147		(14)
87B	Duffryn Yard (Port Talbot)	57	PT	58
87C	Danygraig	47	DG/DNG	37
87D	Swansea East Dock	197	SED	36
87E	Landore	87	LDR	57
87F	Llanelly	107	LLY	72
	Burry Port	17		8
	Llandovery (a)	97		(2)
	Pantyffynnon	177		16
	Llanelly & Mynydd Mawr	117		(5)
87G	Carmarthen	37	CAR	42
	Newcastle Emlyn	157		(1)
87H	Neyland	167	NEY	20
	Milford Haven	127		(2)
	Whitland	217	WTD	22
	Cardigan	27		(1)
	Pembroke Dock	187		(3)
87J	Goodwick (Fishguard)	77	FGD	17

(a) LMS Shed.

On the table. Latterday Prairie tank No 4146 is turned ready for departure on evening suburban duties at Tyseley shed Birmingham in 1952. In the background is Churchward 2-8-0 No 2857 now preserved on the Severn Valley Railway. This was one of two roundhouses (passenger and freight) covering duties in the Birmingham Division. There was also a works which undertook light and intermediate repairs adjacent to the shed.

Overleaf *Hemerdon Summit. Two GWR King class 4-6-0s with No 6023* King Edward II *as pilot bring an express from Plymouth over the summit of Hemerdon bank in South Devon in the late 1940s.* King Edward II *was built at Swindon in 1930, fitted with a double chimney in 1957 and withdrawn in 1963 after running 1,554,201 miles. A special painting by Don Breckon.*

Cardiff Valleys Division (8)

88A	Cardiff, Cathays	58	CVC	60
	Radyr Junction	98	CVY	23
88B	Cardiff East Dock	48	CVED	50
88C	Barry	28	CVB	83
88D	Merthyr	68	CVM	31
	Rhymney	108	CVR	18
	Dowlais Cae Harris	38	CVK	6
	Dowlais Central	78	CVU	2
88E	Abercynon	18	CVJ	32
88F	Treherbert	128	CVT	27
	Pwllyrhebog			(2)
	Ferndale	88	CVF	11

Central Wales Division (9)

89A	Oswestry	129	OSW	69
	Llanfyllin	89		(1)
	Llanidloes	99		(4)
	Moat Lane	109		(7)
	Welshpool	159		(3)(a)
	Whitchurch	169		(1)

89B	Brecon	39	BCN	13(b)
	Builth Wells	49		(2)
89C	Machynlleth	119	MCH	29
	Aberystwyth	19		24(c)
	Aberayron	29		(1)
	Corris	59		(2)
	Portmadoc	139		(6)
	Pwllheli	149		(3)

(a) Includes two narrow gauge locomotives in separate shed.
(b) Includes eight locomotives from Oswestry.
(c) Includes three narrow gauge locomotives in separate shed and eight locomotives from Machynlleth.

Diesel Cars and Department Stock

The eighteen diesel cars in service were stationed as follows: Southall (2), Oxford (2), Reading (1), Bristol (3), Weymouth (1), Tyseley (2), Worcester (3), Cardiff (1), Newport (1), Pontypool Road (1), Landore (1).

Swindon Works had two Departmental locomotives and Bridgwater, Taunton Engineering Depot, Didcot Goods Yard and Reading Signal Depot, one each.

GREAT WESTERN RAILWAY LOCOMOTIVE STOCK 1837–1967

Year	Broad Gauge	Standard Gauge	Total	Year	Broad Gauge	Standard Gauge	Total	Year	Steam Locos	Non-Steam	Total	Year	Steam Locos	Non-Steam	Total	Year	Steam Locos	Non-Steam	Total
1837	5		5	1865	362	348	710	1893	2098		2098	1921	3192		3192	1948	3778	49	3827
1838	17		17	1866	393	407	800	1894	2133		2133	1922	3910		3910	1949	3722	49	3771
1839	20		20	1867	382	453	835	1895	2215		2215	1923	3971	1	3972	1950	3750	50	3800
1840	41		41	1868	377	508	885	1896	2305		2305	1924	4025	1	4026	1951	3685	49	3734
1841	99		99	1869	370	598	968	1897	2392		2392	1925	4021	1	4022	1952	3630	50	3680
1842	127		127	1870	322	680	1002	1898	2470		2470	1926	3975	1	3976	1953	3545	50	3595
1843	126		126	1871	294	770	1064	1899	2560		2560	1927	3944	1	3945	1954	3513	49	3562
1844	126		126	1872	245	853	1098	1900	2644		2644	1928	3874	1	3875	1955	3456	47	3503
1845	126		126	1873	214	976	1190	1901	2734		2734	1929	3853	1	3854	1956	3388	45	3433
1846	140		140	1874	185	1086	1271	1902	2795		2795	1930	3892	1	3893	1957	3276	39	3315
1847	152		152	1875	173	1205	1378	1903	2856		2856	1931	3834	1	3835	1958	3122	35	3157
1848	164		164	1876	336	1292	1628	1904	2875		2875	1932	3727	5	3732	1959	2850	31	2881
1849	170		170	1877	293	1352	1645	1905	2931		2931	1933	3727	6	3733	1960	2612	20	2632
1850	174		174	1878	270	1393	1663	1906	2992		2992	1934	3577	10	3587	1961	2435	7	2442
1851	183		183	1879	246	1431	1677	1907	3051		3051	1935	3543	13	3556	1962	1833	7	1840
1852	192		192	1880	222	1472	1694	1908	3084		3084	1936	3539	24	3563	1963	1275	7	1282
1853	209		209	1881	212	1500	1712	1909	3096		3096	1937	3584	25	3609	1964	586	6	592
1854	243	56	299	1882	206	1549	1755	1910	3107		3107	1938	3582	25	3607	1965	35	6	41
1855	272	70	342	1883	198	1595	1793	1911	3101	1	3102	1939	3672	25	3697	1966	3	6	9
1856	286	76	362	1884	200	1609	1809	1912	3085	1	3086	1940	3667	34	3701	1967	3		3
1857	295	89	384	1885	195	1624	1819	1913	3090	1	3091	1941	3711	42	3753				
1858	298	92	390	1886	188	1657	1845	1914	3106	1	3107	1942	3790	44	3834				
1859	304	92	396	1887	192	1666	1858	1915	3098	1	3099	1943	3818	44	3862				
1860	304	115	419	1888	206	1661	1867	1916	3122	1	3123	1944	3886	44	3930				
1861	315	228	543	1889	198	1687	1885	1917	3080	1	3081	1945	3861	44	3905				
1862	334	279	613	1890	191	1755	1946	1918	3101	1	3102	1946	3865	43	3908				
1863	348	301	649	1891	194	1824	2018	1919	3169		3169	1947	3858	43	3901				
1864	350	332	682	1892	17	2025	2042	1920	3166		3166								

NOTES: Figures are for the December of any year. Between 1903 and 1935 steam locomotive stock totals include steam rail motors. Non-steam figures include the petrol railcar, diesel railcars, Simplex locomotives, petrol locomotives (service stock), diesel mechanical and diesel electric shunters, and the gas turbine locomotives. The 17 broad gauge locomotives recorded at the end of 1892, were 'convertibles' awaiting re-conversion.

7
FIVE LOCOMOTIVE BIOGRAPHIES

MOST Great Western locomotives led busy and varied lives and, though a few had long and much publicised stints at the same depot doing the same duty, some were posted around almost as frequently as methodist ministers. These biographies look at the railway from a different angle.

0-6-0 No 2538

The 0-6-0 wheel arrangement formed by far the numerically largest type of British steam locomotive. Prior to 1883 most of the 0-6-0s built for the GWR during the Armstrong era had had double frames. Thus when William Dean's standard goods engines arrived on the scene their single inside plate frames represented a complete break with tradition. With 260 examples being built between 1883 and 1899 there can not have been many sections of the GWR which at one time or another were not the haunt of these famous locomotives.

As part of Lot 108, Dean Goods No 2538 left Swindon Works in August 1897 having cost the princely sum of £1,133. This was £50 less than many earlier members of the class had cost; inflation was not a problem during these latter years of the Victorian era.

The greater part of No 2538's first two decades in service were spent at Wolverhampton Stafford Road. This famous shed came into being around 1860 when the GWR built a broad gauge depot directly opposite the Shrewsbury & Birmingham's building, with only the Stafford Road separating the two structures. Over the years the facilities were expanded to include a full locomotive works and the depot remained important to the dying years of steam.

At the beginning of its career in the West Midlands, No 2538 was principally kept busy on main line work. It possessed a good route availability and, with ample power for its size, became a useful addition to the GWR motive power fleet. However, as the equally capable but more powerful Churchward 2-8-0s started to appear from 1905, the Dean Goods began to play a humbler role on main line work, and those at Wolverhampton could more often be seen on trip workings and local goods to Stourbridge, Hockley or Bordesley as well as making regular expeditions as far north as Chester and as far south as Banbury. Passenger work now only rarely featured in No 2538's routine, this being more normally dealt with by the 2-4-2T and 2-6-2Ts to Dean's design or by their Churchward successors.

Although allocated to this one Wolverhampton shed for the first 25 years of its life, it was not unknown for No 2538 to be loaned out to other depots, presumably to help out with a temporary power shortage

Overleaf, above *Clear Road Ahead. One of the dramatic and evocative paintings by Terence Cuneo specially commissioned for posters by the then Railway Executive. This scene shows driver and fireman at work on the footplate of No 5037* Monmouth Castle *pounding down the main line from Paddington to Reading. The poster attracted the attention of hundreds of thousands of passengers as they waited for trains and has long been accounted one of the artist's best railway pictures.*

Overleaf, below *Sesqui-centenary celebration. The year 1985 saw widely acclaimed celebrations of 150 years of the Great Western Railway. These included a number of special steam trains headed by a variety of restored and preserved ex GWR classes including King, Castle, Hall and Manor. Newport (Mon) was particularly fortunate as on 10 September 1985 not only was No 7029* Clun Castle *sponsored by Whitbreads to take a train of SLOA Pullmans to Gloucester but Churchward's 28XX class 2-8-0 No 2857, restored from scrap condition on the Severn Valley Railway, was also on display together with a replica GWR freight train which it hauled through the station past admiring crowds.* Clun Castle *is shown leaving for Gloucester.*

109

Previous page, above Coast line local. *Ex Cambrian Railways 0-6-0, now GWR No 892, allocated to Machynlleth, heads south from Harlech with a Pwllheli to Barmouth train in February 1941. Several ex Cambrian engines, all 0-6-0s, were still at work on the coast line and as bankers up to Talerddig summit until the early 1950's.*

Previous page, below Taking water the hard way. *Either the fireman is inexperienced or, more likely, a little slow as the scoop is still in the water trough after the tender tank has been filled. The engine is No 6019* King Henry V *and the train the up 'Red Dragon' in March 1961. This was a somewhat lethargic train leaving Carmarthen at 7.30 am with the main portion not departing from Swansea until 8.45 am. It was, however, a popular service from Cardiff and Newport running non stop from the latter to Paddington arriving at 1.05 pm.*

Opposite Dean Goods No 2538 in *the evening of its days working the Kerry branch freight c1955. It is seen here in the Mule gorge near Middle Mill. This was a regular turn for the engine and the branch was the main reason for its retention in service. It was the last of its class to survive bar No 2516 which has been preserved.*

or as a replacement for a member of the same class away at works. Recorded instances were loans to Banbury in February 1902, Weymouth in June 1907, Llanelly in August 1911 and to Wellington for a six month period at the end of 1917. By this latter date around sixty Dean Goods had been sold to the British Government and crossed the Channel to help out with the war effort in France where many were subsequently seen hauling heavy ammunition trains up to the Front Line. Following the signing of the Armistice, some of the class ventured even further afield into the Middle East while two were even sold to the Ottoman Railway.

No 2538 missed all this excitement, however, and continued its somewhat humdrum existence at Stafford Road right through to February 1922 when its first permanent reallocation, to Shrewsbury, took place. For most of the time here it trundled up and down the joint GW/LNWR line to Hereford on local passenger and freight work and was frequently based out at the sub-shed of Ludlow, situated approximately midway between the two cities, from where it also worked mineral traffic off the former Ludlow & Clee Hill Railway.

No 2538's life over the next 15 years or so proved to be somewhat nomadic and included periods at Banbury (the only time it was allocated permanently to a depot in the London Division), Stafford Road again, Wellington, Worcester, Kidderminster and Stourbridge. It made its first ever formal visit to Swindon Works for overhaul in March 1931 during the course of which Automatic Train Control apparatus was fitted.

In 1939 war again had a dramatic effect on the surviving members of the Dean Goods. More than a hundred of the veterans were requisitioned, some of them within a just a few weeks of the declaration of war. Once again many of the class saw service overseas and included among their number were several engines that had been sent to Europe during the 1914–18 conflict. On the cessation of hostilities a good many of the Dean Goods that survived in France were still at work with some actually being renumbered into SNCF stock. Twenty two of the engines in better condition were sold to China while most of the remainder were shipped home for scrap during 1948–9.

No 2538 again avoided being called up and safely saw out the war years at Severn Tunnel Junction and Cardiff sheds. Within two years of Nationalisation it was transferred to Oswestry and began an association with the lines of the former Cambrian Railway that lasted (apart from six months at Hereford in 1953) until its eventual withdrawal in 1957.

Although freight remained the predominant source of work for No 2538 during this period, it saw occasional use on passenger duties such as the stopping service between Moat Lane and Brecon. Local traffic in agricultural products and coal was not inconsiderable in the heart of Wales and the daily pick-up goods along the ex-Cambrian routes served the Welsh farming community well. A typical example of this was the 9.30am Oswestry to Moat Lane Junction class K train, a duty which three times a week also involved the rostered locomotive working down the byway from Abermule to Kerry, a job which was to directly prolong the life of a handful of Dean Goods.

Seeing Red

Despite their age, the 4300 class (5300 and 6300 series) Moguls were excellent locomotives whilst the erstwhile 9300 series, then on the 'red' classification, saw service in the Oswestry District, but not until they were altered and renumbered in the 7300 series and reclassified as 'blue' engines. None were stationed at Aberystwyth, but several of the class worked in and out of the latter station to and from both Carmarthen and Shrewsbury. On one occasion, one of the 7300 series headed the up Cambrian Coast Express and an alert relief signalman at Llandre spotted the 'red' route mark on the cabside of the locomotive and immediately rang the motive power depot at Machynlleth, stating that an unpermitted locomotive had passed his box. The locomotive was withdrawn at Machynlleth, and a standby engine was attached. All was well, however, as it later transpired that a young and very enthusiastic cleaner had really set to, and had cleaned the fireman's cabside with such vigour that the original 'red' route spot had reasserted itself from layers of grime.
– T. P. Dalton, *Cambrian Companionship*.

This increasingly anachronistic branch had lost its passenger service in 1931 and by the 1950s the only traffic on offer was timber, coal, animal feedstuffs and a certain amount of livestock, particularly in September each year when the Kerry sheep sales took place and several trains of cattle wagons had to be worked up to the terminus. As a result of the severe weight restrictions, Oswestry shed was forced to retain a few of the Dean 0-6-0s for many years after the majority of the class had been withdrawn. Among the lucky survivors were No 2516 (now preserved at Swindon) and our very own No 2538. Yet all good things must come to an end and the thrice weekly freight up to Kerry finally ceased in April 1956. Closure was an inevitable response to a combination of road competition and a permanent way that had deteriorated beyond economic repair.

It was still not the end for No 2538 which by now had become something of a celebrity as the very last Dean Goods in revenue earning service. Not surprisingly, it was now a popular choice for railtours. The first of two in 1956 was organised by the Gloucestershire Railway Society on 12 May and took in a brief tour of lines in South Wales with No 2538 hauling the three coach train from Merthyr to Neath and then on to Caerphilly via Treherbert and Pontypridd. Its appearance on Merthyr shed the night before created a lot of interest, providing a rare opportunity to see a tender engine among the more normal allocation of tank locomotives.

The second trip, on 22 September, was even more interesting and provided the spectacle of two veteran locomotives working together. Coupled with ex-SECR 4-4-0 No 31075 dating back to 1903, No 2538 headed the annual Talyllyn Railway Preservation Society special between Shrewsbury and Towyn, probably the hardest job it had been asked to undertake for many years. Apart from this special traffic there was now no real reason why Oswestry shed needed a Dean Goods on its allocation yet No 2538 was obviously a favourite with the staff there who kept it in very clean condition for its last remaining freight duties down to Brecon.

Withdrawal finally came in May 1957. With an example of this famous class already saved for the National Collection, No 2538's fate was sealed and – after a very short period in store – it travelled to Swindon to be reduced to scrap.

2-6-0 No 4358

The 43XX Moguls were the most numerous tender engines, 307 being built at Swindon and a further 35 by Robert Stephenson & Co of Darlington between 1911 and 1932. Interestingly Nos 7305 – 19 were assembled at Swindon using parts supplied by the private contractor.

They were ideal mixed-traffic locomotives and despite being frequently overworked and overloaded still managed to perform admirably when called upon to handle express passenger or heavy freights. There is the often related, although perhaps slightly apocryphal story of a freight train headed by one of these 2-6-0s actually overtaking the Cheltenham Flyer in which Collett was travelling as a passenger. At the

time he was giving thought to various aspects of the King Class design and this incident is said to have settled the point of reduced wheel diameter for them!

Built at a cost of £2,296, No 4358 left Swindon Works in April 1914 and quickly entered traffic at Plymouth Laira from where it worked east and west on the mixed-traffic duties for which it was designed. As an example of the sort of work it would have handled a typical diagram for a Laira member of the class took it down to Liskeard and back with an early morning local passenger duty. This was followed by another local from Plymouth Millbay to Exeter and then a return trip down the Kingswear branch before heading back home. But the earliest known photograph of No 4358 in action shows it crossing the Royal Albert Bridge at Saltash with a Penzance to Plymouth perishables working in April 1919.

No 4358 remained in the West Country throughout World War I although eleven of her sister locomotives had been sent to Europe in 1917 at the request of the Railway Operating Division of the Ministry of Supply to help with the movement of troops and supplies within France. Despatched from Portsmouth Harbour, all the engines returned safely to England just under two years later having proved to be extremely useful and reliable whilst in the service of King and Country, No 5325 complete with a few bullet holes as evidence of its military duty. No 4358 meanwhile had taken up duty in the London Division at Old Oak Common from September 1919 onwards, also seeing a few brief intervals at Southall prior to its reallocation to Oxley (Wolverhampton) at the beginning of 1924.

Churchward 2-6-0 No 4358 complete with copper capped chimney double heads a down local freight through Birmingham Snow Hill in the 1920s probably when allocated to Oxley (Wolverhampton) between 1924 and 1926. The second locomotive is a double framed 0-6-0 pannier tank most likely a 1076 class rebuilt from a saddle tank.

115

During March 1926 this Mogul was routinely stopped for repairs and put to one side at Oxley awaiting its turn to enter Swindon Works for general overhaul. Clearly Swindon must have been very busy, for it was not until some six months later that No 4358 re-entered service, this time operating out of Worcester initially and then from Chester shed in the period up to July 1930. It then returned to the London Division for a three year spell based at Reading which included two brief postings to the sub-shed at Basingstoke, a small two road depot set in the heart of rival Southern Railway territory, though with its own very Great Western atmosphere and loyalties.

After a further allocation to Oxley between 1933 and 1935, No 4358 moved on to Swansea (Landore). Around this time older members of the class were gradually being withdrawn to provide a stock of major components which could be used in the construction of the new Manor and Grange classes. It is said that had war not intervened all 342 locomotives were intended for conversion; in the event only a hundred were dismantled with No 4358 being one of only a handful of the '4300' numbered series to avoid this fate.

May 1937 saw No 4358 transferred to Neyland, one of the more remote outposts of the GWR network. The last part of the South Wales Railway had opened from Haverfordwest to Neyland in 1856 and Brunel hoped to create a port here at which transatlantic liners would call but

Class 43XX 2-6-0 No 4358 at Neyland depot in 1938. It is still in virtually original condition except for the fitting of a small cast iron chimney. The livery is unlined green retaining Great Western in full on the tender.

the harbour at Fishguard took precedence and Neyland's development never really took off. Even so there was plenty of work to do for the relatively small allocation of locomotives based here and No 4358 could regularly be seen on local passenger and freight duties throughout the Fishguard, Whitland, Pembroke Dock and Carmarthen areas – although it was equally used on longer distance work across the border into England. It was while on one of these forays east of the Severn that this Mogul earned its own particular place in railway history. On 6 December 1940, at the height of the Blitz, Bristol Temple Meads was the subject of the Luftwaffe's attention. The 7.10pm local to Salisbury headed by No 4358 had just left the station when it received a direct hit, destroying much of the train and causing heavy casualties. Although the tender was condemned and broken up, the damage to the locomotive itself was not too severe and following repair at Swindon re-entered traffic back at Neyland during April 1941. The remainder of the war years were less adventurous for No 4358 and it soldiered on with no further incidents of note apart from the fitting of outside steampipes in January 1944.

Nationalisation in 1948 saw little change to No 4358's work pattern and it was not until July 1955 that its final reallocation, to Gloucester Horton Road, took place. Once again it proved a popular choice for local duties, the passenger service across to Hereford being a regular job on which it was photographed several times, while during the summer months it also helped out with the fashionable day excursion traffic of this era, one such instance being a visit to Barry Island in the summer of 1955. A pleasing occurrence in November 1956 was Swindon's decision to paint all their mixed-traffic locomotives in green, and from February the following year many such engines were also fully lined out in GWR style. No 4358 gained its new livery at Caerphilly Works in the spring of 1957. It included a red reversing lever, a red background to the cabside numberplate and a polished safety valve bonnet – and very smart it looked too!

This well-groomed appearance may have led to its selection for railtour duty in May 1957 for on the 18th of that month it double-headed the middle leg of the *Trains Illustrated* Daffodil Express with the legendary 4-4-0 No 3440 *City of Truro*. Taking the train onwards from Gloucester, both locomotives made their leisurely way across to Pontypool Road and then set off westwards crossing the valleys which form the southern watershed of the Brecon Beacons. According to contemporary reports they raised the echoes while lifting their 310 ton train to the two principal summit points, including three miles of 1 in 45 up to Cwm Glyn. This was followed by passage over the famous Crumlin Viaduct although because of weight restrictions *City of Truro* ran across light engine leaving No 4358 to bring the special across on its own. Throughout the Welsh valleys news of the train had spread well beforehand and much of the population, young and old, turned out to watch the two engines' stately progress. Continuing their journey to Neath, Swansea and finally Newport *City of Truro* and the Churchward 2-6-0 handed over to a Castle having completed their day's work, not bad for two locomotives with a combined age of 97 years.

Short Trip

A clerk was to travel as far as Cardiff by the 5.55pm train, Paddington-Fishguard Harbour to prepare customs specifications for parcels destined for Ireland. On arrival at Cardiff, the clerk returned home to London by the first train. Unknown to the powers that be, it used to be the practice to 'scamper' through the work, if possible, by the time the 5.55 got to Reading; thus the clerk could be home by around 8 o'clock.

One night, the clerk jumped out at Reading but, in his hurry, omitted to turn the door handle properly (on the GWR, door handles had to be turned from OUTSIDE the coach). All went well until just beyond the Severn Tunnel when an observant signalman noticed the unturned handle (the door was not swinging open) and 'sent seven' to the box in advance (seven beats on the block bell signifying 'stop and examine train').

The train guard said 'there should be a clerk (rhymed with "work" on the GWR) in that van'. Result – stop everything through the Severn Tunnel while the line was searched for the body; the delay can be imagined. No body having been found, the railway police in London were contacted and a constable sent to the clerk's house around midnight; nothing would shake his story that, feeling ill at Reading, he had left the train and had, most unfortunately, not turned the door handle properly or told the guard. That ended the 'getting off at Reading' business but the clerk never changed his story! – Pat Hart.

Sleepers

GWR sleeping cars were an institution. For much of the Company's history, they were first class only. When lesser mortals were encouraged to spend the night horizontally they were directed into four-berth compartments where often the sexes were divided only by a central curtain. Only a pillow and rug was provided; you were not expected to undress, but nonetheless the Press were sharp in their criticism, especially after World War II.

There used indeed to be a rubber stamp at Paddington, Plymouth and Penzance stating (and imagine the thoughts of husbands sending their wives off on journeys by themselves): 'WARNING: whilst every endeavour is made to allot 3rd class sleeping berths to Ladies and Gentlemen separately, this is not always practicable and may not be possible in the case of this journey.'

Yet thousands used the sleepers as part of their business and holiday lives, three routes being busy for many years: Paddington to the West of England, South and West Wales, and Birkenhead. Many were on board as long as it now takes from London to Inverness. But if speed was not the boast of the GWR at night, its sleepers were usually spotlessly clean and much preferable to those of the LMS even though the latter ran more smoothly.

Passengers for the Scilly Islands, who on summer Fridays eventually had a complete train of sleepers to themselves, going via Castle Cary whereas most West-bound sleepers in the GWR's history went the Great Way Round via Bristol (or Gloucester to South and West Wales), of course had ample time to sleep. But many passengers had little choice but to snatch a few hours of broken rest over relatively short distances, for as is pointed out

continued opposite

Just over a month later No 4358 was on public display again, this time at a Swindon Works Open Day when it was lined up with several other representatives of Western Region motive power; by now it was the oldest member of the class still in service and no doubt this was the main reason for its selection. Less glamorous everyday duties continued but declined with the introduction of diesel multiple units and the falling off of rail borne freight. With the withdrawal of No 4377 at the beginning of 1959, No 4358 became the very last survivor of the original 43XX series until in August it too was condemned with a praiseworthy total of 1,406,215 miles to its credit. Just a few weeks later it was dumped on the scrap lines at Swindon, minus tender, to await its fate.

It was around this time that British Railways had begun to sell some of their locomotives to private scrap merchants for cutting up, the sheer volume of withdrawn steam motive power proving too much for BR's own works to handle. The first private dealer was the now famous Woodham Brothers at Barry who purchased several examples of these 2-6-0s throughout 1959. Unfortunately No 4358 was not amongst these, being sold to John Cashmore of Newport in November 1959 and put to the torch soon after arrival.

0-6-0- Pannier Tank No 3737

1929 saw the implementation of a large scale plan to reduce the hundreds of Victorian saddle and pannier 0-6-0Ts which had formed a major part of the GWR's stock of shunting and light freight tank engines. Churchward's standardisation programme had stopped short of this need and, though he had been responsible for introducing the pannier tank concept, had still not produced a standard 0-6-0PT design by the time of his retirement. This task was left to Collett, who together with his successor Hawksworth, built more than 1,200 engines of the basic type with detail variations. As a result, if there is one class of locomotive that will always be associated with 'things Great Western', The greater family of 0-6-0PTs became a common sight on almost every branch line and goods yard on the GW system (and after nationalisation conquered specialists jobs elsewhere such as helping boat trains up the incline from Folkestone Harbour).

One of a batch of fifty pannier tanks turned out from Swindon Works during 1937, No 3737 officially entered traffic at the adjacent running shed on 11 September. At this time Swindon shed maintained a stock of around thirty pannier tanks, principally for yard shunting duties but also to help handle the numerous short distance transfer freights around the district. Swindon also supplied the locomotives to work the branch between Chippenham and Calne and accordingly No 3737 was sent to the small 3-road stone and timber sub-shed at Chippenham for its first of what proved to be many turns of duty in April 1938.

Between them, the six or so pannier tanks sub-shedded here, together with two 14XX class 0-4-2Ts, coped admirably with the 5¾ mile single line linking the small market town of Calne with the rest of the GWR. Passenger services were mainly in the hands of those engines equipped with the auto-gear necessary for push-pull working. Not being so fitted, No 3737 was generally kept busy on goods traffic in both coal and the well known products of Messrs C & T Harris meat factory. These latter trains, which ran every day except Saturdays, were famous for their specially labelled Siphon C parcel vans complete with yellow side plates and roof boards bearing the legend *Harris's Wiltshire Sausages*.

During the early years of World War II No 3737's work on the Calne branch line was supplemented by the construction of RAF radio schools at nearby Yatesbury and Compton Bassett necessitating the carriage of building equipment, sectional wooden huts and the personal baggage of over 10,000 airmen and airwomen. Just occasionally it would make an appearance on the branch passenger service as part of a balancing working to get it back home to Chippenham. With only two small intermediate halts on the line, namely Stanley Bridge Halt and Black Dog Halt, this would have been an easy duty.

Obviously the selection of which pannier tanks would be sub-shedded at Chippenham was at the whim of the Swindon shedmaster and accordingly for the first eighteen years of its career No 3737 was alternately allocated between the parent and sub-shed with incredible regularity. However by 1947 an additional source of work had been found as a result of several bridges on the Highworth branch being rebuilt to a larger loading gauge, thus enabling the Swindon 57XX pannier tanks, which had previously been barred from the line, to run out as far as the South Marston Siding (2 miles up the branch) with workmen's and freight trains to the Vickers Armstrong factory. For two short periods during 1948 No 3737 was also loaned to Cirencester for duty on the short line across to Kemble Junction. Although a sub-shed of Gloucester the locomotive allocated here was supplied by Swindon

continued
elsewhere the GWR was much slower to get going in the morning than today's railway and the last expresses of the day ran earlier.

So people joined the sleepers at Taunton, Gloucester and even Birmingham, regulars on the latter journey being the dramatic critic J. C. Trewin, who wrote his piece for the *Birmingham Post* and rather than stay in an hotel and waste much of the next morning had a berth reserved on the Birkenhead car.

One of the numerous 57XX 0-6-0 pannier tanks No 3737 stands in Melcombe Regis (Weymouth) station with a Railway Correspondence & Travel Society special to Portland and Easton on 14 August 1960.

Undistinguished End

It had little to do with ownership but was much about the legal entity, the historic traditions and the sheer difference from other railways: even many of those who had voted for the Attlee government were sad when the GWR ended at midnight on 31 December 1947.

Tears or joy, it was something of an anticlimax to find the railway running very much as normal on an overcast first day of 1948. The sun certainly did not sparkle on the sea during the crowded eight minute ride from Teignmouth to Dawlish, depart Teignmouth 11.11am by the time-honoured first train up from Truro, all stations (except between Saltash and Plymouth North Road) to Exeter, taking an incredible (also time-honoured) four and a quarter hours.

We of course continued to use the GWR's large-format timetable (the other railways had long fallen back on extracts from *Bradshaw* as was also the Western Region to do from May), though regular travellers anyway knew many of the times by heart. Depart Paddington for the West of England 5.30 (via Bristol), 10.30 Cornish Riviera (first stop at which passengers could alight being Plymouth), 11.0 Torbay Express (first stop Taunton; it was later to revert to its traditional noon and again be non-stop to Exeter), 1.30 (a very heavy train serving just about everywhere and with numerous branch-line connections), 4.30 (the first indication that the GWR was interested in business as well as holiday passengers cut back to Fridays only because of 1947 austerity as its up morning counterpart was temporarily reduced to Mondays only), 5.0 (via Bristol and taking six and a quarter hours to Plymouth), 6.30 (also via Bristol and in fact only a through coach switched there to a Manchester-*continued opposite*

and on both of these occasions the pannier tank was standing in for the more normal 0-4-2T.

Following this relatively long spell in Wiltshire, No 3737 moved south to Weymouth in March 1956. Almost immediately it found employment on the nine mile branch from Maiden Newton (on the Weymouth to Yeovil main line) down to Bridport, sharing duties with a couple of the 45XX class 2-6-2 tank locomotives. At the beginning of 1958 Weymouth motive power depot was handed over to the British Railways' Southern Region control and all its allocation had their 82F shedplates removed in favour of the less familiar 71G. This reorganisation also meant that the responsibility for No 3737's maintenance switched from Swindon to the SR and in the ensuing years it is known to have visited Ashford Works for overhaul and general repair, travelling via Southampton and Brighton. Strange territory indeed!

29 April 1959 was to prove to be perhaps No 3737's finest hour for on that day the Queen and the Duke of Edinburgh had travelled down to Weymouth in the Royal Train, arriving behind Bulleid Pacific No 34048 *Crediton*. Here pannier tanks Nos 4689 and 3737, suitably prepared and with gleaming paintwork, then worked the train to Portland Dockyard in readiness for Her Majesty's return to Windsor after inspecting HMS *Eagle*. They also both worked the return journey as far as Weymouth Junction, thus providing the unusual spectacle of the Royal Train, with the Sovereign on board, being hauled over a closed branch line by a pair of 0-6-0PTs complete with four-lamp headcode.

Around this time No 3737 was not an infrequent visitor to the Weymouth Harbour lines and for this purpose it was temporarily fitted with a bell on the left-hand side running plate to warn pedestrians of its presence while working that much photographed section through the streets. On other occasions it appeared on the daily goods at Upwey, on the former Abbotsbury branch. Following closure of this line in 1951, the truncated stub to Upwey was treated as a siding and therefore the 1894 Board of Trade regulations prohibiting the use of anything larger than a four-coupled tank on the branch no longer applied. Accordingly, after the departure of the last 14XXs from Weymouth in early 1960, any 0-6-0PT was used and No 3737 was frequently noted on this particular duty. The Bridport branch was still one of its regular haunts, though by this time the diesel multiple units had taken over the majority of the passenger workings leaving only the daily goods service and the one remaining steam hauled passenger train in the hands of a Weymouth 57XX pannier tank.

On 14 August 1960 No 3737 paid a visit to the Portland Docks line again, this time at the head of the Railway Correspondence & Travel Society's Greyhound railtour which had worked down from London behind T9 4-4-0 No 30718. Specially cleaned again for the occasion, the tank locomotive was provided with only three coaches for its complement of some 240 passengers. On the return journey the train was halted on the causeway and searched by the local police who were hunting escaped prisoners. They left empty handed however and the railtour was resumed with the number of passengers undiminished.

No 3737's seven year association with Dorset came to an end in July 1963 with a transfer to Treherbert in the South Wales valleys. It has not been possible to establish whether this was just a move 'on paper' for no photographs or other information seem to have survived as evidence of the reallocation actually having taken place. But, definitely, by the beginning of August 1963 No 3737 was operating from Gloucester (Horton Road) shed on a wide range of duties. Apart from the usual shunting work in the nearby goods yard and local trip freights it also ventured further afield, on a number of occasions being recorded shunting in the former Severn & Wye station at Coleford.

Even at this stage No 3737 was still sometimes rostered for passenger duty and during August 1964 it was photographed at Standish with a stopping service to Chalford in place of the more normal 14XX 0-4-2T. However, this really was the locomotive's Indian Summer for in the first week of September 1964 it was finally condemned and put into store the following month at the former Midland depot at Gloucester Barnwood to await its fate. By November it had been sold for scrap and delivered to Messrs Bird's premises at Risca, a short distance from Newport. Thus a humble pannier tank which had enjoyed a more notable career than most of its contemporaries by being rostered to both Royal Train and railtour duty, ended its days during April 1965, being cut up into several manageable pieces of scrap metal to feed the ever hungry furnaces of the South Wales steelworks.

4-6-0 No 6858 Woolston Grange

Good as the Churchward Moguls were, a more powerful boiler was needed for sustained hard steaming. Thus in 1936, when the time had come to renew some of the older Moguls, Collett managed to please the accountants by using the wheels and motion of withdrawn 43XX locomotives (see above) to contribute towards the construction of the new 68XX Grange class.

Using parts from 2-6-0 No 4373 (condemned during August 1937), No 6858 *Woolston Grange* emerged from Swindon Factory on 5 December 1937 resplendent in unlined Brunswick green livery but with black cylinders, wheels and footplating. For reasons not now possible to ascertain it was not allocated to a shed straight away but spent the first nine weeks of its career running-in on local duties in the Swindon area. When this had been satisfactorily completed the locomotive was dispatched to its first depot at Tyseley during February 1938.

Tyseley shed had been built in 1908–9 to cater for the needs of the Birmingham Division and from the 1930s onwards regularly housed over a hundred engines to cover its freight, local passenger and secondary express rosters. The main express workings in the area were normally dealt with by locomotives from Wolverhampton (Stafford Road) and in fact until the early 1960s when Castles were drafted in after having been made redundant elsewhere, it was rare for anything larger than a Hall to be seen on Tyseley's allocation. Thus *Woolston Grange* was kept busy on a wide range of mixed traffic duties from the West Midlands to most other parts of the GWR system and this work

---

continued

Plymouth train) and the overnights (both with sleepers, first class only) at 9.50 and 11.50.

What a miserable last service! On Mondays to Thursdays, only two trains serving Exeter ran via Castle Cary. The first through train from Cornwall to Paddington was the Cornish Riviera not arriving until 5.0pm. But the austerity conditions after a first taste of peacetime normality bore more heavily on the express than local trains, resulting in what now seems a ridiculously small proportion of trains serving major towns such as Exeter being fast. The all-stations trains however carried large complements of passengers, including the 11.11 from Teignmouth on the first of January, some of them indeed making Intercity journeys.

Slip Coach Excursion

With regard to the recent Pertinent Paragraph entitled 'Excursion Travel de Luxe', we are obliged to Mr T. E. Norman for directing our attention to what – in point of speed – must verily be the most de luxe trip yet scheduled. For on February 26 last patrons of the Taunton Steeplechases were invited to make their day trip on no less illustrious an express than the down Cornish Riviera Limited. For their use an extra third-class coach and a dining car were incorporated in the Taunton slip portion. The arrival time at Taunton in the handbill was duly given at 12.52 p.m. – 143.7 miles in 142 min. – and return fare was advertised as 13s. 6d. The total load of the Limited on this particular day consisted of 15 coaches, weighing 505 tare tons, and the Taunton excursion was well patronised, the extra stock being filled to capacity on starting. – *Railway Magazine*

Rural Crossroads

Deep in the heart of the Worcestershire countryside and serving as an interchange point for Stratford, Birmingham, Cheltenham, Gloucester, Worcester, Oxford and (on the slower services) London, Honeybourne was a great place for watching trains. Not only could one see the Paddington to Worcester and Hereford expresses rushing through with Stars or Saints at their head but also the Birmingham to the South West expresses behind Castles (and until the early 1930s 4-4-0 Counties). Honeybourne was a kind of Midland Railway Trent Junction with all types of trains calling and passengers changing for other lines, yet it was nowhere, a mere hamlet, and that added to the excitement.

Originally Honeybourne was just a junction on the Old Worse & Worse with a 9½ mile branch to Stratford upon Avon. With the completion of the Birmingham North Warwickshire & Stratford upon Avon Railway by the GWR in 1907/8 the scene changed dramatically. This linked with the new Honeybourne-Cheltenham line, providing a new route (rivalling the Midland) from Birmingham to Bristol. The Great Western made the most of this as did the Western Region later on; the *Cornishman* thundered through over Stratford-Cheltenham route, the *Cathedrals Express* over the OWW, though the stoppers from which handfuls of passengers alighted, one or two setting off on long walks but most with a long wait before a connection service, typified this rural crossroads.

increased greatly in World War II. In common with most engines, its cabside windows were sheeted over to reduce glare from the firebox and it was not until just before nationalisation that this was removed, no doubt to the relief of footplate crews.

During the war years No 6858 remained at Tyseley although it was loaned out to Banbury in September 1941 and Stratford-upon-Avon in January 1945. Wartime conditions obviously did not suit this particular Grange well for it is recorded as having been out of use undergoing repair at Swindon Works for five months in 1942 and for a similar time in 1944. Though no doubt in a very run down condition, *Woolston Grange* soldiered on and it was not until six years after the formation of British Railways that it underwent its first permanent change of home, namely to Shrewsbury in September 1954. By this time it was wearing the standard BR mixed traffic livery of lined black, a colour which did not please many GW enthusiasts although, truth to tell, when clean the locomotives carrying this livery did look quite smart.

In July 1955 No 6858 left the Wolverhampton area for Llanelly where its work embraced a wide variety of duties, yet somewhat unexpectedly it is recorded as having arrived at Paddington that summer with a relief for the up Red Dragon. Leaving Swansea at 8.45am this express ran non-stop from Newport to arrive in London by 1.5pm. Not too difficult perhaps for a Castle or a Britannia, but quite a feat for a Grange on the relief train with similar timings.

The South Wales stay turned out to be quite short for in December 1955 *Woolston Grange* was transferred to Plymouth Laira. The Granges proved to be very popular in the West Country, their smaller diameter driving wheels giving them a slight advantage over the Halls when pulling away from the numerous stations at which the majority of the trains stopped, as well as enabling them to tackle the many stiff gradients on the main line between Plymouth and Penzance with relative ease. Living up to their mixed traffic pedigree, they were equally at home on express goods, heavy mineral and stopping passenger trains, and almost without exception performed well when called upon to help out with the hundreds of extra trains that ran each summer weekend throughout the 1950s. *Woolston Grange* was recorded on many such trains, including one on the infamous day in July 1957 when the sheer volume of holiday expresses led to chaos on the West of England main line with almost every block section in Devon occupied. No 6858 left Newquay piloted by No 7823 *Hook Norton Manor* with the 12.30 to Paddington and after a somewhat delayed journey came off the train at Plymouth leaving it to be worked forward by No 1015 *County of Gloucester* and No 5084 *Reading Abbey*. Very few trains ran on time that day, just a year before main line diesels arrived on the Western Region. In addition to these general passenger and freight duties No 6858 often found itself on the celebrated broccoli special trains, composed of vacuum fitted wagons and travelling at fairly high speeds, that ran seasonally from Cornwall to London and the Midlands. It also put in an occasional appearance on the equally important milk trains from the West Country up to the capital.

By now *Woolston Grange* had been repainted in lined green livery, rather appropriate perhaps for in the early part of 1958 it was noted at Marazion with that doyen of Great Western express trains, the Cornish Riviera Express. Nevertheless at the end of the summer timetable that year No 6858 was transferred to Oxford where the Granges and Halls performed all kinds of main line work including express trains to Paddington as well as running as far as Wolverhampton, Gloucester, Swindon and Worcester. In addition they dealt with goods workings to Pontypool Road via Worcester, a three day duty shared between the depots at those two places while from time to time a Grange would also act as the West Midlands sidings passenger pilot waiting to take over from any failure on an up train, although a Hall was more often seen on this particular duty.

In February 1960 No 6858 was reallocated to Penzance but this was quickly followed by periods at Cardiff Canton, Shrewsbury and Tyseley before moving on to Oxley (Wolverhampton) in September 1962. Here its duties were more usually concerned with freight, although appearances on passenger workings were still fairly common. Even so no one could have imagined the extraordinary happenings of 15 August 1964 which earned this particular Grange its permanent place in railway folklore.

Farthest north for a Grange. No 6858 Woolston Grange *stands outside the ex LNWR Hillhouse shed, Huddersfield on Sunday 15 August 1964. Although still in steam the locomotive had to wait a further 10 days before it could return home to Oxley (2B). Note the lack of shed code plate, the Western lamps above each buffer and the damage to the cylinder casing caused by contact with numerous platform edges north of Nottingham Victoria whilst working the train described in the biography.*

123

Trainees

The high standard of train and yard operation required to fulfill the GWR claim of 'one-day transits between important towns', the firmly held belief in Swindon that the mechanical department really ran the railway, and the perpetual reminder of the profit motive . . . these are a few of the impressions that come across in a selection of the memories of those chosen for the Special Training Scheme run from 1921 to 1939 and published privately by one of them, L. King.

Unlike the LNER's better-known training scheme, the GWR's was not based on any formal training but giving those chosen an intense variety of job experience, of course earning their keep as they went. Nearly all the entrants found the GWR a happy railway whose middle managers carried vast responsibilities. Many of them were indeed great individualists or personalities, a few tyrants, some able to imbibe generous quantities of alcohol at lunch without impairing their performance which of course relied on a detailed knowledge of the system and its traffic.

Says Mr King: 'If ever there were a railway system, this one was! A sense of order prevailed. Each morning the "10 o'clock time signal" ran throughout the network, reminding everyone of the importance of "time". A good example was R. W. Higgins, one-time Exeter district traffic superintendent, who had two grandfather clocks, synchronised, in his room; clocksmiths travelled specially from Swindon when they needed attention. The GWR concept of "profit with economy and efficiency" belong to another age.'

On that day No 6858 somewhat unusually arrived at Nottingham Victoria with 8.55am Bournemouth West to Leeds, an eight coach train driven by men from Woodford Halse. An Annesley crew took over and despite leaving two minutes late the train continued on to Sheffield Victoria, arriving there on time – the liberal schedule of 72 minutes called for little effort from the locomotive but as the Annesley crew had never previously been on the footplate of a Grange their efforts were certainly creditable. The arrival at Sheffield was even more noteworthy for No 6858's left hand cylinder dislodged a three feet length of platform coping. This incident was observed by an off-duty loco inspector who quickly made contact with Control to arrange a replacement engine for the onward journey. Unfortunately none was available and the Huddersfield crew, due to take over from Annesley men, were now faced with the prospect of tackling the steep gradients to Penistone with what the driver is reputedly alleged to have called 'this foreign looking contraption'.

He flatly declared his unwillingness to proceed, although the fireman – with the promise of right hand firing – was not so concerned and finally, some 48 minutes late and after having completely disrupted the station workings, *Woolston Grange* left Sheffield northwards on its history making journey driven by an Eastern Region loco inspector immaculately attired in blue pinstripe suit, Homburg hat and briefcase. No 6858's cylinder casing collected a few more dents on the way to Denby Dale but the locomotive still managed to pull back six minutes of lost time when it eventually arrived at Huddersfield. Its subsequent stay on Hillhouse shed initially caused problems for the local railway police who were hard pressed to keep sightseers away but eleven days later it was finally allowed to return home to Oxley as an out of gauge load running via Micklehurst, Edgeley and Crewe, with speed restricted to 35mph.

The last 14 months of No 6858's career were rather less eventful and after a return to Tyseley in June 1965, interestingly its first shed when new, *Woolston Grange* was withdrawn in October that year and stored with several other members of the class at various locations around the shed yard. In January 1966 it was subsequently towed away with sister and numerically consecutive locomotive No 6857 *Tudor Grange* to Cohen's at Kingsbury near Tamworth where within a few weeks of arrival it was unceremoniously cut up for scrap. What a pity not a single representative of this versatile and successful class has survived into preservation.

4-6-0 No 6018 King Henry VI

By the mid-1920s the demands of ever increasing train loads running to faster timings led to the need for Collett to design something a bit larger than his successful Castles. The limiting factor on locomotive development up to this time had been the imposition of a 20 ton axle load restriction by the civil engineer and it was not until the necessary works had been undertaken on certain sections of the main line that the permissible loading was increased, enabling the Kings to be developed.

With a tractive effort some 30 per cent above the Castles, this new 30-strong class of engine took its rightful place at the very top of GWR motive power.

Built at Swindon in June 1928, No 6018 *King Henry VI* spent its first few weeks after assembly running in on short distance local duties. This was normal practice for all new locomotives. There must have been one or two problems, for in early August No 6018 re-entered the works for attention and was not formally handed over to its first shed at Plymouth Laira until 2 September. This was quickly followed by a move to Newton Abbot in March 1929 where *King Henry VI* was destined to remain until just after nationalisation in 1948.

Because of their 22½ ton axle loading the Kings based in the West Country were restricted almost exclusively to the main line services between Plymouth and Paddington via Westbury or Bristol. In this heyday of GWR express workings this included such well known trains of the time as the Cornish Riviera and Torbay Express, the Kings being popular choices for such prestigious duties as a result of their weight-pulling ability and excellent adhesion. Both these qualities enabled the ferocious South Devon banks to be tackled with relative ease, although even a King had to be piloted on heavier trains. While the class were

No 6018 King Henry VI *running in after overhaul hauls an up local near Box on 28 April 1952. The locomotive had been repainted in BR green – a most welcome change from the light blue livery previously carried by the class. Note the second headlamp on the left hand running plate.*

predominantly express passenger engines, they were also regularly seen on parcel trains or vacuum freights at certain periods, as balancing workings to their primary duties.

King Henry VI's work pattern remained fairly constant on the West of England route until shortly after the formation of BR when it was chosen to represent the Western Region in the Locomotive Exchanges in 1948. Owing to their limited route availability and loading gauge restrictions the only 'foreign' line that could take the Kings was the former Great Northern route from Kings Cross to Leeds. On 9 May that year No 6018 appeared at the London terminus to undergo platform clearance tests prior to two weeks of trials alongside a Royal Scot, a Duchess, and a Merchant Navy. Although railway commentators have expressed differing views it is generally considered that No 6018 acquitted itself well, proving capable of a clean start from all stations at which the test trains stopped even under the most difficult conditions.

In November 1948 *King Henry VI* moved to Bristol (Bath Road) partly to cover a circular working from Bristol-Shrewsbury-Paddington-Bristol but the few members of the class based here also worked in the opposite direction to Exeter and Plymouth. The allocation of Kings to Bristol was comparatively brief for by mid 1950 they had all been transferred away, with No 6018 going to Old Oak Common in July. Around this time the locomotive was repainted in the new BR standard light blue express livery with black and white lining. GWR enthusiasts strongly disliked this and indeed it did not suit the Kings who soon were to have their Brunswick Green restored.

Despite now working from the London end of the line, No 6018 was still principally confined to the Plymouth, Bristol and Wolverhampton services. An exception was on the evening of 1 July 1952 when, in sparkling green livery (among the first of its class to be repainted), it worked the ex-LMS Royal Train from Paddington down to Newton Abbot to enable Her Majesty the Queen to visit the Royal Show on the following day. No 6018 also headed the return journey as far as Castle Cary.

By the summer of 1954, when the Bristolian express had resumed its pre-war schedule of 105 minutes for the journey between Paddington and Temple Meads, Kings were again rostered to the train. The operators at first deemed the extra weight of the new BR Standard Mark 1 coaches allocated to the Bristolian – 250 tons for seven coaches Monday to Thursday and over 280 tons when an eighth coach was added at weekends – to be too much for a Castle, so *King Henry VI* was a common sight on the train during this period. On one occasion during July 1955, O. S. Nock was on the footplate of the down Bristolian and he recorded No 6018 as having achieved 102½mph as it passed through Dauntsey. The King's reign on this train was relatively short for within a year or so the increasing numbers of rejuvenated Castles – now provided with four-row superheaters and double chimneys – took over and proved easy masters of the schedule.

Early in 1956 two Kings in quick succession were found to have serious bogie fractures and as a safety measure most of the class were

Poppet Valve Gear

The Great Western Railway Company's engine No 2935 *Caynham Court*, has recently left the Swindon factory, after being fitted with RC poppet valve gear in place of the usual Stephenson gear as fitted to the Saint class.

The motion for the rotary cams is supplied by means of a bevel wheel drive, mounted on the centre of the driving axle, which operates a cardan shaft rotating on the centre line of the engine, and fitted with a universal joint at each end. This shaft couples at the front end to a cross shaft which is entirely enclosed, and in turn operates two shafts, one on each side of the engine, by means of bevel wheels housed in gear boxes. The two outside shafts operate, by means of worm gearing, the cam shafts, which lie across the engine in cam boxes directly over the cylinders.

The reversing gear is worked from the cab by a rotating shaft which lies on the right-hand side of the engine, and meshes, by means of bevel wheels, with a cross-shaft which works a worm and worm wheel, solid with which is a pinion that in turn gears with a rack. At each end of the rack is attached a rocking lever, the other end of which is coupled to the cam shaft. By this means the cam shafts are moved across the engine, so bringing the valves under the control of differently shaped cams. There are nine cams for fore-gear running, one for mid-gear, and three for back-gear.
– *Great Western Railway Magazine*, 1931.

temporarily withdrawn from service at the end of January. Investigations revealed that many had developed fatigue cracks in the bogie, a fault remedied by the welding of strengthening pieces to the frame plates. While this repair work was being undertaken four Stanier Pacifics, Nos 46207/10/54/7 were drafted in to help. Fully fit again, *King Henry VI* was soon returned to service at Old Oak Common and resumed its rightful place on the Western Region top link duties, receiving a double chimney for good measure in February 1958, the last but one of the class to be so treated. During these closing years of the 1950s many famous headboards were to grace its smokebox door including the Cambrian Coast Express, Cornish Riviera, Mayflower, Royal Duchy and Inter-City, this latter duty being shared with Kings stationed at Wolverhampton Stafford Road.

The introduction of the various diesel hydraulic designs from 1959 onwards saw steam working gradually eliminated on the Westbury and Bristol routes to the West with the result that new work had to be found for many of the Old Oak and Laira Kings. One such example was their first regular assignment to the Paddington to South Wales services. This was initiated, none too successfully in the beginning, by Old Oak engines but in the late summer of 1960 it was considered more sensible to base the locomotives at Cardiff and thus Canton received its first ever allocation of Kings in September, No 6018 being one of six sent there to cover these new diagrams. Although principally intended to work the depot's regular turns to and from Paddington, the arrangement of rosters was such that only three Kings were constantly required for London

King class No 6018 King Henry VI *was retained after withdrawal to work an SLS (Midland Area) special from Birmingham to Swindon on 28 April 1963 thus becoming the last King to run in revenue service. It is seen here at Swindon being serviced for the return journey surrounded by Hymek diesels. Smokebox number and shed plates had been removed – the number painted on the front buffer beam and TYS (Tyseley) stencilled on the frame GWR style.*

No 6018 King Henry VI *is back in Swindon Works; 'A' shop on 28 July 1963 – three months after withdrawal. Mystery surrounds the reason behind the careful dismantling being undertaken. Two 38XX class 2-8-0s Nos 3836 and 3826 and Prairie tank locomotive No 6155, are under repair on adjacent roads.*

Dredging
After 1923 the GWR dredged about five million tons of sand and silt annually mainly from the South Wales ports where the combinations of fast-flowing rivers emptying into the Severn and the high tide range led to heavy silting. There were once fourteen dredgers, fourteen steam hopper barges and sixteen 'dumb' hopper barges plus various other vessels. Just one of the worlds within worlds in the docks department.

duty leaving the remainder available for such other workings as the three Cardiff-Shrewsbury duties, the Swindon and Kensington milk trains, or trips to Bristol. One particular train on which *King Henry VI* was photographed several times during this period was the 12.15pm Manchester-Plymouth over the North and West route.

In June 1962 No 6018 returned to Old Oak Common and throughout what proved to be its last summer in normal service was frequently seen on holiday expresses and excursions to the West Country. On one occasion it was noted leaving the carriage sidings at Goodrington with the empty stock of a return working from Paignton to Paddington. This was somewhat unusual as the considerable restrictions imposed on Kings anywhere off the main line normally precluded them from using most sidings and goods loops except in an emergency. Even at this late stage of its career *King Henry VI* was still rostered to some of the more prestigious duties then remaining for steam haulage and this included the weekend working of the Bristolian which ran on a Saturday with a much heavier load and to a slower schedule than the diesel hauled Monday to Friday train.

At the introduction of the winter 1962 timetable only a handful of Kings remained in service and it was gradually getting more and more difficult to find regular work for them. However on 26 October both *King Henry VI* and No 6000 *King George V* were used to haul two special trains conveying guests from London to attend the opening of the new Spencer steelworks at Newport by the Queen. On arrival both engines went on to Ebbw Junction shed for servicing, probably the first time

128

that two examples of the class had been seen there at the same time. As a sure indication that its days as an express passenger locomotive were numbered No 6018 spent several days at the beginning of November, in company with No 6011 *King James I*, acting as a test load for the rebuilding work being undertaken on the Wye bridge at Chepstow. This was followed on the 17th of that month by a return to special duty when it worked a Locomotive Club of Great Britain King Commemoration railtour from Paddington to Birminghan Snow Hill, returning to London coupled inside a Western diesel on the up *Cambrian Coast Express*. There are no further recorded workings after this date and No 6018 was placed in store at Old Oak Common until 21 December when the sheer volume of additional Christmas traffic led to its last ever complete run over the West of England main line to Plymouth when it steamed out of Paddington with the 1.25pm relief to Penzance. Shortly after its return to London official condemnation followed, thus bringing to an end a distinguished career of 34 years, during which it had covered in excess of 1,730,000 miles.

This was not the end of the line for *King Henry VI*, however, for in March 1963 it was given a temporary reprieve and sent to Swindon Works for repair. After receiving a quick repaint as well it was delivered to Tyseley on April 19 and during the following week ran in on local passenger duties, the 6.5pm Birmingham to Leamington and return being a particular favourite. On April 28 it then headed the Stephenson Locomotive Society's farewell King special from Birmingham to Swindon Works, outwards via the Greenford Loop, Southall and Didcot and return via Didcot, Oxford and Leamington. For this very last run *King Henry VI* was smartly turned out – the smokebox number and shed plate had been removed and the number painted on the bufferbeam in true GWR style together with the shed code TYS stencilled on the frames.

With the final journey over, *King Henry VI* was withdrawn for the second time and left its temporary home at Tyseley a few days later bound for Swindon. Cut up in the infamous C shop during September 1963 No 6018 was one of ten Kings that at least retained the dignity of being dismantled at its place of birth rather than by outside scrap metal merchants.

A Busy Weekend at Cardiff

In the early evening of Saturday 27 January 1934 the final excursion train carrying the last of the estimated 21,277 returning supporters home from the Wales v England International Rugby match departed, and the Great Western operating authorities breathed a collective sigh of relief. Everything had worked without a hitch. The rebuilt and resignalled Cardiff General station and its approaches, from Ely in the west to Newtown in the east, had passed a severe test a bare twenty days after completion.

This rebuilding and resignalling scheme, the largest and most complex of its type that the Great Western had then undertaken, was but one of the Company's major

investment programmes in South Wales undertaken during the twenties and thirties. They included similar rebuilding at Newport (High Street), Briton Ferry and Swansea (High Street) together with new marshalling yards, upgrading of shipping facilities and modern locomotive sheds. Taken together they resulted in great improvements to both the main line and the branches in the industrial valleys. The times were uncertain and troubled, but not only did the Company look to the future, it also conducted such projects with a skill and efficiency that many envy today. Such certainly was the case as far as the Cardiff project was concerned.

Commencing in the west the lines were quadrupled from approximately one and a half miles east of Ely

---

No Hurry

Passengers landing or embarking at the Ports of Plymouth and Avonmouth can obtain Special Reduced Fare Tickets to and from London and certain other principal Stations on the system.

Tickets from Plymouth to London are available for seven days, and passengers may break their journey at any Main Line Station en route. Application for the necessary authority to break the journey must be made to the Station Master at the Docks or Millbay Station. On payment of a small additional sum passengers can also obtain Tickets to London by the Cathedral route, enabling them to visit the interesting Cathedral Cities of Exeter, Bristol, Hereford, Worcester and Oxford; also Stratford-upon-Avon, &c.

Friends desiring to meet passengers by steamer, or to see them embark, can, in many cases, obtain Single Fare for the Double Journey Tickets upon the presentation of a voucher obtainable from the Shipping Company.

station, and an additional up goods loop was also added eastwards from Leckwith Road bridge. At the same time the lines between Ely and Leckwith Road were diverted to a site immediately adjacent to the south of the old main lines and raised on embankments, and bridges were built to allow the abolition of three level crossings at Moors Lane, Sanatorium Road and Leckwith Road. New mechanical signal boxes of 37 and 135 levers respectively were built at Leckwith Road Junction and Canton Sidings. The former box controlled the newly built junction between the main line and the ex-Taff Vale Railway line from Radyr Junction to Grangetown. Cardiff General station was rebuilt to provide three down platforms numbered 3, 4 and 7; three up platforms numbered 1, 2 and 6, and a bay platform (numbered 5 and situated between platforms 3 and 4) at the west end for arrivals and departures in the Swansea direction. In addition the scheme included up and down 'middle' lines and an up goods line for through traffic. The Riverside station retained its identity at this time, but was rebuilt as an island platform for up and down traffic from Clarence Road in Cardiff's dockland. (This island platform later became platform Nos 8 and 9.) The station layout now allowed departures to the up main to be made from Nos 1 and 2 platforms, and the up goods line; to the up relief from Nos 1, 2 and 6 platforms and to the up goods line, and also to the up ex-Taff Vale line from Platform Nos 4 and 6. Access to Nos 3 and 4 platforms could be made from the down main, while from the down relief both these platforms and No 7 could be reached, together with the down 'middle' line. The down ex-Taff Vale line had access to Nos 4 and 7 platforms. Finally running eastwards from the station two additional running lines were built on the north side of the original main lines as far as Newtown West signal box. As is well known the former mechanical signalling in the station area was replaced by electrically powered signalling, which included colour light signals, electrically operated points and track circuiting. The East signal box, which contained 153 levers was opened on May 28 1933, while the West signal box, which replaced one of the same name, and Penarth Junction signal box, had 339 levers and was opened on 7 January 1934.

The design of these new signal boxes was unique being in line with the architectural thinking of the times rather than in the traditional style of the Company. Both were three storied, had steel frames with red brick infill and were faced with a multi-coloured sand faced brick. The ground floor contained the power supply; the first floor accommodation for relays, cable runs and so on and gave access to the interlocking frame for maintenance, while on the top floor was the operating room with interlocking frame and block telegraph instruments. There was a central bay window on this floor to give the signalmen an unobstructed view of the area under their control. In the locking frame, the locks for interlocking were separate from those for track circuits and other controls.

All running signals were controlled directly by track circuits, of which there were 169, each being automatically replaced to 'danger' by the passage of the train. For the main line 88 two aspect signals (green and red for stop, green and yellow for distant), were installed. These signals were visible at over 2,000 yards in bright sunlight, a necessity in this case since the layout faced approximately east-west, and the rising or setting sun at certain times of the year could be directly in a driver's eyes. In addition to these main line signals, 144 goods, shunt, call-on and backing signals were installed, together with 29 route indicators and finally 141 point machines. This whole complex project took place alongside the existing layout, which operated unhindered during its progress, apart from the inevitable temporary speed restrictions, and reached its climax on the weekend of 6–7 January 1934 with the change-over to bring into operation the new signalling and track layout.

As until recent times the traffic through Cardiff fell into two main groups. Firstly there was the main line between London and West Wales and secondly the local traffic to and from Queen Street station, Penarth and Barry as well as, at that time, Cardiff Docks via Riverside station. In total some 306 passenger and 140 freight trains were dealt with in a twenty four hour period. Then, as now, there was little interchange for ordinary passenger services between these two groups, although through trains from the South Wales ports, diverted from the main line at Bridgend and Penarth Dock and regained the main line at Cardiff West signal box. It is also perhaps worth mentioning the local service between Cardiff (Riverside) and Pontypridd via the main line and St Fagans, and to recall that this service ran on a modified route during much of the Cardiff rebuilding. At an early stage the direct junction from the Riverside lines to the main line disappeared, and it was impossible to bring into use the new junction at this stage since Penarth Junction signal box occupied the site of this new junction. The service was therefore diverted via the Penarth relief lines and East and North curve junctions, between which a loop linked the Cardiff to Grangetown line with that of the ex-Taff Vale Radyr to Grangetown line, before rejoining the main line by way of the new Leckwith Road Junction.

All ordinary passenger trains stopped at Cardiff General station and a considerable amount of engine changing and tail work was normal. In addition there were numerous movements to and from the locomotive and carriage sidings, the former alone accounting for over 170 such movements daily. Thus the change-over from two mechanical signal boxes of 36 and 115 levers to the new power box while at the same time bringing into use the whole new permanent way layout was a huge undertaking.

The work was divided into three stages. The first, commencing at midnight on Saturday 6 January, involved the disconnection of all the points and signals on

the up and down Riverside to Penarth lines and Nos 6 and 7 platform lines and, except for the block telegraph for platform Nos 3 and 4 the old West signal box was taken out of use. The signals were immediately removed, and upon completion of this task signal contractors from the Westinghouse Brake & Saxby Signal Company moved in and began connecting up the new points and light signals into the new West signal box. The second stage involved the disconnection from the Penarth Junction signal box of all points and signals on the up and down Penarth relief lines, Nos 4 and 5 platform lines, and the up and down engine and carriage lines. The block telegraph for platform Nos 3 and 4 was moved from the old West signal box to the new West signal box, and the block telegraph for the up and down Penarth relief lines was also moved to the new West signal box from Penarth Junction signal box. As before, all the old signalling equipment was removed and the signalling contractors then moved in to connect up.

The third and last stage of the change-over involved the transfer of the remaining block telegraph apparatus

Pengam Junction east of Cardiff with a South Wales – West of England express hauled by Hall class No 6927 Lilford Hall passing on the up main line. The branch to the left is the Roath Dock branch. Even in the late 1950s this was an almost one hundred percent GWR scene in spite of the maroon painted coaches, LMS style. The last GWR type pannier tank class (84/94XX) is on the left, signals and signal box are typical and the then important yard is at the height of activity. Note the single bolster wagons for carrying rail for relaying work.

to the new West signal box and the physical removal of the Penarth Junction and old West signal boxes. During this phase traffic operations were maintained by groundmen on the main line until the connecting up of the remaining work was finished. Priority in this phase of the work was given to providing through facilities from the up lines through the station and access to the fish platform and loading dock. (These were situated at the west end of the station and to the north of platform No 1 beyond the up goods line.) On completion of this work

131

Cardiff General station as reconstructed, together with adjacent works. GWR Development Works 1933.

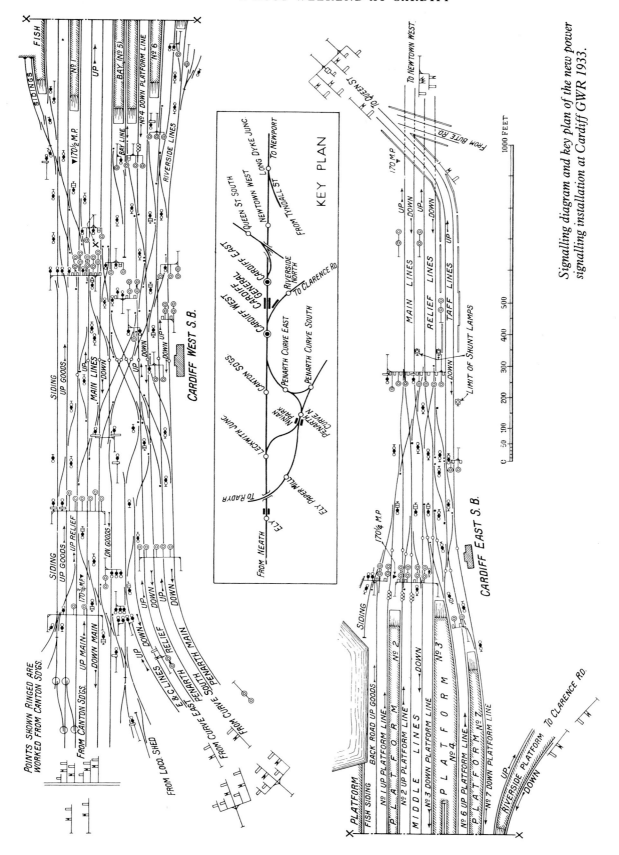

Signalling diagram and key plan of the new power signalling installation at Cardiff GWR 1933.

133

the main line connection to the engine shed, the depot and carriage sidings remained to be completed, and when these were finished the operations, with one minor exception, were complete. Dismantling and removal of the old signal boxes began at the start of this phase, the old West signal box being cleared and ready for dispatch by half past five that evening. Penarth Junction signal box was considerably larger and it took another twelve hours to complete its removal. Unfortunately this box stood foul of both the down goods and down main lines and until it had been removed this junction could not be laid in; in fact it was finally laid and connected up on the following Sunday morning.

The planned time for this exercise was from midnight on Saturday to 6pm on Sunday, a mere eighteen hours, but so well was the work organised, and so efficiently was it carried out, that the work was completed by 2pm. During this time some 94 normal engine movements were dealt with, as well as the numerous accompanying shunting operations, in between which had to thread the crane and the Signal Department train, loading the two old signal boxes and picking up 27 old signals, 27 old ground discs, together with 13 sets of facing point apparatus.

Those who took part in this mammoth exercise, which relieved a very bad traffic bottleneck and provided Wales' capital with a main line railway station of which it could be proud, and which still stands largely unaltered to this day, would, if they had been asked, probably have shrugged and said it was 'all in a day's work'. But they, no doubt, took a quiet pride in what by any consideration was a job well done. The Great Western certainly knew how to instil pride and loyalty in its men, and in so doing reaped in South Wales, as elsewhere, a great benefit from a grateful, satisfied public.

Port Service
Opened in 1910, the direct line from Filton Junction gave access to Avonmouth from Bristol and South Wales as well as London without touching Bristol. The *Railway & Travel Monthly* reported that the line was inaugurated on 12 May in connection with the sailing of the Canadian Northern Railway's liner *Royal Edward* from the new Royal Edward Dock at Avonmouth. Two special trains were run from Paddington direct to the Avonmouth Docks. The opening of this new linking-up line reduces the distance from London to Avonmouth to 120 miles and therefore presents an excellent opportunity for the GWR to inaugurate a two-hour schedule, at exactly 60 miles an hour. The first special train, conveying the third class passengers, left Paddington at 11.5am and arrived at Avonmouth at 1.30pm, whilst the second train, with the saloon and cabin passengers, left at 4.20pm, arriving at the ship's side at 6.32.

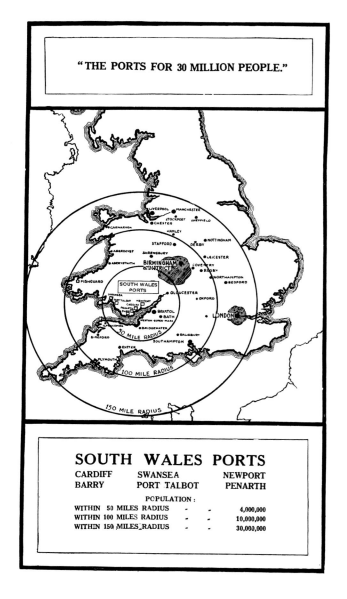

"THE PORTS FOR 30 MILLION PEOPLE."

SOUTH WALES PORTS

| CARDIFF | SWANSEA | NEWPORT |
| BARRY | PORT TALBOT | PENARTH |

POPULATION:

WITHIN 50 MILES RADIUS	-	-	4,000,000
WITHIN 100 MILES RADIUS	-	-	10,000,000
WITHIN 150 MILES RADIUS	-	-	30,000,000

South Wales

South Wales is a country of contrasts, deep narrow valleys formerly with collieries scattered along their sides, steel works both in the valleys and along the coastal strip, wild moorland, ports and seaside resorts. All this was served by the Great Western plus, prior to 1922/3 13 independent railways which were amalgamated with the GWR. The LMS had a foothold by virtue of the LNWR Heads of the Valleys and Sirhowy Valley lines plus the Midland's purchase of the Swansea Vale Railway.

Fortunately the bulk of the loaded traffic was down the valleys where lengthy coal trains trundled slowly towards the ports hauled by relatively modest size tank locomotives controlled only by the engine's steam brake and a 20 ton brake van.

Some railways also ran intensive passenger services from Newport and Cardiff up the valleys to the larger towns. Those to Merthyr, Rhymney and Aberdare inter alia survive to this day.

The main line, originally broad gauge, serves Newport, Cardiff, Port Talbot, Neath and Swansea and, since 1906, the cross-channel port of Fishguard.

Almost certainly a posed picture but this does epitomise the 'Valleys' and coal traffic. Two down loaded coal trains and an up empty wagon train on the Taff Vale line south of Taffs Well station. Both locomotives are 56XX class 0-6-2Ts built specially for the South Wales coal traffic. Rather unusually one is facing down the valley, they normally worked chimney first up the valleys. The Taff Vale was a very early line to serve the coalfields and was opened in 1840/41. The viaduct, 'Walnut Tree', was a latecomer and carried the Barry Railway line from Tyn-y-Caeau Junction to Penrhos Junctions with the Rhymney and Alexandra Dock Railways. It was opened on 1 August 1901. Walnut Tree viaduct was demolished between 1969 and 1973.

135

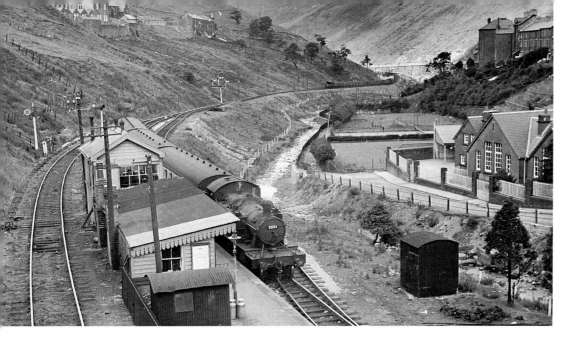

The GWR branch from Bridgend to Abergwynfi was opened on 22 March 1886 and closed to passengers on 13 June 1960. It was at the head of a remote valley on the River Avan. Small 2-6-2T No 5556 has just arrived at the terminus with a train from Bridgend on 2 August 1951. The goods line to the left led to Avon Colliery.

Pentyrch Crossing south of Taffs Well, Taff Vale Railway with a 56XX class 0-6-2T No 6643 on an up train of coal empties in 1954. The single line crossing the TVR main line diagonally is the Melingriffith Tramroad which ran from Taffs Well Junction north of the station to Melingriffith tinplate works near Radyr.

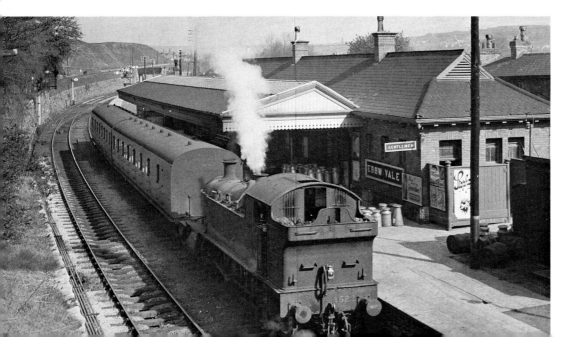

Ebbw Vale was on the site of a very early railway, the Monmouthshire Railway and Canal originally opened in 1798 and worked by the GWR from 1 August 1875. Passenger trains were withdrawn from 30 April 1962. 45XX class 2-6-2T No 4522 is waiting to depart with the 10.03am to Aberbeeg consisting of a 2 coach 'B' set on 26 April 1948. Note the milk churns on the platform.

Some of the South Wales lines escaped from the industrial valleys and traversed some wild and beautiful scenery. Ponsticill Junction, Brecon & Merthyr Railway was on the B&M mainline from Newport to Brecon and the junction for Merthyr. It was alongside the lower end of Taff Fechan reservoir. The 1.19pm to Merthyr stands in the loop platform behind 0-6-0PT No 9642 and another member of the class No 7771, is entering the station with the 12.15pm Brecon to Newport. The date is 24 March 1951. Passenger services to Merthyr were withdrawn on 13 November 1961 and between Brecon and Newport on 31 December 1962.

Nantymoel, another branch with a train service from Bridgend. 0-6-0PT No 7770 heads the 3.00pm to Bridgend on 25 September 1951. The branch was opened in 1865 and closed to passengers on 5 May 1965.

Castle class 4-6-0 No 4082 Windsor Castle *on a North to West express near Llanvihangel on 1 August 1953. Before the introduction of BR Mark 1 stock coaches were both LMS and GWR. The leading vehicles are LMS and there appears to be some GWR ones at the rear. No 4082 is in fact No 7013* Bristol Castle *in disguise as the real* Windsor Castle *was in shops in February 1952 when it was required to work King George VI's funeral train. So No 7013 was hastily substituted and renumbered/renamed.*

8
FAST WORK
IN THE MARCHES

THE driver brings his head in from the window opening and dodges across the Castle's cab between his mate's swings. 'Smell anything?' He leans well out on the left side, his eye divided between watching for bridge arches and scanning the wheels and motion. The engine is pounding up the bank above Llantarnam, barely doing forty, the regulator well open and making a fair old crackle at the chimney. She is ready for shopping, beginning to kick on the curves. She tumbles hard into low rail joints, and there are tell-tale wisps of steam where there should not be any. Canton has made a brave show of cleaning her paintwork and scouring the brass, but the baked-on oily grime on the underside of the boiler tells a truer tale of accumulated miles. Nationalisation is but weeks away.

The driver eventually focusses on the intermediate coupled wheel boss which has a hazy look about it. 'Think we've got a warm one there. Don't put any more on, we'll probably need a fresh one at Pontypool. Knock off the heat, too.' He crosses the cab again, eases the regulator well back and winds the reverser nearly into full forward to ease the loading on the suffering axlebox bearing. With this light working speed falls rapidly on the 1 in 95, but now Pontypool South's distant is in sight. The 8.55 from Cardiff rolls up the outside road, past the Bristol portion waiting in the platform and braking gently. Through the scissors into the platform, the fireman looking back to see the last of their eight coaches clear the switches. He calls 'Right, mate,' and with a rush of air the driver brakes her to a stand.

He is down the cab steps into the six-foot in a jiffy, feeling the big end with the back of his fingers (cool), the coupling rod boss (warm) – but he can feel the heat from the wheel boss without touching it. She is undoubtedly finished for today.

He climbs up again and on to the platform. The station inspector is at the rear end supervising the attachment of the five Bristol coaches, and the driver has to walk back, dodging passengers and barrows. 'Need a fresh engine, Owen. Hot box.'

The inspector cusses inwardly and dives for the phone to speak first to the shed and then to Control. 'The only thing they can give you quickly is the 53 that came in with your Bristol part. They haven't started to clean the fire, so they'll fill the tank and send her straight back. She'll be over in a few minutes.'

The driver looks grim. 'A 53? Is that the best they can find? What's the Bristol load, five? That makes us thirteen up, which will be about 400 tons. That's way over the top for a 53.'

Opposite *No 6943 Farnley Hall calls at Abergavenny Junction with the 4.10pm Hereford–Cardiff. The connection for the LNWR line to Merthyr Tydfil hauled by LMS Class 3 2-6-2T No 40145 stands in the up loop. Abergavenny Junction lay in the middle of a seven mile climb to Llanvihangel and bank engines were provided here if required. The date is September 1952.*

'Sorry, that's all they've got, unless you'd like a 28, and you'd have to wait for that, anyway.'

A shrug of the shoulders, and 'Looks like we're landed with it, then. Let's hope she can take some punishment. Ask Control if they can give us anything better at Hereford.'

'Will do. Meanwhile hook off and put your engine in the bay. I'll speak to North box.'

As driver and fireman wait at the head of the train with their gear they watch No 5343 back down from the shed, a column of smoke telling of valiant efforts to build up a respectable fire again. A few ribald pleasantries are exchanged with the shed crew and a quick glance at their new mount. She is grubby but the paint tells them that she is not many months out of Swindon after overhaul. A cleaner with a coalpick is busy in the tender pulling coal down to the front; it looks reasonably lumpy, but heaven knows what might be underneath. The fireman goes down between to couple while the driver stows their gear and looks at the fire; it is built up thick enough but is green and unburnt despite the blower's roar. Water is just below the top nut, with the pressure at 170 and climbing very slowly.

After the brake test the ejector pulls the vacuum gauge slowly round to 25 inches; from the platform whistles blow, a flag waves at the back end, and the driver turns to pop the whistle and yank the regulator handle open. It is 9.58 when it should have been 9.41. He has set the reversing lever some way short of full gear – he estimates it is about 45–50 per cent, and she hesitates a moment before getting hold of the train. He tells his mate 'Shut the door and don't put any on her for two or three minutes, until the fire is well burnt up' and checks the delivery from the sight feed lubricator. As they gather speed down the bank to Little Mill the pressure gauge falters a bit but then starts to recover; in the dip, on goes the injector and the fireman starts feeding coal to the now-hot fire as the driver gives her more steam for the hump before Nantyderry. Pressure lags a little but once over the top she begins to really roll the train. But not for long; down goes the regulator handle and the driver rubs the brake to steady things on the Penpergwm curve to something not too much above the sixty limit, bearing in mind the ensuing seven mile climb to Llanvihangel. It is just the breather the boiler needed, the safety valves are just beginning to sizzle and as she puts her nose to the bank the water is bobbing near the top of the glass.

Still the lever has not been touched since leaving Pontypool. As Penpergwm station platform comes in sight the driver opens the regulator again on to the main valve and the little 53 shakes herself and starts to talk. With the Sugar Loaf looming ahead, he has now got to make a quick decision on whether to stop at Abergavenny for a shove over the last four miles of the bank, which are at 1 in 82/95. Speed is already falling, but the engine seems in good shape and even if they only crawl over Llanvihangel it will be quicker than stopping for a banker. Water level is pretty steady against the injector; if it stays that way they will comfortably survive when she tips over the top and starts down for Pontrilas. So he hangs on grimly and gives the regulator handle another

Saintly Saints

The *Saints* seemed so appropriately named, so steadfast, so ready to meet any challenge. Only the old-fashioned cabs betrayed their age. *Moguls* or *Halls* ran on everything, grimy goods trains, mineral trains, stopping trains, even local trains sometimes, when a tank engine had had a failure and nothing else was available. But *Saints* – even on the Penzance to Kensington milk train – would elevate the service somehow, persuade the platform staff that such a veteran deserved prompt work at station stops.

Although they remained in their last days in the North where for so long they showed the flag between Saltney and Chester, and took the Grand National specials and the Isle of Man boat trains (I almost forgot about these) right through from Shrewsbury to Birkenhead avoiding Chester, it is not 2926 *Saint Nicholas* flashing down Chirk Viaduct and stopping alongside the Glyn Valley Tram that I recall, but *Clevedon Court*, squeezed into a pair of spurs (where latterly a *Mogul* would repose) at the east end of Reading's down main platform.

Occasionally *Clevedon Court* would emerge for water, then scuttle back again like a crab, or possibly attach a van to some Weston express at the platform. Why it sat there sizzling all day
continued opposite

Pontypool Road station up platform looking south. The Bristol portion of a West to North express would have been standing beyond the scissors crossing and the Cardiff train run through this to the part of the platform in the foreground of the picture. The bay platform is just visible on the left.

tug until it is very nearly fully open. He gives a steady blast on the whistle approaching the box to say that he is going through. The bark is tremendous and staccato, and the coal is being sucked off the shovel almost before it can be aimed on to the blinding fire. The line veers to the right to avoid the mountain flank; by the summit speed is down to something like twenty, and they are going more like a pickup freight, but they have made it and dropped no more than three minutes.

Now the driver shuts off, pulls the lever back to something more like a running position, and gives her the first valve. With the change of gradient the water drops below half glass, and with the incandescent fire sending the pressure up the fireman briefly puts the second injector on to calm her. By Pandy with the River Monnow for company she is bettering sixty and the regulator comes down to the drifting position. By the bottom of the bank she is up nearly to seventy and becoming quite lively, but with a grin and shout of 'Hang on' he opens the regulator again as the engine leans to the curve. There is an envious glance at a Hall on a down freight in the loop at Pontrilas as they sweep by at 65. Now it is a case of holding what speed they can against the collar, past St Devereux and Tram Inn to the gentle but dragging final rise to the long closed Haywood box; they surmount it at close on sixty.

From here it's all downhill into Hereford and the driver takes it coasting; with braking for the heavy slacks at Red Hill Junction and Rotherwas there is no point in doing anything else. The fireman has shut off the train heat in readiness for an engine change. So they roll down Hereford platform and stop more by habit than intention at the water column. The station clock says 10.30, so they have made up three minutes.

Waiting in the Salop bay is a 'Saint', No 2937 *Clevedon Court* whose fireman is standing by the column ready to hand up the bag. 'What do we want water for,' calls the fireman from the 53's cab, 'haven't you brought that engine for us?'

'No, we're a hooker-on to Shrewsbury for you. Control orders. And don't forget there's no water at Ludlow.'

continued

long was because *Clevedon Court* was the Reading station pilot, ready to dash off at a moment's notice and surpass expectations as on one occasion occurred with the Bristolian, the crack express for *Kings*, for which the track was carefully kept cleared.

Although I have only once been held up by a failed GWR engine, failures do occur, even on the Bristolian. *Clevedon Court* rose to the occasion, taking the train from Reading to Bristol in 72 minutes 28 seconds. The time allowed for the 82.4 miles was precisely twenty-eight seconds less – for a *King* or a *Castle* expected to be travelling through Reading at 75mph or so, not starting from a stop. – George Behrend, *Gone With Regret*, one of the classics of later year publications by an author who brilliantly conveys the railway's changing ambiance.

141

Public Participation
For the first time in the history of railways a signal box, completely equipped, will be thrown open to the public . . . The public will be given an opportunity of having the unique experience of operating the levers which control the signals and switches. – Introduction to the brochure *A Great Western Railway Signal Box* issued free at the GWR's exhibit (a complete signal box) at the British Empire Exhibition, Wembley, 1925.

Hereford station down side on 7 April 1958 showing 43XX 2-6-0 No 6352 (86C) taking over the 8.00am Birmingham Snow Hill to Cardiff. Note the tidy platform and the mobile water tank filler by the footbridge.

That raises spirits somewhat, and the fireman clambers over the coal, pick in hand, to put the bag in and then bring some more coal forward. His own driver is meanwhile going round the engine with his feeder, checking that all is cool and offering her a drop of oil here and there. Standing precariously on the coal, the fireman is thrown briefly off balance as the Saint buffers up. Now it is a warning to the man on the platform and even as he is shutting off the water the bag is thrown off with a splash.

Back in the cab, the fireman has a quick look round the firebox, the coal burning bright and clean with no sign of clinker, and fires a dozen shovels ready for the next stage before putting the heat on again. The two drivers confer; the leading man will do all the braking and the 53's man tells him with a grin not to overdo it. Hereford cuts the eight minute station time by two and they get the rightaway at 10.46, eleven down. They are booked 72 minutes non-stop for the 51 miles to Salop, a hard road mostly against the collar as far as Church Stretton and then tumbling down the rest of the way on a fairly sinuous alignment which only the brave – or foolhardy – take very fast. The Saint has screw reverse, so the 53's driver can happily take it a little easier and afford to shut off steam to make more adjustment on the reversing lever. It soon becomes clear that the men on the Saint intend to pull their whack and more.

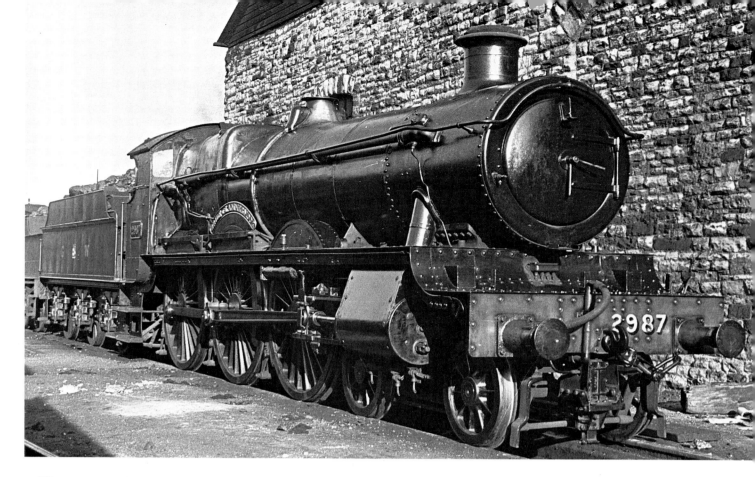

Saint class 4-6-0 No 2987 Bride of Lammermoor *on Hereford shed 6 November 1948. It was one of the earlier members of the class originally built as a 4-4-2 in August 1905 (as No 187* Robertson), *for comparison with the French built compounds. It was renamed in April 1907, converted to a 4-6-0 in July 1912 and withdrawn in October 1949. It retained a lever reverse throughout its life.*

Flanges squeal round the curve to Barrs Court Junction, and then they are away in earnest. On the Mogul the driver sets his lever at about 30 per cent and reckons that will see them through Dinmore with variations in the regulator opening. She is steaming nicely and the fireman is finding the smallish grate easy to fire on the uniform slope. The easier grades past Shelwick Junction to get them up to forty; coming round from the Worcester line to join the North and West is Saint No 2987 *Bride of Lammermoor* on a passenger, with its crew seeing the twin columns of steam and smoke, the sharp bark telling them of great effort, gives them an encouraging wave. By the time the two tracks separate for the single bores of Dinmore tunnels they are making 65. Up through the 1,054 yard tunnel itself it is all noise, smoke and a display of pyrotechnics until they emerge again into daylight at 55 plus.

The next thirteen miles, to beyond Woofferton, are reasonably easy, and the driver on the Saint is determined to make the most of it, looking back to the 53 and smilingly urging its crew on with a beckoning gesture. But the driver on the train engine has pulled the lever back a notch while his mate gets the water well up in the glass; the fire is incandescent and on a light rein only needs its palate tickled with six shovels at regular intervals. Before Ludlow they are bowling along at something close to 75, the little 53's wheels and motion twinkling at unaccustomed speed. The sharp rise from Saltmore takes enough speed out of them that they would normally shut off for the curve into the station and pay lip service to the speed restriction. But today is *not* normal; Ludlow troughs are OUT, literally, for relaying, and there is a 15mph restriction over the

143

Qualities of Coal

As a rule, the best bituminous South Wales coal is used on engines intended for fast and heavy passenger trains, and a mixture of hard Yorkshire, North Wales, or Staffordshire, with second grade South Wales coal for trains of less importance. What is known in South Wales as smokeless steam coal is of no use whatever for locomotive purposes, on account of its dry character. It is very rich in carbon, and its calorific value is exceedingly high. With a steady, continuous draught, such as is obtained in steamboats, it gives the best of results; but in locomotives, where the draught is intermittent, the punching effect of the blast produces the same result as poking an anthracite fire. On the other hand, when a bituminous coal is used, the punching of the blast has the desired effect of keeping the fire open, and turning the binding qualities of the coal to the best advantage. The Northern coals have different characteristics altogether. These are not so rich in carbon, but more so in hydrogen, and are therefore swifter burning. For light work, the hard coal makes an ideal fuel, and a mixture with a slower burning coal gives excellent results for heavy work. Instructions are given to the coalmen to put on suitable coal for particular trains, but, owing to the inadequate accommodation on the stage, or irregular supply of first and second grade coal, it sometimes, though fortunately not very often, happens that a shunting engine gets best coal, whilst an express engine gets such a quality as to render the lives of the engineman and fireman not exactly a bed of roses. – From *The Working of a Running Department*, 1907.

new track. The driver checks his watch as they run through the station, braking, and at 11.11 notes they are now only five down. But this slack could hardly be in a worse place, and will cost them all of four minutes. Maybe they take it a little charily, for there is an uncomfortable lurch near the beginning that makes them wonder whether they will be making closer contact with the nice new ballast.

Now comes the hardest part of the journey as the line climbs up the broad valley of the Teme and the narrow valley of the Onny towards the watershed at Church Stretton, and it is no fun beginning it at fifteen – well, about twenty, truth to tell. The driver on the 53 takes the opportunity to drop the reversing lever down a couple of notches, and as soon as the train is past the end of the restriction both engines are opened up to accelerate on the mile of 1 in 160 up to Bromfield. Where they would have been doing a mile a minute, and despite some lovely chimney music, they are doing barely forty. The fireman is now shovelling eight at a time to meet the heavy demand on the boiler; the driver reckons it is perhaps a bit much, and shuts off to pull her up one notch. So they come up to the main road level crossing at Onibury doing rather over fifty; cars and lorries are waiting on both sides, more than normally because of the longer section time as a result of the slack. Now there is the mile-and-a-half of 1 in 112 before Craven Arms Crossing's distant, and even with a touch more regulator speed falls off to little more than 45. The splendid view of Stokesay Castle slides by on the right but they hardly notice it.

The next interest is the running of the Central Wales train, the 7.45 from Swansea. It is due away from Craven Arms fifteen minutes before they are due through, but with that long single line you never know. The distant is off, which is a good sign, and on the slight downgrade into the station they recover to fifty. Due through at 11.18, it is actually 11.21. No sign of the Swansea – it must be away ahead of them. The driver hopes that the margin is adequate! Now they are climbing again, first at 1 in 130/105 and (with two short easements) finishing with nearly two miles of 1 in 112, and the overall pace gradually slackens. Even the Saint's slower exhaust beat is audible from the 53's cab above the noise of its own exhaust, encouraging its driver to nudge his regulator a bit nearer full open for the final miles. Marsh Farm Junction box, snug amongst the woods, slides by as they clatter over the Much Wenlock branch points. On the left, the Long Mynd dominates the valley; Wenlock Edge towers on the other side but recedes behind nearer hills. The final pull to the summit drags them down to a very noisy forty and they accelerate down through Church Stretton station at 11.30, now right on time. Would that it were as straightforward to recover time with a single engine! No sign of the Swansea – thank goodness.

There is no point now in tearing down the hill to Shrewsbury; they are allowed seventeen minutes for the nearly thirteen miles and will probably have to wait at Severn Bridge for the platform if they are more than a couple of minutes early. On the 53 the driver closes the regulator to the drift position, braces himself to let the reversing lever down a couple of notches and surveys his command. The water has come down

144

Shrewsbury Joint station on 14 May 1949. Saint class 4-6-0 No 2942 Fawley Court *passes through with an up freight. On the right an LMS Class 5 is taking water.*

to about a third of a glass, with pressure only slightly down. His mate has shut the damper and opened the firedoor to keep her quiet, leaving the flap up. He has already shut off the steam heat ready for detaching, and is now filling the tool bucket from the sprinkler pipe for a quick wash.

On the steep fall to Dorrington (it is mostly 1 in 100) speed rises into the seventies and the little 5ft 8in wheels are fairly whirling round. Some gentle braking is forthcoming from the Saint for the curves before and after Condover. The quarry structures at Bayston Hill tell the drivers that Shrewsbury is at the end of the next straight, and the Sutton Bridge Junction distant at caution suggests that the station was not expecting them to be on time. So the driver of the Saint brakes hard and then eases right off to crawl towards the home. Coming up to the bridge carrying the moribund Shropshire & Montgomeryshire line from Shrewsbury Abbey over the Great Western's tracks an unusual sight greets them. A Dean Goods comes puffing up to the bridge with a mineral wagon and brake in tow and heads for the interchange sidings at Hookagate. 'First

7000
Older readers will probably guess the subject from the number: Paddington's long-lasting telephone number in pre-dial and STD days. It was as well known as the times of express departures.

145

Superior guard, 1899.

time I've seen anything on that line for years', comments the Mogul driver to his mate, 'and the last time it was a wheezy old North Western coal engine. I thought they'd closed it.' The home does not clear until they are about a hundred yards from it. Gently does it now until he opens up to pull round the curve and into the down through platform; he stops just short of the starting signals and fully destroys the vacuum. The two engines will hook off, draw forward by Crewe Junction box and then set back to Coleham shed for disposal, where their crews will leave them to the tender mercies of the ashpit men and go to the messroom to refresh the inner man. An LMS 'Jubilee' will take the train on to Manchester after the C&W examiner has had a look at the coaches and the reservoir strings have been pulled to allow a 21in vacuum brake onward.

It was a shame about the 'Castle', but it happens. The 53 has stood up manfully to her sudden task and in partnership from Hereford has done her fair share of regaining time. The men are quite happy with their morning's work, which will be a talking point with their colleagues for a month or more. And it will all go down as an official inter-company statistic: 8.55am Cardiff–Manchester handed over to the LMS at Shrewsbury right time, in spite of everything.

No 2937 *Clevedon Court*

Following several years of trials with three prototypes and the construction of fifteen basically similar engines but with two differing wheel arrangements, Churchward eventually settled on the 4-6-0 configuration as the basis for future GWR express passenger locomotive development. He thus progressed with two versions of the 4-6-0 design in order to establish the relative merits of a two or four cylinder layout. The latter version was ultimately developed into the highly successful Star class while production proper of the two cylinder type began in 1906 with ten of the equally accomplished Saints, Nos 2901-10. The class finally reached 77 in number, this total including conversions of all the earlier 4-4-2 examples.

Turned out from Swindon Works in December 1911 No 2937 *Clevedon Court* travelled down to West Wales to take up duty at Fishguard shed, becoming the first member of the class to be allocated there. This comparatively small depot had been opened only five years previously to coincide with the introduction of the Southern Ireland steamer services and was often referred to as Goodwick, this being the name of the adjacent station. Its early years at Fishguard were shared with No 2938 *Corsham Court* and No 2940 *Dorney Court* and together they helped work the sometimes heavy boat trains as well as other South Wales expresses.

By the summer of 1914 No 2937 had moved on to Wolverhampton (Stafford Road) and took its place on the important two-hour expresses between Birmingham Snow Hill and Paddington. One of the most difficult

trains on this service was the 2.50pm up from Birmingham which not only carried a fair load through to London but also a three-coach section that was slipped at Banbury. The Saint's performance on these almost 400 ton trains was frequently remarkable, their Wolverhampton drivers having no qualms in working them flat out over the uphill sections of the route.

In December 1917, *Clevedon Court* was transferred to Bristol where its work continued on top-link duties, almost having a monopoly of the west to north trains which it took as far as Plymouth. This lasted until September 1921 when it moved to a new home at Exeter. By this date most of the longer distance trains in the West Country were in the hands of the larger Stars but Exeter's Saints managed to retain one main line duty well into the 1920s. This was the West of England postal service over the entire distance between Penzance and Paddington via Bristol. No 2937 frequently appeared on this train which left the Cornish terminus at 6.00pm and ran right through to London with a change of crew at Exeter. The men lodged at Old Oak and then returned on the corresponding down train, again being replaced at Exeter. On arrival at Penzance in the early morning the locomotive would pass the rest of the day tucked away at the back of the shed. The Exeter Saints had another important duty in the early 1920s, this being the haulage of the *Cornish Riviera Express* over the short stretch between Truro and Plymouth.

Clevedon Court returned briefly to Goodwick in the summer of 1925 but following the South Wales reorganisation of 1926 Fishguard lost its entire allocation of

Saints with a large batch of the class being centred on Landore shed in Swansea. Within a short time of its arrival here the locomotive was sent to Swindon for repair, an operation which took some five months, the greater part of which was actually spent waiting its turn to enter the works at what was clearly a busy time. On completion of its overhaul No 2937 did not return to Landore but was posted to Bristol Bath Road quickly followed by further moves to Gloucester and Reading in the period up to December 1929. The Saints at this latter depot were regularly used on the semi-fasts up to Paddington but were just as equally seen on the cross-country services between Westbury and Weymouth.

At the beginning of 1930 *Clevedon Court* was operating from Shrewsbury over the West to North line again, its two cylinder layout and Churchward arrangement of the Stephenson link motion giving it a slight edge over the Stars on this route where there were heavy gradients and little opportunity for fast running. The Salop Saints were also available for working south to Wolverhampton and north to Chester when required.

After a brief spell at Oxford, No 2937 was reallocated to Wolverhampton (Stafford Road) again in August

Saint class No 2937 Clevedon Court *stands in the up bay at Hereford in 1953. A Midland class 3F 0-6-0 is just visible behind the signal box, no doubt waiting to work a train to Brecon. The engine is in its early BR livery of 'LNWR' lined out black as applied to secondary passenger engines and by now has been allocated a 4000 gallon tender. The headlamps on the buffer beam are actually tail and headlamps as the engine will have been running light from the shed.*

1931, the very month in which the first of the Saints was withdrawn, the unfortunate locomotive being No 2985 *Peveril of the Peak*. Many observers thought the writing was now on the wall for the rest of the class but *Clevedon Court* was to show there was still plenty of life left in them yet, a point it emphasised on two separate occasions following its transferral to Reading in October 1932. Both instances involved the engine, which was minding its own business on relatively mundane station pilot chores, being pressed into top class express duty following the failure of the rostered motive power.

The first of the noteworthy episodes occurred in April

147

1936 when the regular King expired at Reading with the down *Cornish Riviera*. Fortunately a correspondent of *The Railway Magazine* was on hand to see *Clevedon Court* take its place and subsequently pass through Taunton at full speed on its way to Plymouth just ten minutes late. The second incident also featured an ailing King, this time on the down *Bristolian*, which had run hot. No 2937 was backed on very quickly and set about making up lost time, the crew apparently having full confidence in the capabilities of their theoretically unsuitable engine to keep up with the King's schedule. In the event they were proved correct for the net time from Reading to Bristol was 5½ minutes ahead of schedule and this included a maximum speed of 90mph through Dauntsey!

After this somewhat energetic interlude at Reading, *Clevedon Court* was transferred to Cardiff in May 1938 and then to Pontypool Road shortly after the outbreak of World War II in November 1939. At this latter shed the Saints frequently took turns with the Castle Class 4-6-0s on some of the heavier passenger work between Pontypool and Shrewsbury, trains which often comprised sixteen or seventeen loaded coaches. The operating authorities must have been very pleased indeed to have such able locomotives as the Saints to call on in times of need.

Clevedon Court's nameplate almost certainly with a red background to its brass letters. Even though the engine is very much in the winter of its days – it was withdrawn June 1953 – the wheel tyres are very thick with many thousands of miles left in them.

In May 1942 No 2937 made its final move to Hereford where it continued on very much the same sort of work right through to Nationalisation in 1948, although the introduction of Hawksworth's Counties and Modified Halls during the latter part of this decade ultimately displaced the Saints from regular main line express duty and their final years were spent on semi-fast and stopping trains as well as occasional appearances on relief expresses in the busy summer period. In common with many other locomotives of the time, *Clevedon Court* was repainted in the lined all black mixed-traffic livery that had been adopted by the newly formed British Railways. The Swindon works' painters added a few touches of their own and this included a red background to both the name and numberplates as well as thickening the lining around the splashers to simulate the brass beading that the class had carried prior to World War I.

As gradual withdrawal of the Saints continued, enthusiasts generally took more interest in their day-to-day workings and these were frequently recorded in the railway Press, giving us a good insight into how these relatively elderly engines occupied their last days. One of the first of these observations was on 16 September 1950 when No 2937 and No 2920 *Saint David* took an excursion from Hereford right through to Bournville. The train of eleven bogies and two vans was routed via Droitwich and Bromsgrove and made a fine spectacle ascending the Lickey Incline banked by 0-10-0 No 58100. It was said to be the first recorded instance of ex-GWR locomotives working a train up this celebrated bank.

Surprisingly it was only two months later that *Clevedon Court* repeated this historic journey, this time running light engine with No 2944 *Highnam Court* from Bromsgrove to Bournville after having brought in a football special in connection with the FA Cup tie between Hereford City and Bromsgrove Rovers. In the summer of 1952, No 2937 made a by then rare appearance at Paddington as pilot to Hall No 6985 on the 4.48pm from Hereford, its more normal duties at this time keeping it confined to cross-country routes, a slightly unusual example of this being the 6.30am from its home city to Abergavenny on 7 April 1953.

On 12 June that same year, literally just a few days before withdrawal, No 2937 headed the 1.10pm Cardiff to Birmingham as far as Hereford and according to one observer the start from all the stations, including those on rising gradients, was very clean and crisp indicating that the legendary strength of the Saints had not deserted them even at this eleventh hour. Perhaps *Clevedon Court's* very last working took place the following day when it was noted on the Hereford portion of the 6.10pm Worcester to Paddington express. It was the end of an illustrious career spanning 42 years.

Within a matter of weeks No 2937 was condemned and parked outside Swindon works in company with No 2945 *Hillingdon Court*, both engines awaiting their last journey into the cutting up shop for dismantling.

9
SNOW HILL DAYS

ONCE, when the child's fare from the city boundary to Snow Hill was a penny ha'penny and the buses were real ones with outside staircases winding round to the upper deck, you could have a Saturday afternoon watching trains and two whole bars of chocolate for sixpence. Those were the days when the conductor had a proper bell which he rang by pulling on a leather cased wire when he was inside or thumping a plunger on the platform. The number 4 stopped adjacent to the tram terminus outside the Great Western Hotel; or, coming the other way, across the road close to the Great Western Arcade and Barnby's wonderful toy shop, its windows alive with wares from Hornby, Bassett-Lowke or Bing. If you were lucky there was a Hornby *County of Bedford* in one of those red boxes stacked behind the wooden glass fronted counters, and a real County on the railway down below – rushing out of the cut and cover tunnel into No 5 platform at the head of a down Bristol via the North Warwick line or an Oxford semi-fast. The very last County of all No 3834 *County of Somerset* was a Tyseley engine: it lasted until November 1933.

The late 1920s and early 1930s were heady times for small boys taken to Snow Hill for a Saturday afternoon treat. It seemed a long walk to the platforms, under the great arch through the hotel, across the car park with its huge wrought iron gates and down one of two wide flagstoned passageways with their goods lifts for the porter's trolleys and the sound of a train thundering in or out; all under cover of course. The passageway linking the up and down entrances to the platform steps had two of those very Great Western platform ticket machines in smart red livery; they accepted one's penny with a dong-g and issued a paper ticket carefully marked on each side with the hours and designed to be clipped in one of those spaces to ensure that ONLY an hour was spent. Fortunately none but the fiercest of the guardians of the steps actually bothered. But no one, no one at all, passed through those sliding grill gates without the supervision of the resident ticket collector.

The down island platform was the favourite for watching trains – probably for two reasons. Parents with younger children on Saturday afternoon treats (everyone worked on Saturday mornings) found Wyman's bookstall and seats a plenty within yards of reaching the bottom of two flights of steps; older children on their own and interested in numbers or photography took the long walk up beyond the Great Charles Street bridge to the windswept areas beneath open canopies. Here one could feel the thunder of exhausts as the Stars, Castles or Kings left for Wolverhampton, hear the rattle of couplings as the 72XX 2-8-2

Engine Name
A certain lady of distinction was travelling home from Paddington on one of those renowned two hour express trains to Birmingham, often worked by a Saint or Star class locomotive. The train had just left Leamington Spa when the ticket collector entered the first class portion of the dining car, and almost apologetically approached the aforementioned lady and inquired if he could see her ticket. Having duly punched her ticket, he assured her the train would be on time at Wolverhampton. Just before moving on to the next table the lady passenger asked him if he knew the name of the engine, as her small son would certainly want to know when she got home. The ticket collector assured her he would endeavour to find out, and within minutes returned saying, 'Madame, the name of the engine is '*Lady of Quality*'. – T. P. Dalton, *Cambrian Companionship.*

tank took up the slack on a Banbury ironstone train bound for Stewarts and Lloyds at Bilston or watch a Bulldog come up the bank from Hockley with the afternoon semi-fast to Stratford: or perhaps the Dudley push-and-pulls with 64XX tanks sandwiched between auto trailer cars coming in and out of the bays. Later these latter would be streamlined railcars. There was a sector table pivotted at its apex at the end of each bay platforms 3 and 4 but in living memory no one had seen it move; officially it went out of use in 1929.

The Wyman's bookstalls on both the down and up platforms were presided over by ladies who had been there almost for ever and what wares *they* possessed. In those days Birmingham had four daily broadsheets, the *Post*, *Mail*, *Gazette* and *Despatch*. These were piled alongside the London papers including the relatively new tabloids, the *Daily Sketch* and *Daily Mirror*. Add to these *Punch* for mother or occasionally father and that wonder of wonders the *Railway Magazine*, with its different colour cover every month at a shilling, and even more desirable the GWR 'engine book' at the same price. Then, if the accompanying adult was an indulgent uncle or aunt and a birthday approaching, there was the possibility of acquiring one of those individually hand-fretted wooden jig-saw puzzles made specially for the Great Western by the nearby Harborne based firm of Chad Valley. They were good value at half a crown when *that* was a lot of money.

Those seats by the bookstall were just right. Here the whole excitement and atmosphere of the station could be claimed. The first indication of an approaching train was a loud clang from the depths of the tunnel. This came from a warning apparatus comprising a bracket with a spring loaded plunger bolted to the rail several yards to the rear of the down main home signal. When depressed by an engine's wheel flanges it caused a flat lever to strike against a suspended metal sheet in the form of a clapper gong. It was very effective in its purpose warning drivers on a rising gradient that they were approaching this vital signal

Britain's Mightiest. A spotters view of Snow Hill. King class 4-6-0 possibly No 6002 King William IV is leaving platform 6 and about to cross over to the down main line on a Paddington–Birkenhead express. The King will come off at Wolverhampton with the dining car and three or four coaches as the class was not then permitted beyond due to weight restrictions. Note the red headlamps and the centre pivot signal arm. The picture was taken by a small boy aged 12 with a box camera.

The end of platform 6 looking down to the north box, the carriage sidings and Hockley tunnel, was a favourite spot for young enthusiasts, the lucky ones with Kodak or Coronet 5/- box cameras. Here one could see it all – arriving trains such as this afternoon express to Stratford upon Avon behind Bulldog class 4-4-0 No 3399 Ottawa with the water tank for station pilots behind the cab roof, the through freights, trips and Banbury ironstones to Stewarts and Lloyds works at Bilston, and noisy Wolverhampton bound expresses mostly hauled by impressive Kings. In those days if you were in GWR uniform you could wander the tracks with impunity – no orange jackets just a careful eye and ear.

Compartment Lunch

The dining-car attendants came round fastening long tables taken from the ends of the coaches, and placing them against the compartment doors where they fitted into a special attachment, the other end resting on a single leg. The silverine cutlery, all with the railway's crest, was spread upon white napery.

Do not ask why the luncheon fish was invariably a nice piece of fresh turbot; it always was, just as breakfast included finnan haddock for certain, with kippers an alternative that could not be counted upon as they could on certain other companies' lines. Somehow even the menus were part of Great Western tradition, the company proudly pointing out in 1928 that their *table d'hôte* luncheon cost 3s while that of the Canadian Pacific was 7s 11d. Exactly why they compared their service to the CPR was not stated!

For 3s you got roast beef and horseradish sauce; potatoes; cauliflower, followed by compôte of fruit and custard; cheese and salad; biscuits. But not just any biscuits. They came round in a tin called 'Railway Assortment' containing more variety of Huntley & Palmers than I have seen in one tin since. Of course there was no need to state which railway, for the tin had a picture of a *Star* and train on the side, and anyway, Huntley & Palmers made Superior Reading Biscuits, whilst the Southern put their catering out to contractors. – George Behrend, *Gone With Regret*.

which was often hard to spot – even though it was a colour light – due to the smoke and steam hanging about from departing trains. In later years the iron sheet was replaced by a piece of rail altering the sound to a less impressing 'ping'. The colour lights were far from new as they were put in when Siemens Bros completed the installation of the new power box at Birmingham South in 1913. The down main distant was fitted with three fixed route indicators giving drivers an indication of which platforms (1 or 5) or the through road, they would be taking.

Suddenly a down fast, perhaps the Eastbourne-Birkenhead due at 3.10pm with dark green Southern Railway coaches, exploded (it seemed just like that) out of the tunnel and rushed into the platform behind an Oxford Star, the train's tail lamp usually stopping a good twenty yards from the twin staircases. Crowds disgorged and made their way past in a phalanx to queue on the steps whilst they SHEWED their tickets – Great Western tickets were never shown – and filtered through the gap in the sliding trellis gate guarded by the collector in his brown wooden hut. Down the platform a green upright tank on wheels was trundled out from close to the refreshment room to the train's diner, a hose uncoiled and one end pushed into a pipe on the coach. The contraption had a huge hand wheel which made the whole thing look rather like a kitchen mangle; this was turned with gusto by the porter in charge. To the uninitiated it was a great mystery but if you knew about railways it was drinking water being supplied to the dining car's kitchen. It needed to be a quick operation as the stop was only five minutes. The Birkenhead – and indeed most trains – pulled far enough down platforms to leave room behind the rear coach to see across to platforms 7 and 12 and the departure of the up expresses to London or Oxford. The staccato exhausts as the big engines moved their passengers into the dark tunnel (with its twinkling electric lights) conveyed that feeling of awe and power which made the Great Western seem much fiercer than the LMS down at New Street; GWR engined barked and made funny noises while those at the other station merely chaffed and woofed. The centre roads too were full of interest with old and new pannier tanks on the Bordesley Junction to Hockley trips and the 72XX 2-8-2 tanks, 28XX 2-8-0s or RODs on the through freights: Banbury had four 2-8-2 tanks for the ironstone services, Nos 7218, 7236/8/9 and Oxley another four, Nos 7226/7/34/7. Unlike New Street there were no avoiding lines. Everything GW had to go through Snow Hill.

And, oh the automatic machines! Graceful pillarbox red columns gave one bar of wrapped Nestlé's milk chocolate for a penny. A four-tiered cast iron giant, also in red, offered more variety: Fry's chocolate cream, Sun Maid raisins (popularly known as Sun Raised Maidens), one single Churchman's cigarette neatly packed in a green cardboard casing with silver paper – but no cigarette card – and matches. And then the green metal box on four legs. This had a sloping front on which lay large raised letters and figures with a metal pointer on a central axis. One inserted a penny, moved the pointer to the appropriate letter, pulled down a handle and blow by blow punched out a name on to an aluminium strip which came out of an appropriate slot. It was fine if one wanted Charles

or even Rosemary but a penny's worth would not allow either to live at Newcastle upon Tyne. Up in the high level connecting lobby between the platforms, adjacent to the red ticket machines was, in later days, a scale model of *King George V*, in Bassett-Lowke parlance probably gauge II. This had its driving wheels on rollers connected to a timed electric motor. Boys hung around to see which adult would set the wheels in motion for a penny. Last were those dreadful machines where a nickel-plated derrick crane with a huge grab was encased in glass, the grab resting on some particularly horrible sugared sweets and cheap objects d'art half buried in them. A real con, for few who invested their penny were able to move the grab by hand controls to pick up something worthwhile.

As one grew older the sense of adventure broadened. There were trips to Stourbridge to stay with a railway minded friend often on the somewhat misnamed Birmingham and South Wales Express starting out of No 3 or 4 bay often behind Bulldog No 3353. Although this train carried coach roof boards proudly proclaiming its glory, it stopped frequently at such stations as Smethwick Junction (the last connection with the LNWR departed in 1915), Stourbridge Junction and Kidderminster before making off for Cardiff via Worcester (Foregate Street) and Hereford. From 1933 after bridge strengthening between Handsworth Junction and Stourbridge Junction these trains had Saints, two

The fast from London behind No 6016 King Edward V *is running over the junction for the North Warwick line at Tyseley and the fireman has just used his last shovelful of coal before watching out for the Bordesley Junction distant signal which is likely to be on if he is on or ahead of time. Meanwhile the signalman and booking boy are waiting to check the train's red tail lamp prior to giving the 'two pause one' train out of section to the box in the rear at Acocks Green. The two three arm bracket signals control movements on the up relief lines to Leamington Spa out of Tyseley station and those from the North Warwick line. The tracks to the far right of the picture lead to the 'down through sidings' which were the approach lines to and from Tyseley sheds.*

153

regular performers being 2976 *Winterstoke* and 2981 *Ivanhoe*. Stourbridge Junction was another good spot to watch trains and until 1935 there was the steam railcar to Stourbridge Town with a half fare return of one penny. The Town branch in those earlier years was a peculiar affair of two parallel single lines, one for passenger trains to the terminus and the other going on down a steep grade to Stourbridge goods yard. Sometimes the trip freight engine was a saddle tank, something unknown at Snow Hill. It was always an old open cab engine. The railcar was gas lit and often, in the quieter time of the day, it was possible to get a very hot footplate ride. One peculiar feature carefully pointed out by a friendly driver was that the headlamp was supplied by the Loco Department and the tail lamp by the Carriage Department.

The Birmingham and South Wales Express returned during the afternoon, this time into one of the up platform bays at Snow Hill, the stock being shunted back into the up carriage sidings where there was also a turntable. Adjacent to those bays and similarly on the down side, there were those remarkably sturdy poster boards displaying both double and quad Royal posters of remarkable colour and beauty, a powerful image of a King at speed with the new Centenary stock with the Company's monogram at each corner, a GWR restaurant car scene with a couple sitting on carved arm chairs, the blue Devon sea behind them, the lower half devoted to a straight line map with a large rectangle proclaiming 'popular 2/6 luncheon on all routes', a rural Shrewsbury 'an historic and picturesque town in a charming county' or Weymouth 'the English Naples'.

The up platform was also the place to see a fascinating working. An express would be waiting in No 7 or No 12 and suddenly a local drifted in behind it stopping at the bracket signal before the scissors crossover on No 8. At No 11 there was a calling on arm at the platform entrance. The quiet scene of slowly loading passengers was interrupted by the hordes of people flowing down the platform from the far distance. Snow

Stourbridge Town railmotor. Steam railcar No 55 coming into Stourbridge Junction from Stourbridge Town probably in 1933/34 during the summer holidays. One of the joys of Snow Hill was the ability for a few pence to get to other centres of traffic such as Stourbridge Junction with its open cab 0-6-0 saddle tanks shunting the yard (they were rarely seen in the Birmingham area) or Wolverhampton where engines were changed going to and coming from the north. The Stourbridge Junction trip could, if luck was there, include a hot ride in the driving compartment of the railcar where one could be right out of sight of authority.

Hill platforms were long: 1,200ft. Another advantage of watching trains on the up side was the occasional appearance of the partially streamlined King No 6014 *King Henry VII* on the 3pm London, or the feeling of Great Western express power over the ages around 3.50 when the 4.5pm to Oxford and Reading stood in No 7 behind a Star and the 3.55pm Birkenhead to Paddington direct in No 12 behind a King: old and new across the platform face.

In the mid 1930s two other things came to the notice of the Snow Hill watcher. The Great Western brought in a new and revolutionary train service between Birmingham, Stratford, Gloucester, Newport and Cardiff (General). This was effected by the use of new streamlined diesel railcars (44 seats plus a buffet) with a supplementary charge of 2/6 over and above the third class rail fare. Smart in chocolate-and-cream livery cars 2, 3 and 4 caused a minor sensation. There was even a suitable jig-saw puzzle available from Wyman's bookstall. There were two trains each way Mondays to Fridays leaving Snow Hill at 9.5am and 3.40pm.

Brand new and the modern image. GWR AEC railcar No 2, streamlined elegance of the 1930s, stands outside the works at Tyseley shortly after its introduction on the Snow Hill–Cardiff services. Some wag at Tyseley suggested that its colour was wrong – it should have been blue and cream like the corporation's buses. On the right is Bulldog No 3320 Meteor *awaiting attention whilst on the left on the exit road from the freight section of the shed is an unknown 43XX 2-6-0. Note the brass numberplate on the rear of the tender.*

Leamington locomen. Driver Albert Daniels and Firman Walter Skelsey stand proudly by the side of 2-6-2T No 4110. One of their other regular engines in 1938 was No 8100 one of a small sub class of 51XX locomotives with smaller diameter driving wheels, 5ft 6in and a higher boiler pressure of 225lb/sq in.

Opposite, above *Work on widening at Small Heath, 1907.*

Opposite, below *Platform 12 in April 1960; apart from liveries very little altered from Great Western days. The 5.45pm to Worcester via Stratford upon Avon, Honeybourne and Evesham is waiting to leave behind Hall class 4-6-0 No 6935 Brownsholme Hall. Looking at this scene it is almost impossible to believe that the Kings would all be gone in three years and all Great Western steam in five.*

Then there was the appearance of a new stationmaster. GWR stationmasters were always IMPORTANT PEOPLE but the Snow Hill maestro was more important than most. The new incumbent was Arthur Hammond Elsden, a little man with a little man's temperament – very efficient. The waxed moustache and pill box hat made the booking boys at the north and south signal boxes blanch at the twice daily inspections. To the general public, the sight of this immaculate, often red faced official patrolling the platforms and meeting the important trains was comfortably reassuring. Certainly during this period Snow Hill was one of Birmingham's prize possessions. It was renowned for its cleanliness and efficiency. Arthur Elsden was a true Great Western man; the job was done properly and he was respected. Even the white glazed bricks in the subways and toilets were washed down every week. And the tunnel horses used to shunt wagons in and out of the fish platforms were well disciplined too; it has been said that they knew what the signals meant as well as any railwayman. They *never* moved into the path of an oncoming train.

1937 saw the school train to Warwick. This was the 8am out of platform 12, all stations except Bordesley always behind a 51XX 2-6-2 tank getting to Warwick at 8.48. The long walk to the school absolved 'train boys' from morning chapel though there was a special compulsory attendance at 1.45 instead. If one was early enough at Snow Hill it was sometimes fun to catch the 7.45 Paddington, which always had a Stafford Road King, alight at Leamington and come back on the 8.28 all stations to Warwick at 8.32. This meant dodging the ticket collector but that was easy enough as he worked his way down from the rear van and rarely began his travels early. Home was by the 4.42 which was always a Saint, mostly Nos 2902 *Lady of the Lake*, 2914 *Saint Augustine* or 2924 *Saint Helena*. For some reason this always had a corridor strengthener as the first coach. The train ran virtually empty until Tyseley where it picked up the local Girling factory workforce at 5.24 running packed to the doors to the far end of Snow Hill's down platform whence it ran empty stock to Wolverhampton. There was one memorable occasion when one of the least desirable train boys, with a tendency to bullying, was lured into a compartment in this corridor coach (the front of the train stopped far along the platform at Tyseley and was rarely invaded by the Girling workers), heaved onto the rack and strapped there by seven pairs of braces. He was left in situ and ended up in the Wolverhampton carriage sidings rather late. After this episode the Railway Police in plain clothes (but wearing bowler hats making their presence quite clear when they leaned out of the windows!) travelled on the 4.42 for a while but no one got led by the ear down into the bowels of Snow Hill station.

Then, as time moved on there were new experiences; one evening after college a walk along the up platform to see what was going on at the north end and there in No 10 bay stood the evening pilot, Leamington Saint No 2924 *Saint Helena* which had come in at 6.50pm turned on the table in the up sidings and was making itself useful before returning at 11.05. The local services were good in those days. A chat with the crew,

156

an invitation on to the footplate and driver Albert Daniels along with his fireman Walter Skelsey became friends. Daniels would then have been around sixty and a teetotaller. Skelsey 40–42 was chalk against cheese; he liked his pint. The first footplate ride with the pair was from Wolverhampton (Low Level) on No 4924 *Eydon Hall* (TYS) heading the 7.57pm all stations to Snow Hill going on to Leamington at 9.10. Later the ploy was to meet them at Stourbridge Junction on the arrival of the 4.35 from Leamington getting in at 6.03. This turn had a lay over in the spur beyond the down platform at the Junction and a 7.35pm departure gave Skelsey time enough to nip down to the 'Labour in Vain' for a couple of quick ones. Daniels was an extremely well read man and was a delight to listen to. Cheerful from the pub Walter became an excellent firing instructor and, in due time, even Old Hill bank was left in amateur hands. The engines were usually one of the new 2-6-2 tanks Nos 4110 or 8100 where a 'third man' was out of sight. Discipline was stern but fair. Albert Daniels always asked to see the train ticket: the GWR was not to be swindled!

Birmingham Snow Hill as many will remember it. Standing at platform 7 is the 12.30pm Wolverhampton to Paddington (dep. Snow Hill at 1.20pm) calling all stations to Oxford! then Didcot, Reading and Paddington on 15 August 1951. The locomotive is one well suited to such a task, a Grange class 4-6-0 No 6839 Hewell Grange. The enormous clock, now preserved, can be seen above the second coach and the up and down main lines used mainly by freight trains are between platforms 5 and 7.

The very strictness of Snow Hill's ticket collectors sometimes inspired an illicit ride, perhaps to Dudley and back on the autos or to Wolverhampton Low Level where the clutter was so great that it was easy enough to get over to the up platform without any problems. Ticket collectors did not travel on suburban services. One summer Saturday in 1939, two impoverished articled pupils made an illegal journey from Snow Hill to Craven Arms and back for a penny. Work finished at 12 noon giving plenty of time to catch the 1.15pm all stations to Wolverhampton behind 5156 (TYS) getting in at 1.49. Across the platform in the Low Level bay was the 2.10 to Wellington stopping everywhere; this was a bonus as it had Wellington (WLN) shed's one and only Bulldog No 3414 *A. H. Mills*, which was filthy. Wellington to Craven Arms took an hour and a half but the small wheeled 2-6-2 tank No 4403 (one of five kept at WLN for the Much Wenlock branch) got away smartly at 3pm leaving an LNWR coal tank with two red coaches for Coalport in the adjacent bay. Only two trains a day ran through to Craven Arms. This was the second, making twenty one stops including Platforms and Halts crossing the Severn Valley line from Bewdley to Shrewsbury at Buildwas. Fifty minutes wait at Craven Arms with the LNWR shed at the west end of the down platform then to Shrewsbury behind a Salop engine No 5916 *Trinity Hall*, getting in at 6.13 and allowing a couple of glasses before the departure of the 7pm all stations to Wolverhampton behind 5167 (WSR). The 8.18 arrival gave time to watch a gleaming No 6005 *King George I* replace SALOP Star No 4061 *Glastonbury Abbey* on the 8.35 to Paddington. The 8.50 all stations except Priestfield got us back to Snow Hill at 9.28, two minutes down behind Tyseley's No 4978 *Westwood Hall*.

Snow Hill's Signalling

Modernisation came to Birmingham Snow Hill in 1910; not only was the station rebuilt but its signalling too had a complete renewal. Those who knew it in the next halcyon half century of Great Western steam found an atmosphere hard to be repeated anywhere. There were two new signalboxes, South Box, at the exit to the cut and cover tunnel, and North Box on stilts controlling the exit and entrance from the Hockley tunnels including the carriage sidings and engine lay over area. South Box had 96 levers, North Box 224.

The boxes were described as 'electric power signalling installations', and were equipped by Siemens. They were, however, extraordinarily traditional, 'inasmuch as constant current control associated with mechanical and electrical interlocking has been abandoned in favour of mechanical interlocking combined with electrical check locking, one result being that it has been found possible to very considerably simplify the somewhat complicated electrical connections necessary at Didcot [North Box opened a few years earlier at considerable expense]. Another important consideration in regard to the Birmingham installation is that the electrical gear and appliances for actuating the signals and points have been designed to adapt, without undue modification, the standard Great Western signal and point fittings to allow of their operation by electrical agency . . . The erection of the signal cabins and the provision of all points, locking bars, plunger bolts, signal posts, arms and fittings devolves on the Great Western Company's own staff.'

Thus there was a compact, modern frame, North's being 12½in wide, 4ft high, and with 224 levers 37ft 6in long, but whole gantries as well as many individual lower semaphore signals (some with illuminated route indicators) that resulted in a unique combination of electric yet utter Great Western signalling well after most boxes controlling arrays of semaphores were indeed outdated.

The only absolute block in the station was the track serving platforms 1 and 2; this was due to the curve coming out of the tunnel round the back of the South Box. All the other roads had permissive block working allowing more than one train in the section. Train describers were in use in all boxes from Tyseley South to Handsworth Junction. Signalmen asked 'Line Clear' and described the train: North Warwick, Main Line, Bordesley Cattle Pens, Tyseley Carriage Sidings, Hockley Yard, Stourbridge Extension, Great Bridge Branch, and so on.

The South Box main distant signal was a lower arm on Moor Street's down main starter; this was 'cleared' together with the South Box colour light Home Signal in the tunnel even though 'Line Clear' had not been obtained from the North Box. It only took trains on the down main (the through road) as far as the 'swing signal' (down main starting signal suspended from the roof girders) as there could be a train occupying the tracks ahead, waiting line clear at the down main advanced starting signal. Trains going into platform 5 would run as far as the down starting signal suspended under the platform verandah. In all cases there were only depression bars – no track circuits. There were scissor crossovers at the North end controlled by the North Box as follows: platform 5 to down main, down main to platform 6, up main to platform 7, platform 8 to up main. Again there were no track circuits but the signalman at the North Box was advised by the 'Gantry Man' who had a cabin above the up and down main lines on a bridge spanning all the tracks accessible by ladder from platform 6 when trains were 'clear of the scissors'. This was a job for a 'Green Card Man' – someone fallen by the wayside because of poor health – yet without the aid of track circuits there would have been instant chaos if the 'clear' sign were given prematurely and points were pulled with something still on the scissors.

Each box was of course open continuously with the three shifts of men. North Box double manned early and late, one man only on nights: there was a booking lad on each shift, the South Box a booking boy early and late turn but not on nights. Signalling classes were held in a room deep below the station, where there was a complete model railway with points and signals worked from miniature frames. Unofficially the lads were allowed to work North Box at nights after the cleaning was over and things had died down. All under the watchful eye of the signalman. It was good grounding and discipline was strict. Signalmen had to be addressed as 'Mr' and besides cleaning the lads had to make tea, wash up, cook the breakfast and run errands.

Windows in the South Box would rattle while trains were coming up the grade through the tunnel. If they stopped rattling the signalman knew that the train had failed! This meant the provision of a green wrong line order to authorise an assisting engine (the duty pilot) to back down on to the front of the train and drag it out of the tunnel. In addition to the clapper gong there were lights on the downside wall, to let the train men know which way they were going after a failure. Trains were never divided as the grade was 1 in 47. There was indeed a sand drag at the Moor Street end just in case.

There were two extra pieces of excitement for the South Box signalmen, the arrival of bullion for the Bank of England and the 'Money Engine'. Bullion would arrive on the rear of a down London and the van detached by the shunting engine from Tunnel Sidings, run round and propelled to the Bank of England lift in the tunnel. This was direct access to the Bank situated directly over that section of the cut and cover. On Thursdays the 'Money Engine' would arrive from Tyseley and shunt the down siding to be loaded with staff wages and return to Tyseley with a locomotive inspector and a railway policeman.

The South Box lad worked in the telegraph office on Sundays taking messages and telegrams about the station to different offices. The old single needle instruments were still there in the late 1940s. There was also an extensive pneumatic pipe system in the station and offices. Telegrams were put into a cylinder which was placed in the tube and sucked up the pipe noisily to its destination.

A booking lad in North Box in the late 1940s was Keith Steele who vividly recalls making up the fires, cleaning out the ashes, sweeping and polishing the floor, dusting, as well as the duties mentioned earlier, between logging the train movements in the register. There was also the heavy cleaning: Monday, clean all the windows inside and out, Tuesday the brasses, Wednesday the frame with an oil rag and the gas stove, Thursday black lead the two stoves, whiten the hearths and clean the toilet, Friday scrub the floor – two buckets of hot water off the big pilot engine and carbolic which was used for cleaning coaches. Damp tea leaves had to be put down

when sweeping the floor because a signalman suffered from asthma.

There was a ringing out bell in the middle of the North Box which also had an illuminated platform number when a train was ready to depart. Lads had to cancel this and advise the signalman at Handsworth Junction and Wolverhampton South when down expresses left. The South Box lad similarly advised Tyseley South and Leamington Spa. While doing this lads had their backs to the frame, but it did not take long to understand every movement whether you saw it or not.

Mr Elsden, the stationmaster, visited each box every morning. At North, it was 'Good Morning Richards, Good Morning Duggan'; all the lad got was a nod of the head. He would then put on his 'pince-nez' glasses, take his gold fountain pen from his coat pocket and sign the train register.

Arthur Hammond Elsden was typical of a breed of stationmasters who made their importance felt. A small man, he was always resplendent in his frock tail coat with fancy lacing up his sleeves, razor sharp creases in his trousers, shoes so polished you could shave in them, cut away white stiff collar complete with a diamond pinned tie and to crown it all that Great Western pill box hat. On his way out he could remark 'the air was a little blue this morning Richards', comment on the swearing at the shunters, not an unusual occurrence. One of the first up trains from Bewdley which often ran late was nicknamed the 'Red Necker'. It came in front of, and to connect with, the crack 9am Snow Hill to Paddington express and Mr Elsden's neck went red if it was late.

The approach to Snow Hill from the North photographed from a signal gantry. The North box perched on its stilts is middle right and various types of GWR signal are visible including the cruious backing signals with two holes in the arm. The photograph was taken in October 1936 when the GWR roundel (seen on the side of its 51XX class 2-6-2T) was newly introduced. There is a freight in the down centre road behind a 72XX 2-8-2T – probably an iron ore train from Banbury to Stewarts and Lloyds at Bilston. Note the wooden post, wooden arm bracket signal behind the clerestory roofed coach.

10
HOW CUT-OFFS MADE
THE WESTERN GREAT

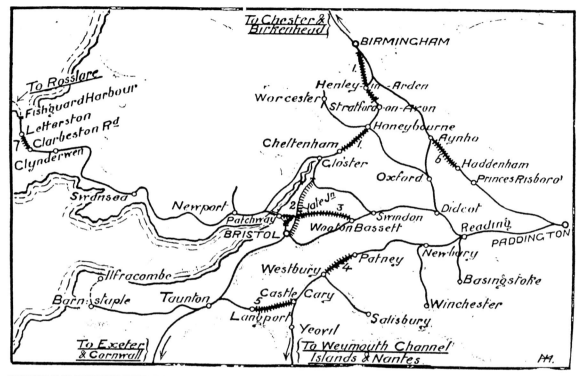

SKETCH MAP SHOWING TWENTIETH CENTURY SHORTENINGS OF THE GREAT WESTERN RAILWAY'S MAIN ROUTES
Reference on Map:—

1. New lines forming part of the direct Birmingham–Bristol route via Stratford-upon-Avon.
2. Running powers over Midland Railway, completing the direct Bristol–Birmingham route.
3. South Wales Direct Railway and shorter alternative London–Bristol route.
4. Connecting Link, forming shorter route to Weymouth District.
4 and 5. Connecting Links forming the short route to Taunton and the West of England.
6. The Haddenham–Aynho line, completing the shortest route between London and Birmingham.
7. Link forming the completion of the Express route to Fishguard.

WHOEVER applied the term 'Great Way Round' to the GWR was certainly accurate as well as witty. Although there was a route from Oxford via Banbury the company still routed some of its 'expresses' to Wolverhampton via Worcester. Despite the opening of the Severn Tunnel in 1886 the principal route into South Wales was still via the extra fifteen miles required to pass via Gloucester, and the only route to the West of England was down the original main line and through the congestion of Bristol. It was fortunate for the receipts of the company that there was virtually no competition on its most lucrative routes between London and Bristol and South Wales because it could certainly not have competed on the basis of speed. True, by the end of Victoria's

Devil's Work

A railway-loving parson was commiserating with a clerical friend who had been prescribed a living in a not altogether desirable place. 'Why,' he exclaimed as though his colleague were being banished to Outer Mongolia, 'it is not even on the Great Western.'

The Severn Tunnel was the first cut-off to be built by the Great Western reducing the distance to South Wales by some 15 miles. The pioneer mixed traffic 2-6-0 No 4301 is on the climb out of the tunnel at Patchway with a freight train which is banked in the rear. The line is divided between Patchway and Pilning, the up line, built when the tunnel was opened, is at an easier grade than the original then down line.

reign competition was hotting up for the Devon and Cornwall traffic. Finally, on the London to Birmingham route it was a case of 'no match' with the LNWR for passenger traffic and, in a different way, for freight.

Yet in a little more than a dozen years this picture was totally changed; it was as if the GWR finally shrugged off the conservatism and stupor of the broad gauge years and became a truly great railway. In the ten years from 1900 the GWR opened a little over 250 miles of brand new main lines and upgraded around 90 miles of secondary lines to main line status. And what lines they were! As far as possible the new lines were constructed to easy gradients and curvature for high speed running and they were provided, in the most important cases, with plentiful loop lines for local passenger and freight trains. (The figures include the joint ownership with the Great Central.)

The new route to South Wales was probably the most important. The GWR had a prodigious traffic in coal and coke from South Wales into England, and prior to the opening of the Severn Tunnel in 1886 this all had to pass via Gloucester or Worcester, irrespective of destination. Hauling traffic for London and the Home Counties via Worcester was obviously expensive in sheer mileage, but working via Gloucester was little better with all trains for those destinations having to ascend the steep gradient through the Golden Valley to Sapperton Tunnel. Trains were invariably banked up these steep climbs and the heavier coal trains were double-headed as well. The advent of larger locomotives was obviously not the complete solution and the severe congestion around Bristol, followed by a stiff climb from Chippenham to Swindon offered only a minimum of relief. Thus an 1896 Parliamentary Bill sought powers for the South Wales & Bristol Direct Railway following a fairly easily-graded route from Wootton Bassett, just west of Swindon, to Patchway, on the northern edge of Bristol. Work commenced in November 1897 and, to achieve the required gradients, included the

4,444yd Chipping Sodbury and the much shorter (506yd) Alderton Tunnels. The new route was complemented by new freight marshalling yards at Stoke Gifford, a mile or so east of Patchway. Intermediate stations were provided at the principal villages and towns, such as there were. The line opened from the east end to Badminton for local goods traffic on 1 January 1903 and was opened for through goods traffic on 1 May of that year, with passenger opening following on 1 July. The new route was 25 miles shorter than the Gloucester route from Swindon to South Wales and three expresses between Paddington and Cardiff were immediately introduced on 2h 55m timings. The impact on freight, especially coal, was dramatic and contributed substantially to the increase of one-fifth in average train loads in the century's early years. And the much heavier trains a single engine could handle over the route east of Stoke Gifford gave savings in banking engines and train crew working hours. The new route provided the essential link, that must have been foreseen by Gooch when he championed the Severn Tunnel. South Wales now had a main line as good as any in the land. As will be

Bulldog class 4-4-0 No 3407 Madras leaves the English portal of the Severn Tunnel, after a, no doubt, very smokey journey; it is heading a Cardiff–Bristol express in the mid 1930s. The block section of 4 miles 54 chains to Severn Tunnel West somewhat restricted the line occupancy and it was not until the pressure of war that the Ministry of War Transport permitted intermediate block signals to be installed, immediately doubling the line capacity.

The South Wales and Bristol direct line was next to be opened in 1903; it immediately provided a quicker route to the principality albeit restricted by the Severn Tunnel bottleneck. The 8.00am Neyland to Paddington is going well up the 1 in 300 through Chipping Sodbury behind No 7004 Eastnor Castle in July 1956. The stations on the new line were all well laid out with platform loops to allow expresses to overtake stopping trains.

The South Wales and Bristol direct line was next to be opened in 1903; it immediately provided a quicker route to the principality albeit restricted by the Severn Tunnel bottleneck. The 8.00am Neyland to Paddington is going well up the 1 in 300 through Chipping Sodbury behind No 7004 *Eastnor Castle* in July 1956. The stations on the new line were all well laid out with platform loops to allow expresses to overtake stopping trains.

The last of the long cut-offs, the Birmingham direct line, was opened in 1910. A portion of the southern end was jointly owned with the Great Central although this section always seemed more GW than GC. The 4.10pm Paddington–Birkenhead is seen at Saunderton summit in 1938 behind No 6008 King James II. *The up and down lines between here and Princes Risborough take separate routes to ease the grade on the up line which can be seen coming in on the left at a slightly lower level.*

seen later on, another link within South Wales complemented the Badminton route in a way which was perhaps more typical of some of the grandiose ideas of the old Brunel era.

Great things were also happening in the West Country and while some of the work going on there was contemporary with that on the Badminton line, the entire scheme spread over a much longer period. Unlike the Badminton scheme the new route to the West of England made use of various portions of existing branches or secondary routes joining them with stretches of new construction to create an entirely new main line from Reading to a junction with the former Bristol & Exeter main line at Cogload to the east of Taunton. The first stage of the work, started in 1897, was the doubling of the Berks & Hants line (from Reading to Devizes) to the west of Hungerford and realignment to ease curves. A new line, connecting out of the Berks & Hants at a new station at Patney & Chirton, was constructed to cover the 14½ miles to Westbury where it joined the former Wilts, Somerset & Weymouth route from Chippenham to Weymouth. This part of the route was opened for goods traffic on 29 July 1900 with passenger traffic following on 1 October. Apart from a rebuilt station at Westbury the new route also had a number of intermediate stations to serve local communities including Lavington which, in later years, gave its name to the whole section. Again the passenger department was quick to grasp new opportunities and three through Paddington-Weymouth fast trains were introduced on 1 July 1901.

The next stage was the 'cut off' between the Wilts, Somerset & Weymouth and the Bristol & Exeter. The principal new work was what came to be known as the 'Langport Cut-Off', a 15½ mile line linking Castle Cary with the B&E Yeovil branch at Curry Rivel Junction, a mile west of Langport. This involved substantial earthworks, the cutting of Somerton Tunnel, and embanking the line west of Langport above the flood plain of the Somerset Levels. The final stage was a three mile link between Athelney and Cogload to avoid the poor alignment of the Yeovil branch between Athelney and Durston. The route was fully opened to goods traffic in May 1906 with passenger trains following on 2 July. Unlike the Badminton line the new route, shortening the journey to Taunton by some twenty miles and again avoiding congestions round Bristol, was primarily for passengers, though of course also used by the fast perishable and milk trains feeding London's growing demands.

The third of the London-orientated new routes introduced a new factor because much of it was controlled by a Joint Committee established by the Great Western and the newcomer to London – the Great Central. In 1897 the GWR had obtained powers for a new line between what was to become Old Oak Common West Junction and High Wycombe, a distance of 23 miles, where it joined the route of the former Wycombe Railway from Maidenhead to Aylesbury. Added to this were Parliamentary powers obtained by the Great Western in 1905 for a link out of the joint line from Ashendon Junction to Aynho Junction on the Oxford-Banbury section of the then main line to Birmingham. While it is arguable that the GWR obtained many of the facilities of this new cut-

164

off at the expense of the Great Central, the latter was going through a very uncomfortable period with the Metropolitan and it got a very good main line into London as its part of the bargain. South of High Wycombe the route was engineered very much with an eye on the prospects for local passenger business and, as on the Badminton line but in greater profusion, stations were provided with loops to serve the platforms, thus allowing expresses to readily overtake local services. The route from Princes Risborough, via Thame, to Oxford also benefitted from upgrading to provide a faster London to Oxford service over a route some eight miles shorter than that via Reading. Like the new West of England route, it was opened in sections so that some traffic could get started. The first section from Old Oak Common to, in effect, Princes Risborough was opened to goods traffic on 20 November 1905 with passenger services following on 2 April of the next year. It was to be another four years before the final link in the new direct Birmingham route was completed with Ashendon Junction to Aynho Junction opening to goods on 4 April 1910 and passenger traffic on 1 July of the same year. The GWR now had a London to Birmingham route that was not only some nineteen miles shorter than the old route via Reading but,

Star class No 4049 Princess Maud *hauls a partially fitted freight through West Ruislip at the southern end of the GW and GC Joint line in the winter of 1949/50. London Transport's newly opened Central Line extension is to the right. By now the Oxford and Reading Stars were beginning to be replaced by new Castles relegating the Churchward greyhounds to secondary work and relief expresses.*

probably more important, was two miles shorter than the competing LNWR route from Euston. The rapid provision of the 'Two Hour' service to Birmingham at long last enabled the GWR to compete properly for business between London and the West Midlands.

The final one of the quartet of cut-offs knitting the GWR into a well integrated railway before the outbreak of World War I was a very different animal. The Cheltenham & Honeybourne Railway and the Birmingham & North Warwickshire Line were constructed to provide a shorter and improved route between South Wales and the West Country and the Birmingham area. Like the West of England scheme some use was made of existing lines by improving and doubling the existing Stratford branch between a new East Junction at Honeybourne and the deviation of the new North Warwick line from the old route at Bearley. To the south of this improvement work twenty-one miles of new line were constructed to link Honeybourne and Cheltenham while to the north the North Warwick line provided a shorter, faster, link into Birmingham. The new sections opened for through traffic over a year with the Cheltenham & Honeybourne opened throughout for passenger traffic on 1 August 1906 and the North Warwick following for goods traffic on 9 December 1907 and, finally, passenger traffic on 1 July 1908. Away to the south, and after some argument with the Midland Railway, a new chord linked from Yate South Junction to the Badminton line at Westerleigh Junction, allowing GWR trains to regain parent metals after exercising running powers over the Midland south of Gloucester. The new route allowed an improved passenger service between Cardiff and Birmingham and offered major improvements for services from Bristol and the West of England. Although the gradients were steeper than had been achieved on the other cut-offs, the route still offered significant advantages for freight traffic which was able to avoid the heavy gradients and increasingly severe congestion between Stourbridge Junction and the Birmingham and Wolverhampton areas.

The last of the big cut-off schemes followed a little behind the others and has an air of the grandiose ideas so beloved of Brunel and which sometimes carried on into later GWR history. The Swansea District Line was conceived as a high speed avoiding line to whisk Fishguard boat expresses clear of the heavily graded line between Neath and Cockett, to the west of Landore. With Fishguard in mind as a major deep-water Transatlantic port the whole thing has echoes of Brunel's original ideas for fast packet boats connecting with his London railway at Bristol. Much work, at great expense, was done to develop Fishguard for this role which would expand on its initial job as an Irish ferry port and the Swansea District Line was the finale. Linking Skewen, just east of Neath, with the Llanelly Railway about 3½ miles north of Llandillo Junction it was authorised in 1904 and opened to all traffic on 14 July 1913. Although it was steeply graded, in comparison with the Badminton line, at 1 in 120 it offered major advantages over the serpentine 1 in 52 climb from Landore to Cockett. In true style, it boasted a couple of stations with loop-served platforms but the rise of Southampton prevented its real development. But it was also built with an eye to the

The North Warwickshire line under construction in 1906 near the junction with the GWR main line at Tyseley. Note the very temporary tracks and the contractors tipping wagons. The vertical boiler steam crane appears to be of a wider gauge than 4ft 8½ins!

Lost Case
A rather curious case was decided the other day at the West London County Court. The Great Western Railway contended that a child's toy, in the form of a miniature motorcar and propelled by pedals after the manner of a velocipede, was really a velocipede, and therefore chargeable at the rates for such unwieldly articles. The judge, however, decided that the article in question was a toy, and therefore should be conveyed at the usual rates for goods coming under that description. – Railway & Travel Monthly, 1910.

Birmingham was connected with the west of England and South Wales by two new lines, Tyseley to Bearley and Honeybourne to Cheltenham. Saint class 4-6-0 No 2924 Saint Helena *approaches Stratford upon Avon with a West of England Wolverhampton train (possibly the Kingswear portion of the* Cornishman *running separately as four coaches have roof boards) in the long summer of either 1947 or 1949. The signal box is S&M Junction which controlled the curve up to the Stratford upon Avon and Midland Junction Railway seen in the background. With ten coaches the Saint will need a pilot (from Stratford shed) to conquer the banks up to Bearley, Henley in Arden and Earlswood.*

developing anthracite coal field around Llanelli and as a relief route for freight from that area. In this latter respect there is little doubt that it was a major success – so much so that at times difficulty was encountered in trying to timetable the odd few boat trains which did actually use it.

After World War I the great years of railway expansion were gone. But short cut-offs were in place by 1932 to route through trains around the bottlenecks of Westbury and Frome on the 'new' West of England route. Well it seemed as if days of grander schemes had gone until the GWR announced in the 1930s the grandest of them all – a new inland route from Exeter to Newton Abbot.

Deviating from the existing line at Exeter City Basin and rejoining it at Newton Abbot, the new route was intended to avoid the weather perils of the Dawlish sea wall. The war brought things to a halt, but some bridges were widened and strengthened and earthworks completed – some still stand, a monument to a fascinating 'might have been'.

Though built for speed, the cut-offs of this century did not have such sound foundations as the trunk Victorian routes, and especially in the early years of nationalisation, there was much trouble and extensive diversions caused by landslips and spreading clay. Today two of the four

Birmingham Moor Street was built in 1909 to accommodate the North Warwickshire line locals; it was also used on summer Saturdays by holiday trains. Hall class No 5946 Marwell Hall of Exeter shed (83C) has just arrived with a relief from Kingswear during the summer of 1960. Note the traverser in the foreground used to release locomotives from local trains.

principal cut-offs are used by heavy traffic: the Badminton and Lavington (now generally referred to as the Castle Cary) routes. Only one daily train takes the direct route north from Paddington to Banbury, while the Cheltenham link with the North Warwick line, which once carried queues of heavily-laden summer Saturday holiday expresses from Wolverhampton and Birmingham to the South West, has long been closed, though a fraction survives in preservation.

Taunton

Taunton was one of those junctions where you realised that GWR passenger trains earned much of their revenue carrying things rather than people, and that among the people the vast majority were making journeys of less than twenty five miles. Nearly all day long the station hummed with the aggregate of pretty humdrum activity, highlighting the sense of occasion when an express roared through non stop or came to a halt occupying the whole busy platform length.

Three main lines (from Paddington, Bristol and Penzance) and four branches (Yeovil, Chard, Minehead, Barnstaple) converged on Taunton, and since the main lines carried local as well as expresses that meant there were basically ten kinds of passenger trains, not allowing for the non-stops as a separate category or taking into account the summer weekend expresses on the Minehead and Barnstaple branches.

The sixty or so stopping trains from the seven different routes (Castle Cary in the case of the Paddington line) brought in kids going to school, shoppers, office workers, hospital visitors in far larger numbers than those changing to the expresses, though most locals were of course timed to give 'up country' connections. The Minehead and Barnstaple locals waiting in their bays were well loaded, conversation reflecting the social and economic life of the strips of countryside through which they ran, before say the twelve coach 1.30pm from Paddington drew in and a handful of posh folk, helped by porters, sought any remaining corner seats in which to continue their journeys.

Arriving locals were always handled expeditiously, especially those from Bristol and Weston-super-Mare, Castle Cary (usually lightly used auto cars) and Chard since they frequently terminated at the main or relief down, Post Office and parcel vehicles occupying the only bay, and needed getting out of the way quickly.

Out would come a mixture of local people with shopping baskets, brief cases, satchels, flowers for relatives in hospital, and occasionally produce for market, followed by one or two with cases and trunks to be transferred to an express. The guard opened his van doors instantly, the first barrow was wheeled in to take crates of rabbits, milk churns, packages of fruit and flowers and whatever else the local countryside was currently producing, ice cream empties, mail bags and assorted private parcels. By the time the passengers had dispersed, the van doors were closed and the train shunted out, its existence ended and attention turned to another.

Often, however, there was the complication of a truck of cattle, a gas cylinder wagon, a six-wheeled milk van (or later tanker), a horse box, gas vehicle, or some other 'carriage traffic' to be taken off and shunted separately. Even if there had been no expresses, the signalmen in the boxes at either end of the station and the station pilots would have been kept busy. Most freights went by the goods avoiding line, but seldom was the station totally dead.

Even if there were no train or shunting movements, knots of passengers, postmen and mail bags, barrowfuls of parcels always rewarding to look at, day-old chicks and protesting calves, were waiting. Only on Sundays were there long hours of slumber, but in summer the Sunday Minehead locals were the best loaded of any.

The biggest inward rush was of course just before school and office starting time, the evening return being more spread out. The morning arrivals included three within five minutes, two of them often side by side, along the quadrupled track from Norton Fitzwarren. Then the subway seemed as busy as that of a Southern suburban station. Even among those making journeys of less than twenty five miles, there were many who changed here, from one branch line to another. Very few of the locals ran through, each service being self contained in GWR days.

A feature of the expresses that served Taunton was that almost more passengers joined for the continuing journey West than were going up to London or Bristol or beyond. Since those alighting from up country were often met by local people, and porters were out in strength, two hundred souls might be on the platform as an important down express drew in. The same was of course true at Exeter and Plymouth, expresses being well used all the way to Penzance as the places of London or northern passengers were taken by those making journeys within the West. In the Intercity age, after periods when BR boasted it was not interested in 'local' traffic, trains which leave Paddington crowded get progressively emptier as they journey west.

But, even when joined by fewer passengers, it was still the important up trains that brought the greater ritual, the silk hatted stationmasters and station inspectors on parade. 'Next stop Paddington,' had a great thrill about it as the driver rapidly went round his locomotive with oil can and the fireman brought more coal forward for the hard work ahead. Who could not resist the feeling of envy as the newly-joined passengers accepted their second or third luncheon sitting ticket from the chief steward promptly going through the train . . . so much more convenient than at Paddington where, to make sure

you could get a seat, you had to visit the steward on the platform.

Twice a day in each direction you could sense the lull, the tension as the signals, homes and distants, came off for 'runners', the up and down Cornish Riviera and Torbay Expresses, consecutive trains in both directions when only five or six ran by the Berks & Hants all day long whose missing Taunton meant a miserable service for the Somerset capital. Middle of the day passengers to Town had to take the Great Way Round.

Runners were of course far more frequent on summer Saturdays. Then and then alone the locals were put in the shadow, seen as nuisances, indeed as time went on curtailed (especially the Castle Cary auto cars) because they occupied valuable track capacity. Those that ran were disposed of with even greater alacrity, the lunch time from Chard with its bare dozen passengers even on the year's busiest day being moved on so rapidly as though it were in disgrace.

The two major holiday traffic arteries of course joined at Cogload Junction, with quadrupled track through Taunton on to Norton Fitzwarren. Many, many trains which had good runs this far now found themselves caught in a queue, and many of the down 'runners' in truth crawled through the station, overtaking other expresses they should have left behind a long time ago. Main and relief were both used by expresses to Norton Fitzwarren; it was the six or seven minute section up from Wellington to Whiteball that effectively rationed what could be sent west.

Up runners, however, nearly always had a clear road, even if they had been bottled up much of the way from Exeter; many again overtook another express at Taunton. The stopping one would come to a standstill, and while it was still being attacked by the throng on the platform all signals for the central up main platform dropped and you heard the compressed screech of the runner's whistle approaching at full speed. At Reading, Swindon, Taunton, hearing an approaching express, regulator full open, a minute after the last distant arm dropped and experiencing the mobile coal power station thunder through with its hundreds of tons of metal and wood and hundreds of passengers was one of the Great Western's greats, and as has been said elsewhere a much higher proportion of expresses missed such stations in the 'great days'.

On summer Saturdays nearly everyone had luggage, and there was a constant movement of barrows around the platforms and through the subway. Hundreds rather than dozens joined the all-stations to Minehead and Barnstaple, and the Yeovil trains took many to and from the Channel Isles. Most locals other than the Castle Cary auto cars and the Chard line ones were strengthened. Finally, there were the through expresses for Minehead and Ilfracombe via Barnstaple, including that by the North Warwick line from Wolverhampton.

Once there were daily slip coaches for Minehead and

The north end of Taunton station on 8 August 1955 with an auto-train on the Yeovil service. It is the usual formation of a wooden bodied trailer probably gas lit, and a class 54XX 0-6-0PT No 5403 from Yeovil shed (82D), still lettered GWR, seven years into nationalisation.

Ilfracombe, but ordinary through coach working ended in the twenties, only whole trains (or half ones) going through. Half ones because the Wolverhampton and sometimes a Paddington divided at Taunton going down and joined going up, placing unfamiliar pressure on a layout not geared to it (as at Newton Abbot). It was fascinating, but seemingly endless because especially on the up they could never do it in the time allocated and from the far down end of the platform you could see one, sometimes two side by side, following trains held up if the main up platform were also in use.

In BR days, summer Saturdays brought regulation seat tickets and a ban on platform ones. In the great days hundreds of boys of all ages took full advantage of their penny's worth, and though the hour of your arrival would be dutifully recorded none of the ticket collectors sought to surcharge you if you exceeded your nominal hour by several more. The train spotters helped inform each other and were often aided by the staff including a shout from the West Box signalman if something unusual was happening; there was always someone in the know who could unravel the magic of the train's reporting number on the smokebox door. But then the destination boards, even for the Minehead and Ilfracombe expresses, told their own story, Kingsbridge, Newquay, Falmouth, Perranporth, St Ives all being ticked off each Saturday.

Yet after all the Saturday excitement it was good to rediscover Taunton as its normal self, stoppers predominating, the sounds and smells of the countryside brought to the very platforms, the station pilots chugging to and fro with the odd van of this or that.

171

Dartmouth and the River Dart provide the back drop to Kingswear station on 18 September 1957. The up Torbay Express is leaving behind Castle class No 5053 Earl Cairns whilst No 7029 Clun Castle still with its single chimney and Hawkesworth tender, stands on the turntable road awaiting its next duty. Note the typical corrugated iron roofed GWR water tower on the left and the goods yard still in use behind the departing train.

No 4077 Chepstow Castle climbs up the 1 in 66 out of Kingswear towards Greenway tunnel with an up express in September 1961. The single line to Goodrington is one of the few regularly travelled by Castles and even the occasional King.

11
THREE WEST
COUNTRY JOURNEYS
(Early 1950s)

Kingswear – Exeter

We finish our business in Dartmouth at noon, walk through the GWR's only station without trains (tearing a couple of excursion bills off the piles looped with string by the booking office window) and down the floating landing stage to board the SS *Mew*. Bells ringing as though it were the start of an ocean journey, the glorified ferry (a railway cartage van and a couple of cars on the top deck) sets off at 12.5. We see coal being unloaded from a ship at Kingswear, a Grange class locomotive making up a coal train for Torquay gas works. And having taken water, a Prairie tank backs onto our train, three chocolate-and-cream coaches, the 12.15 for Wolverhampton as the destination boards proclaim.

The Prairie tank makes light though noisy work of the climb with gorgeous views of the estuary and its wooded banks up to Greenway tunnel, but the business-like start is misleading since in our first hour we will achieve less than thirteen miles. A good ten minutes are spent at Churston. We whistle but are brought to a dead stand at the home while the signalman lets the down train, a connection off the 5.30am Paddington-Penzance (an eleven-hour job that) in first. We go in, see the down off, and wait. Then a 1400-class tank that runs the Brixham branch propels its auto-car down towards Kingswear, trailing a fish van which eventually it adds to our train, behind our first-class carriage. Punctually at 12.30, six minutes after the down was scheduled to leave, we energetically continue our journey, the fish probably earning as much per mile as our handful of passengers.

One extra person joins us at Goodrington Sands Halt but we see a packed beach – and sidings full of old stock that brought visitors down on Saturday and will take others back next Saturday. Many more join us at Paignton, however, and even more at Torquay where the two minutes we are allowed are fully occupied, passengers taking advantage of the only through train of the day to Stratford-upon-Avon and Wolverhampton (one of only two even to Birmingham) searching for their reserved seats.

Unlike those going to London on the Torbay Express an hour earlier, we have still not finished with branch-line affairs, for we stop half way up another climb at Torre, and then at Kingskerswell – an hour after leaving Kingswear. Next Newton Abbot where we are at platform five from 1.22 until 1.30. Those eight minutes compare with the sixteen that most through coaches from the Torbay line take to be attached to the main train at Newton; but then these coaches are unusual in being added at Exeter to which we work independently. The eight minutes are in

Via Castle Cary

The Cornish Riviera Limited express commenced running on 21 July via the Castle Cary and Langport line. Carriages are slipped from the down train at Westbury to give an accelerated connection with Weymouth, and at Exeter to afford an improved service to that city and the South Devon health resorts.

Each seat in the train is numbered and, as was the case last year, passengers may secure a seat upon payment of a fee of 1s. Tickets of different colours are used to differentiate between the various portions of the train: thus those for the Cornish portion are red, for the Exeter portion white, and for the Weymouth coaches blue. In normal working a dining car and five other vehicles form the Penzance portion, the number of seats being 268, but a spare coach is provided, bringing the available seating accommodation to 340. In the Weymouth and Exeter slip portions of the train there are 104 seats, but in each case the number may be reduced, if the traffic is light, by detaching the second coach.

A feature of this train, as in former years, is the provision of attendants for the convenience of ladies travelling alone or with children. Indeed, everything possible is done to secure the comfort of passengers on the journey.

fact magical ones and the enthusiasts among the regulars detrain to enjoy them. For during them both up and down Cornish Riviera pass through.

The down is usually first. Even in summer, mid week it sometimes runs non-stop to Plymouth in its allocated four hours, going through Newton's down main, platforms three and four. If it needs a banker it pulls up on the platformless down through and the extra loco that has been waiting on the slow is shunted over in a trice. The up always takes the platformless up through, running through gently if non-stop and beginning to gather speed if it has stopped to detach a banker outside the station. As soon as it clears Hackney we have our starter, and usually the distant arm lowers as it clears Bishopsteignton just as our eight minutes are up.

At Teignmouth we pick up more local than through passengers; the same at Dawlish, depart 1.48. Though the Prairie tank has donned express headlamps throughout, only now do we cease stopping at all stations and make a spirited dash to Exeter, though because this is a convenient shoppers' service we call at St Thomas (about fifty get out) before pulling into St David's platform six at 2.8. Time now to see the fish truck taken off in one direction, the Prairie tank disappear in the other, to cross the bridge and see our opposite number the down Wolverhampton or Cornishman be divided into its Penzance and Kingswear portions, before our Penzance section arrives at platform five at 2.19 non-stop from Plymouth. Its locomotive (a Castle) picks us up and places

The west end of Exeter St. Davids on Sunday 26 March 1950. 51XX class 2-6-2T No 4176 leaves with the 5.00pm. Exeter–Kingswear local made up of four corridor coaches. The fine bracket signal was only superseded by colour lights in May 1987. The whole train is in period livery, the engine in 'LNWR' lined out black with the original large emblem and the coaches in red and cream. A backing signal complete with route indicator is on the left of the last coach.

us at the front of the combined train as another Prairie tank cautiously backs down platform one onto the three Kingswear coaches left behind by the Penzance-bound service. They're due out at 2.25 after eighteen minutes in the station; we're away first at 2.22 after only fourteen. Two and a quarter hours since we left Dartmouth, but we all know the serious work begins now, next stop Bristol Temple Meads with three hundred passengers, first service of afternoon tea already being called.

Newton Abbot – Penzance

The hooter at the locomotive works blows off exactly as the guard sounds his whistle. It is 7.40 and once more Newton Abbot based number 4077 *Chepstow Castle* sets off for Penzance. Six coaches and a van, sixty or so passengers, Lyons cakes for all intermediate stations to Plymouth other than Bittaford Platform, and a lot of miscellaneous packages. Every day the train is a lifeline for a section of Devon humanity. Many use it to get to work just between one station and the next. A solicitor's clerk gets out at Totnes where a BBC man for Plymouth is among the regulars buying his ticket along with those for the day's first up train, the only Totnes-Newton Abbot auto-car working. *Chepstow Castle* announces the time and parents urge their children on as she works full out climbing Tigley Bank. The sun gains strength and there once more is the Kingsbridge connection across the platform at Brent. And a few minutes later three diminutive schoolgirls at Bittaford platform bound for

The Royal Duchy, 1.30pm. Paddington to Penzance climbing to Dainton on 17 May 1958 behind No 7027 Thornbury Castle. *The leading coach, probably a Saturday strengthener, is Hawksworth and the remainder of the train BR Mk 1 stock. The whole train has a very Great Western appearance as at this period the coaches on the principal expresses had reverted (sadly temporarily) to chocolate and cream livery. Although in the GWR building programme No 7027* Thornbury Castle *was one of those built under BR auspices. It is now preserved.*

Royal Tatties

Many are the stories of how the Great Western coped with Royal trains and the crowds of people who wanted to travel to witness a Royal event, but perhaps the most memorable occasions were during the war.

Once King George VI and the Queen were on their way from Paddington to Cornwall when Plymouth was being bombed. The train was held for safety within the short Mutley tunnel until the all-clear sounded.

Later on the same journey it was thought safer to make them leave the Royal train for a time, and later again the train was for safety stabled at a point on a branch line with a curve. Disaster: because of the cant water would not flow into the King's bath and GWR ingenuity was used in summoning local resources to top up the water tanks.

Years later when the Royal train spent a night at a scenic but quiet point on the Fowey branch, the Queen Mother heard that the driver – the same one as halted the train in Mutley tunnel during the bombing – was about to retire.

The Queen Mother insisted in clambering down the step ladder carried for emergencies and walked along the ballast to the engine, where the driver told her that he was going to spend his retirement gardening and growing Tatties.

'I like growing them too,' said the Queen Mother, adding on her way back to her saloon accompanied by C. W. Powell the operating superintendent from Paddington that she did not have many opportunities to do things privately like that.

Plympton. Never a crowd, but always a few passengers all the way down, Cornwood where the bus is slow providing the best business including the librarian for St Budeaux who will change at Plymouth North Road. Here the 7.40 Newton connects into the Saltash auto-car which in turn connects back into it at Saltash, enthusiasts occasionally getting value for money by making the double change.

We arrive at North Road, when all the workers and school children rush off, at 8.48 and do not leave until 9.10. Though the locomotive, stock and crew are unchanged, now it is quite a different train. Instead of taking people to work, it is carrying those going about their working-hours business plus many going to Cornwall to visit friends or just on a day out. And unlike the previous service, the 'Owl' 11.50pm from Paddington, all stations except Dockyard Halt and St Budeaux platform from Plymouth to Penzance (from Paddington it is a marathon 11.50pm to 11.00am), we are semi-fast. We are indeed one of the day's key trains down the backbone of Cornwall, carrying people who matter like the railway's own district officer, planners, journalists, church officials, you name it. More than any other train, this says Cornwall and you can tell much about the state of the country's economy and social and political life from it. All the way down the stationmasters will be on parade to meet us and make a point, and at every junction the branch train will provide a decent connection.

At Liskeard we catch a glimpse of the Looe train at its terminal platform at right angles to the main line. At Bodmin Road the locomotive of the Wadebridge train twice gives three loud whistles that echo up the Glyn Valley as it runs round. At Lostwithiel only two or three cross the platform to join the Fowey auto-car, but several dozen for Newquay cross the bridge at Par, and the Falmouth train (Looe, Newquay and Falmouth all have standard two-coach branch-line non-corridor sets) has every compartment well used. This is Truro's rush hour, the up Cornish Riviera overtaking the Cornishman at the same time. With about 1,600 daily passengers and local trains that start for Plymouth and Penzance as well as Newquay and Falmouth, Truro is Cornwall's busiest station, though in these pre-road bridge days more passengers use the suburban service at Saltash.

Three expresses with Castles. Though ours is a purely West Country affair (no connection east of Exeter), we have no need of inferiority complex! As many get on as off at Truro, and there will still be connections waiting at Gwinear Road for Helston and at St Erth for St Ives after we do brisk business at Redruth and Camborne. We skirt Mount's Bay and pull up under the ugly roof at the buffer at Penzance. Even here the stationmaster greets us as the fireman unhooks *Chepstow Castle* after her 111-mile run starting hundreds of people's days in all manner of ways. And every day there will be a few newcomers enjoying the scenic treat, the glimpses of Atlantic and English Channel, of castles and mine stacks, and perhaps be surprised by the number of busy freight yards, clay dries and the general level of activity along the whole route. *Chepstow Castle* retires to Long Rock for turning, watering and resting before the return trip carrying many of the same passengers back home.

Bodmin Road, junction for Bodmin and Wadebridge, (now downgraded to 'Bodmin Parkway' with a minimal bus connection to Wadebridge), in 1956 with No 4908 Broome Hall *on a down express (possibly the Penzance portion of the Cornishman.)* The branch platform on the up side is now host to the Bodmin Steam Railway.

The 6.03pm to Newton Abbot leaving Lostwithiel, junction for Fowey, on 11 June 1956 behind No 6821 Leaton Grange. Lostwithiel Crossing Signal box is just visible through the steam. This is very much a period picture with World War II gas mask cases in use as camera bags or for rations etc.

Newton Abbot – Christow

Eight or nine times a day a small group of country folk cluster around the primitive shelter on Newton Abbot's number nine platform, outside the main station. We reach it beside the Railway Inn and join the auto-car headed by a 1400-class 0-4-2 tank. We swing away from the main line picking up our token from Newton Abbot East that looks even vaster from this angle and pass alongside the thriving freight yard and then run beside the Stover Canal the railway superseded many years ago. Teigngrace Halt sees no business today, but the clay sidings either side of us at the level crossing are busy, and as we approach Heathfield there seems a whole world of activity in sidings serving the lignite mine and even the pottery siding is full.

We alight, wait to cross the tracks until the up train from Moretonhampstead has run in and then make our way to the Teign Valley bay, where a third 0-4-2 and auto-car wait. Passengers scurry to and from all three trains. No thoughts of closure yet, though there are no signs of pre-war trimmings such as the seasonal non-stop through Newton Abbot from Torquay to Bovey Tracey, or the occasional extension of a Teign Valley train to serve Bovey. At 10.42 the Moretonhampstead and the Newton Abbot are off, about twenty five passengers each. Three minutes later the beaming guard slides the doors closed between the entrance vestibule and the two compartments with longitudinal seating of the Teign Valley car, and we enter that private world of a branch off a branch.

We catch a glimpse of the illuminated panel in the signalbox; this was about the last piece of GWR modernisation hereabouts before the

Teign Valley Trains. On 15 February 1958 0-6-0PT No 7761 is seen at Christow station with an Exeter–Heathfield train whilst 0-4-2T No 1451 waits with the corresponding service the 12.49 Heathfield to Exeter. Note the second locomotive headlamp facing inwards on the pannier tank next to the toolbox – a traditional Great Western practice. All four coaches are particularly clean as are the locomotives – the 0-4-2T in lined green and the pannier tank in plain black still with the old emblem.

outbreak of war, and handy it is proving with the lignite and other traffic. Our wheels screech round the sharp curve and we see that there is still an ambulance train with large red crosses on it occupying one of the two sidings of Stover Camp. Chudleigh Knighton Halt sees a couple of passengers, but only parcels business at Chudleigh. The Christow freight is on the other track at Trusham, its Mogul having positioned a rake of trunks full of products from the concrete works to be picked up on the return. Ten wagons a day here. Occasionally the down through goods, run for route training purposes (since when the Sea Wall is closed at Dawlish even the Limited comes this way) stops to help clear the traffic. But if that happens it might mean holding it two hours or more since for all its track circuitry Heathfield cannot cope. But then all over the GWR freight and especially mineral trains are routinely held hours on end waiting for a path.

Then briskly alongside the Teign, dum dum der dum der de, dum dum der dum der de, the guard now sitting with his five passengers discussing the universe. He suddenly jumps up and shouts 'Plastered'. The brakes jam on. He is thrown down the car but animatedly repeats 'Plastered' and jumps out. The driver, fireman and guard go gathering mushrooms! Mushrooms have plastered the field. Ninety seconds later we're on our way examining the guard's specimens, and he shows them off to the stationmaster, the solitary employee and so general factotum despite his hat.

Then into Christow, alongside the refuge siding where once they had to back the Limited to cross its opposite number. The village the station purports to serve is miles away, but the threatened Devon General bus service has not yet started and a dozen join for Exeter. We are the only ones off and when we explain our interest the stationmaster tells us everything about his charge and takes us over to the signalbox. 'Passengers aren't much but the minerals booming,' he says. The signalman adds that while the complex sidings on both sides were laid out to be worked from the Exeter end, in fact nearly all shunting is on the Heathfield one. Only through route-training freights, one daily each way, go in the Exeter direction with its steep gradients and long tunnel from which every inch of a locomotive emerges dirty as though no rags had been applied for weeks. The only signalbox between here and City Basin Junction on the main line at Exeter is Longdown and it only crosses trains in emergencies (see *Great Days of the Country Railway* page 185). Routinely all trains asking clear to Longdown are 'blocked back' effectively making Christow – City Basin Junction one long section.

'So everything has to go out via Heathfield.' Everything includes stone traffic which arrives from the quarry by aerial ropeway, barytes from the mine, charcoal. Between them a dozen to a score of daily wagons, while coal and fertilisers of course come in. 'We're really very busy though you might not guess it from the number of passengers. Only the mornings to Exeter and early evenings back are well used.' And since the fuel crisis of 1947 a short evening working from Heathfield to Christow has been curtailed, the engine spending over an hour simmering in the bay at Heathfield to harbour the nation's coal reserves.

Station Doubts

The GWR named its stations more consistently than most railways. This often helped (or at least warned) those in the know, but puzzled strangers.

A special point to beware of was that if a station was named after two places it served neither conveniently, while if the name included 'Road' you could be sure it was even further away from the place whose name it boasted. Many Roads (Claberston, Grampound, Pontypool) were famous institutions and supported small communities much in the way that remotely-situated junctions sometimes did. Because it could not be approached by road and was a changing place only, Bala Junction did not figure in the timetable other than in a footnote: 'Passengers to and from Bala change at Bala Junction by most trains'.

Halts were unstaffed, usually with the most rudimentary shelter and no means of heating or communication; Platforms were often little better but had a porter on duty who issued tickets and handled passenger parcels (no goods) at least part of the day, though a few had been proper stations before downgrading.

If the GWR had more than one station in a town, each was named, but sometimes just the place name (such as Barnstaple and Dorchester) was deemed sufficient where there were rival establishments.

We watch the freight we overtook at Trusham come in and start shunting: a very slow game of chess and they are still playing it when nearly two hours later, after a walk up to the village and a visit to the pub, we return to become the only passengers using the Exeter to Heathfield lunch-time train. In fact this is the only train (other than a Saturday evening down that returns via the main line) that goes through to Newton Abbot. You can catch a fast connection or wait on board to follow half an hour later. We of course opt for the latter and are surprised that over twenty Heathfield folk (six mothers with prams) join us.

Engineering Instructions

The Great Western thought of just about everything, and the

INSTRUCTIONS
For the Guidance of
INSPECTORS AND STOREKEEPERS
in the
ENGINEERING
DEPARTMENT

set out to cover just about every eventuality. In the volume for 1933 were 1,234 such instructions, of which the following are a selection of this diversity.

★

551 All clocks should be kept to Greenwich time, which can be ascertained at stations at 10 a.m. daily. As far as possible, the winding and regulating of clocks should be done by the same person, who must be competent to perform the duty properly.

★

1135 Applications from persons of foreign nationality to visit railway or dock premises and works carried out thereon are to be referred to the Divisional Engineer before facilities of the kind are granted, giving the name, nationality and home address, and a copy of their statement of the object of their application.

One wonders what industrial spies wrote!

★

Well-tended lineside allotments still live in the memory. But how many knew there was, or thought about, the bureaucracy behind them?

633 Land within the permanent way fences may be left to Company employees for the purposes of garden ground at an annual rent (*note* 1933) of 3d or 4d per perch, the higher rate to be charged when the rent for outside public allotments in the locality is relatively high.

634 Agreement (Form No 4800) must be signed in respect of all garden tenancies.

639 Rents payable by Company's Staff (salaried and waged) in all Departments will be deducted through the paybills.

637 The Company will not undertake the construction of small buildings, such as tool houses, on land let for garden plots, but, where the Divisional Engineer agrees, such buildings may be erected by the tenants at their own

risk, the Company to be expressly relieved from all liability arising from the existence or failure of such buildings or any fire that may occur to them.

★

The Great Western looked after the welfare of all of God's creatures.

651 Where game-preserving rights have been granted to adjoining landowners, care must be taken not to destroy nests of game birds when burning grass on the railway embankments.

★

Well – not quite all!

654 The presence of rabbits in slopes of cuttings and embankments is undesirable, and permanent way men are to keep down the numbers of these animals as far as practicable, but the use of steel spring traps for the purpose is forbidden.

★

405 W.C. white pans, with hinged seats are to be used for general requirements at stations and offices. For workmen's lavatories, W.C. pans, white inside and cane outside, with fixed wooden inserta seats are to be provided.

The reach of the Company was even unto the smallest room!

★

406 Each ladies' lavatory is to be provided with an ordinary hat and coat hook.

An early example of sex discrimination?

★

1127 Before transmitting complaints of alleged defective mackintoshes, a test should be made by placing the back of each garment over a bucket in such a manner as to hold water and allowing a pool, say 2in. deep, to stand in the garment for a period of 12/24 hours, repeating the experiment over the seams and shoulders, the material being rubbed underneath occasionally while the water is standing upon it.

★

558 Private persons are not to be permitted to take photographs of any engine or carriage shed or any work affecting the Locomotive Department until sanction has been obtained from the Divisional Engineer.

This regulation was surely more honoured in the breach – thank goodness!

How many of us, one wonders, ever gave a thought as to where the shrubs, trees and flowers in those once beautiful station gardens came from?

687 A nursery for the rearing of shrubs is maintained at Gloucester, and particulars of shrubs, etc., will be circulated in October. Requests for shrubs, trees, etc., should be addressed to the Divisional Engineer.

★

110 To find the speed of a train, note the number of seconds the train takes to travel a quarter-of-a-mile, divide 900 by this number of seconds and the result will give the speed of the train in miles per hour.

And this in the age before calculators!

★

Above all however the Great Western had a Corporate Image, and it was not confined to its locomotives and Rolling Stock.

459 Annually, on the 1st June, proposals for cleaning, painting, limewhiting, etc., for the ensuing year must be sent to the Divisional Engineer as follows . . .

★

However

476 Firebuckets are to be repainted by the Chief Mechanical Engineer's Department at Swindon, and must not be included in station repainting proposals.

★

But notwithstanding that little interdepartmental foible.

464 The standard tints for the painting of stations, bridges, etc., are as follows:

No 1. – Stone.   No 5. – BridgeGreen.
No 2. – Stone.   No 6. – Steel Grey.
No 3. – Stone.   No 7. – Bright Red.
No 4. – Chocolate. No 8. – Deep Red.

467 Woodwork at stations should, as a rule, be plain painted. Graining and varnishing should only be adopted when local considerations render it desirable, for example at the more important stations.

470 Standard tints for distemper are:
Rooms where a green effect is desired:
Upper portions of walls to be coated with "Dark Italian Green" distemper G1.
Lower portions of walls i.e., the dado or below chair rail level, "Privet Green," G2.
Rooms where a blue effect is desired:
Upper portions of walls to be coated with "Cambridge Blue" distemper B1.
Lower portions of walls i.e., the dado or below chair rail level, "Italian Blue," B2.
Rooms where a cream effect is desired:
Upper portions of walls to be coated with "Cream" distemper H1.
Lower portions of walls i.e., the dado or below chair rail level, "Neutral Brown."
In certain circumstances, it may not be convenient to use a light and dark tint, e.g., where the bottom portions of walls are panelled, etc., but when the two tints are applied, a black line, about 1in. in depth, should be drawn between the two shades of colour.

471 The following colours are, as a general rule, to be adopted for distempering or painting walls of rooms occupied by the Hotels and Refreshment Rooms Department:

(1) Cream, H1.
(2) Two shades of Grey, H2 and 3.
(3) White, H4.

473 Gas, water and other mains above ground in workshops should be painted in accordance with the colour list given below:

Blast Mains	Black
Gas Pipes	Stone
Water Pipes	Chocolate
Water Valves	Red
Hydraulic Pipes	Blue
Compressed Air Pipes	Yellow
Acetylene Gas Pipes	Green
Oxygen Pipes	Red
Fire Hydrants	Red
Main Gas Stopcocks	Red

493 Station Name Boards should be repainted in the Company's standard colours, *viz.*, black ground with white letters, as often as may be, in the opinion of the Divisional Engineer, be necessary irrespective of the periodical repainting of the stations, in order that they may be noticeable and easily read by passengers in trains passing them. Halt Boards on Road Motor Routes must be painted in a similar manner.

★

408 New mat wells, or existing wells under repair, must be made to accommodate the Company's standard size of mats, *viz.*

2ft. 0in. by 1ft. 6in.
2ft. 6in. by sft. 0in.
3ft. 0in. by 2ft. 0in.
4ft. 0in. by 3ft. 0in.

★

Finally their reach even extended to things maritime, and a few years later would even extend into the air . . . The Great Western was not JUST a Railway Company, it was an integrated transport system, and we all benefited from its reach and vision.

582 When unable to proceed to sea owing to weather conditions, Masters of Dredgers and Hopper are to obtain the signature of the Dock Master to a statement in the log to that effect. When, however, the Dock Master is satisfied that the weather is suitable for the craft to go to sea, his decision will over-rule that of the Master of the Dredger or Hopper, and he will undertake the responsibility for his action and report to the Dredging Inspector.

564 Mooring chains at the Principal South Wales Docks should be of 2⅝in. diameter, except at Cardiff East Dock, Swansea South Dock, and Prince of Wales Dock, where chains of 2¼in. diameter are to be provided. At the smaller docks cables should be of 2in. diameter . . .

12
CAMBRIAN HOLIDAY
1937

WHICHEVER route you take, past Ruabon's spoil tips and Telford's majestic Pontcysyllte aqueduct on through Deeside Llangollen to Bala Junction (change for Bala and Blaenau Festiniog) and Dolgelley or over the Cambrian's hilly main line through Welshpool and Newtown, Machynlleth and Dovey Junction, the crossing of Barmouth's great trestle can scarcely fail to impress. Once there, provided of course that you do not try swimming in the estuary tide race, everything is fine for the family; beach, mountains, a comfortable apartment house kept by Miss Richards whose brother is by chance a signalman and the railway visible from the attic bedroom window. It is better not to pronounce on which is the prettier route for a benevolent Great Western allows its passengers to go either way for the same fare.

At 11am, No 3450 *Peacock* (CNYD), a Bulldog, bustles out of Ruabon and up to Acrefair trailing five corridors; it is the (not very good) connection off the 8.33am from Birmingham to Birkenhead and this is a summer Saturday. Down then to Llangollen with its S curved platform and footbridge actually overhanging the River Dee on the down side. On through Glyndyfrdwy (to put down only – on request to the guard at Ruabon) – then Corwen at 11.38 where an ancient one time LNWR 2-4-2 tank has come in with an LMS train from Denbigh. The 10.15 from Barmouth (SO) is waiting to depart behind Mogul No 5303 (CNYD) and both trains are away once new tablets are available. Past Bala Lake to Llanuwchllyn, over the top at isolated Garneddwen Halt even more remote than Talerddig, and down to Dolgelley. The old 4-4-0 from Croes Newydd shed is no stranger here. This time the river is the Mawddach, about to widen into its estuary; the tracks from here on were once the property of the Cambrian Railways: they literally met the Great Western head on. So at Penmaenpool, where the wooden toll bridge is the last road over the river, it is no surprise to find a small shed just beyond the level crossing and the single platform station; it is almost hidden under the rocks and houses an occasional Mogul from Croes Newydd and a regular 48XX 0-4-2 (MCH) tank for the local push and pull service. On through rock cuttings alongside the now blue river to Arthog at the base of Cader then round the curve into triangular Barmouth Junction, whose refreshment room is the local pub serving the local hamlet and railwaymen alike. There is no connection for the Coast Line southwards so *Peacock* has but a two minute wait before moving out past the signal box on to the stone embankment and then the 800yd along 113 span estuary viaduct with its swing bridge at the end; one of the finest views in West Wales is staggering. At 1.26 they

Llangollen station alongside the River Dee at Easter 1936. An unknown Bulldog is leaving with the 12.36pm to Birkenhead and Paddington. The four coach train, 2 + 2 split at Ruabon – the respective portions being added to the 1.00pm to Chester and Birkenhead (9.10 am ex Paddington) and the 1.08pm to Paddington – due 5.05pm. A busy time at the junction.

The Duke/Bulldog rebuilds appeared on the Cambrian from 1936 and worked many of the trains either singly or in pairs until the late 1950s. No 9028, the last to be rebuilt, is seen between Machynlleth and Dovey Junction in 1949. Although this is technically BR days nothing has yet changed – the number on the bufferbeam, GWR livery (albeit a filthy engine) and stock. Note the thicker copper capped chimney applied to most of the class in lieu of the graceful cast iron one carried on the boilers when they ran with true Dukes.

Moat Lane Junction

What memories of this remote junction between the Cambrian's main line and then down through Llanidloes to Brecon!

Memory number one is undoubtedly of the embarassment of the red-faced young soldier as the refreshment room assistant who could not read the writing of his love telegram passing it round the assembled throng to prove how impossible her task was. Especially in World War II, many passengers passed merry hours here waiting for delayed connections.

Memory number two is of a thunderstorm breaking just as a 'short' from Llanidloes arrived, ten minutes before an up main line service was due. Though the GWR spent much on raising the standards of the Welsh lines it absorbed at Grouping, this did not include providing a shelter on the up platform. Often a branch train would be shunted up towards Newtown (double track this section) and backed into an up bay, where passengers could rejoin it to shelter from the elements waiting for their train to Oswestry or Shrewsbury. On this occasion, passengers were spared an instant soaking in the cloudburst by being allowed to stay aboard during the shunt. 'Better be a dead than a wet passenger,' someone was heard muttering, exaggerating the risk of backing over unlocked points.

are in Barmouth and it is time to get the luggage down. Over the footbridge out into the station yard turn right over the crossing, right again and it is Miss Richards'.

A weekly runabout ticket covering the sweep of Cardigan Bay from Pwllheli to Aberystwyth with short detours to Dolgelly and Machynlleth costs ten shillings so there is a good opportunity to explore these fascinating pieces of the old Cambrian Railways and the numerous narrow gauge lines as well. Festiniog, Talyllyn, Corris, Vale of Rheidol are all musts. Planning is important bearing in mind that there is only one train on Sundays. Half an hour checking the station's timetable boards shows that most of the hoped for itinerary can be covered though it will mean digging hard into pocket money for rides on the narrow-gauge lines carrying passengers and talking nicely to the stationmaster at Machynlleth about the Corris – very much an unknown quantity.

This is a job for Monday, taking the 2.23pm from Barmouth behind one of the new Dukedogs No 3214 (MCH) passing Dean Goods No 2464 (MCH) on a down Pwllheli train at Barmouth Junction. A mixture of ancient and modern, though it is hard to call a Duke boiler on a Bulldog frame modern. Even so these are attractive machines, though a pity they have sealed the fate of those lovely 2-4-0s which served the coast line well. Then it is round to single platformed Fairbourne with its Cambrian home signal, still with a white spot on the red arm, across the level crossing with a glimpse of the 15in gauge railway down to Penrhyn Point and perhaps the Bassett-Lowke 4-4-2 *Count Louis* before the long slog up to the high ledge cut into the Friog cliffs of ill repute and through the avalanche tunnel. Down again to Llwyngwril with its army camp and up along the cliff once more then down to a marshy river estuary. Another army camp at Tonfanau then the straight stretch beside the rocky sea defences to Towyn where a pick up freight waits in the yard with empty gunpowder vans for Minffordd behind Dean Goods No 2435 (OSW). On the left, once under the bridge, is the Wharf station and yard of the Talyllyn Railway whose 2ft 3in gauge trains run up the Afon Fathew valley to Dolgoch Falls and a hamlet called Abergynolwyn. There is no sign of activity here so a separate journey will have to be made to find out how or if the trains are running. Through the sand dunes, past the golf links and it is Aberdovey then a stiff climb up behind the town through a tunnel to Penhelig Halt, another tunnel and along the Dovey estuary squeezing along the cliff edge on a shelf past Abertafol and Gogarth Halts to sweep right into marshland Dovey Junction where there is a ten minute wait to pass the 3.34pm to Aberystwyth headed by an old Duke 4-4-0 No 3284 *Isle of Jersey* (ABH). It is an on time arrival at Machynlleth at 3.38pm. Then a quick look round.

Some trains start from here; others split for Aberystwyth and the Barmouth-Pwllheli line; some terminate. There is a medium sized shed housing engines for the coast line and bankers or pilots for the heavy climb up to Talerddig and, as a bonus, the 2ft 3in gauge Corris Railway purchased only a few years ago by the Great Western from one of its associated road companies. This is not on the runabout ticket. In fact a cursory look at the goods yard gives the impression that it might not run at all: there is certainly no sign of an engine and precious little stock. The questions are, where to check? Who to ask? Of course, it has to be the stationmaster.

The stationmaster at Machynlleth is an important man meriting a fine house and a pill box hat. A porter is good enough to lead the way. A respectful tap on the door 'two boys for you Mr Thom-as'. A courteous reception for Mr Campbell Thomas is a kindly man. Certainly it is possible to ride on the train 'but care is needed now'. Mr Thomas himself is going up tomorrow, 'that will be a suitable day?' Meanwhile would a look at the shed be of interest?

The 10.40 ex Barmouth headed by Dean Goods No 2535 arrives at Machynlleth at 11.54am four minutes down; stationmaster Thomas is on the platform waiting. Into the yard and there, with half a dozen empty slate wagons, two with an inverted V for slabs, and a wooden four wheeled van is 0-4-2 saddle tank No 3 (Falcon), a cheerful driver/fireman and Mr Pryce Owen the guard, 'Meet Mr Corris' says Mr Campbell Thomas. No 3 has come down from her shed at Maespoeth Junction about two thirds of the way up the Corris Valley. The guard suggests that the best place to ride is one person on either side of the V 'to get the views you see. It will be bumping now, so hold on tight.'

Over the Dovey bridge on grass grown track No 3 begins to pant as the train clicks and clacks its way alongside but below the Corris road

The Corris Railway, purchased by the GWR in 1930 ran a thrice weekly freight service until part of the embankment near Machynlleth was washed away by floods in August 1948. Kerr, Stuart built (4047 of 1921) 0-4-2T No 4 stands in Corris station in 1940. Note the Royal Leamington Spa poster under the station roof.

Automatic Exchangers

Nowhere was the GWR's feeling of superiority over its rivals stronger than in North Devon on summer Saturdays. The map's thick red line from Taunton to Barnstaple might in reality only be a hilly, single-track branch, but through trains took this shorter route from London, and other expresses came from Swansea and Wolverhampton.

Up to half a dozen summer Saturday trains in each direction ran with express headlamps and, thanks to the work carried out by the GWR before the evil pact with the SR agreeing that neither would spend a penny more on improving their respective routes to Barnstaple, long non-stop runs were indeed possible with speeds of up to forty miles an hour through the crossing stations.

While the signalmen at the Southern's crossing stations on its route to North Devon had to hand wedge points in order to back the tails of expresses into the refuge sidings, the GWR's loops accepted the maximum of two locomotives and nine carriages. And while the Southern men had to exchange tokens by hand, the GWR's proudly used the automatic exchangers when they could.

Distant signals were only pulled for automatic exchanging, which meant the signalman had to time himself carefully, since once the signal was off he had to walk well beyond the platform end to set up the apparatus. Usually it worked perfectly, on the Minehead as well as the Barnstaple line, but occasionally a token would be flung into the vegetation down the embankment and the fireman walk back to collect it.

Before World War II a Friday and Saturday down express usually made its advertised non-stop journey all the way from Taunton to Barnstaple Junction, taking the loop completing the triangle out-
continued opposite

separated by a wall, on the right hand the Afon Dulas. The scenery is wooded and magnificent; at Fridd Gate there is a little building like a toll house but once a station and No 3 stops for Mr Pryce Owen to open the gate. The engine slips on restarting but this must be nothing new as the driver, Mr Humphrey Humphries, leaving her running, gets down from the cab with a can of sand, drops this judiciously on the rails, waits for No 3 to catch up with him and jumps back on. Later one hears that when the grass is longer or the rails even more slippery the guard rides shotgun on the loco's buffer beam with the can. Past the Old Mill at Dol-y-Dderwen where the hills beyond the road sweep down with a startling suddenness and round twisting curves to Escair-geiliog. Here the valley narrows with road, rail and river running closely together amid the trees. A little further at Pont Evans Mr Campbell Thomas stops the train and suggests a short walk 'to see the river in the sunshine'. It is well worth the scramble. Water at Maespoeth where No 4, a Kerr Stuart saddle tank waits in silence; two engines are a luxury here.

Through more fields to Corris (five miles beyond and 300ft above Machynlleth) and a station with an overall wooden roof, the original passenger terminus. Very Great Western though passenger services were withdrawn when the GWR got its hand on the line. Beyond, the whole character changes, the train running between the houses in slate lined cuttings before reaching open meadow land the single platform at Aberllefenni so close to a wall that the cab almost grates against it.

On the way back, at Corris station, the train has a Crosville bus for company and the station mistress who is Mr Humphries' sister brings out the tea. Another stop at Maespoeth for water and a picture of No 4. Handshakes all round at Machynlleth then back to Barmouth on the 5.34 behind a Dukedog once again (change at Dovey Junction). The Barmouth train (all stations and halts) is headed by Cambrian 0-6-0 No 894 (MCH) which makes light work of the switch backs with only four corridors.

Next morning there is a quick trip to Dolgelly on the 9.25am auto train with No 4839 (MCH) leading, this goes on to Bontnewydd but the runabout ticket does not. Back on the 10.25 (the same train) reaching Barmouth at 11.01 in plenty of time for a snack before catching the 12.25 to Portmadoc double headed behind Aberystwyth shed's Duke No 3270 now unnamed (*Earl of Devon* until 1936 when this was lost to new Dukedog No 3205 which in turn lost it to Castle No 5048 in 1937) and Dukedog No 3214 (MCH). This is an all stations train stopping at every halt so progress is tedious. Dyffryn-on-Sea, Llanbedr & Pensarn (for Shell Island) past castle keep to Harlech where Cambrian 0-6-0 No 894 is waiting with the 12.10 Pwllheli to Barmouth at 12.53. The signalman already has the tablet for the next section and is waiting on the platform so there is no delay. Tygwyn Halt, Talsarnau with its wooden trestle over the small estuary, Llandecwyn Halt, Penrhyndeudraeth, still by the sea then a stiff 1 in 50 climb up to Minffordd to where the Festiniog Railway crosses on an overbridge before rolling down into Portmadoc with its shed (five 23XX and one 32XX all allocated to Machynlleth) just beyond the up platform end at 1.22pm.

A walk through the town to the Harbour station to find the Festiniog Railway. Shortly a double Fairlie appears over the Cob from Boston Lodge works, in good time to take the 3pm to Blaenau Festiniog; a red engine, FR No 10 is named after the bard *Merddin Emrys*. The trip is another story but there is time at the Great Western terminus to see the rows of empty narrow gauge slate wagons in the exchange sidings and the 4.25 for Bala with a 58XX and two coaches. The FR train gets back to Minffordd at 5.27pm to make a connection with the 5.15 from Pwllheli at 5.51pm behind No 2283 (MCH). There should have been plenty of time to make this connection at Portmadoc – twenty minutes – but the FR train is ten minutes late and it is not worth the possibility of further delays. The Collett 0-6-0 makes poor time with the all-stations train which gets home to Barmouth at 7.7pm, seven minutes late.

The Afon Wen trip is an afternoon one taking the 2.15 from Barmouth, another all stations train of five coaches headed by Cambrian 0-6-0 No 892 sub shedded at Portmadoc: this gets in at 3.25 passing the Portmadoc only 3.15 from Pwllheli behind MCH 2-6-2 tank No 4549. Before long there is an eldrich shriek in the east and LNWR 4-6-2 tank No 6957 arrives round the curve of the LMS branch from Bangor, one of only three left on that shed and a relief as this class is just being superseded by new Stanier 2-6-4 tanks. The stock is part corridor, part suburban and only four coaches. No 6957 backs out, runs round and leaves again at 4pm allowing plenty of time to pick up the 4.15 to Barmouth only behind No 894. A bit of luck here: a Cambrian goods in each direction.

Saturday is spent at Barmouth as the holiday trains and other extras make this a busy place with almost anything going. Sometimes a Chester Aberdare appears. Trains terminate, others run through to Pwllheli in one direction and Ruabon or Machynlleth and beyond in the other. Some start from the north bay adjacent to the down platform, others from the new platform to the south of the level crossing.

There is an almost constant procession of trains (allowing for the single line section) between Barmouth and Barmouth Junction. On summer Saturdays one gets an extra bonus with engines from the east and south which terminate here making trips to the Junction triangle to turn. There are two excellent spots for photography. The first is opposite the end of the south bay, on the edge of the sand dunes where trains are running slowly and are just about stopped by the 1/100th second (nominal) shutter speed of an old bellows Kodak. The other is more dramatic, on top of a rock just off the road and looking down over the embankment at the back of the harbour in one direction and the estuary with its great bridge in the other. Here one can see Cader Idris, the Mawddach estuary and, in the far distance Barmouth Junction station with trails of white steam as trains move off in three directions. Looking carefully at the miniscule engine drawn up in either of the down platforms the first sign that anything is on the move is a small puff of white steam and then, if the wind is right, the faint sound of a very Great Western whistle. More puffs, this time from the chimney and the toy

continued
side Barnstaple GW. The Friday train was lightly used, the stock working down to return next morning. The Saturday one seldom had a vacant corner seat.

After the war, even the fastest summer Saturday trains stopped at Dulverton and South Molton. But every day's first down and last up freight, empty stock workings at the end of busy Saturdays, and during the war military specials, still called for automatic token exchanges, the fireman watching anxiously over the arm extended from the locomotive dashing through the loop.

Steam Launch Lunch
The Great Western Railway Company's twin-screw Steam Launch *St David*, stationed at New Milford, is available for hire by private parties for use within the limits of Milford Haven at an inclusive charge of £3 3s per working day of 8 hours, or £2 2s for remainder of working day after noon.

The number of passengers not to exceed 30 persons.

On previous notice being given, arrangements can be made for refreshments to be supplied at a moderate tariff.

Applications for the use of this vessel should be addressed to the Station Master, Great Western Railway, New Milford Station, or to Captain Sharp, Assistant Marine Superintendent, Great Western railway, Neyland, R.S.O., Pembrokeshire. – From 1905 timetable.

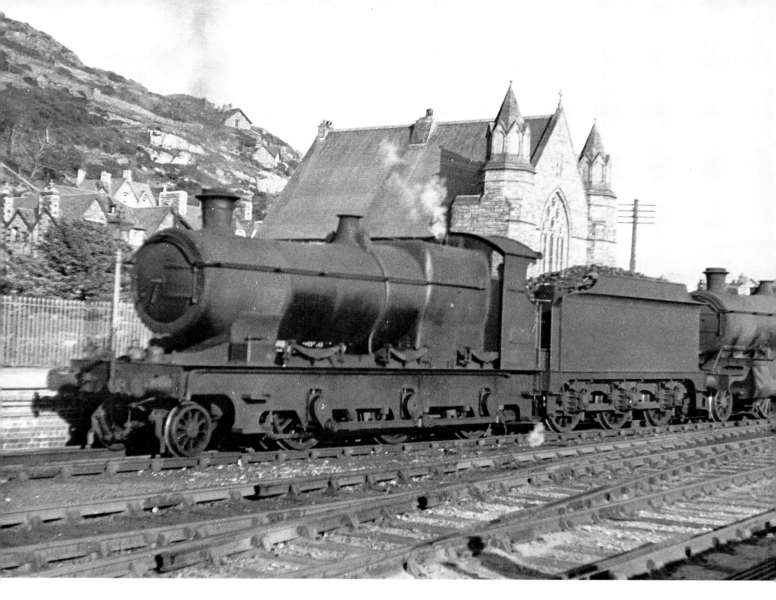

Aberdare class 2-6-0s worked from Croes Newydd, Wrexham, to Barmouth on the freight service. A member of the class is seen coupled to a class 43XX 2-6-0 in the south bay at Barmouth in August 1936 probably awaiting a path to Barmouth Junction for turning.

like train moves slowly – very slowly past the signal box on to the stone embankment. By now the steam is a flowing plume but as the engine passes the fixed distant the driver shuts off and lets the train roll seemingly under its own momentum to comply with the speed restriction. A murmur increases to a faint roar as the train moves slowly over the spindly wooden bridge ending with a metallic echo as it runs through the steel swing section (swung once a year to protect the river's rights and where they made *The Ghost Train*) to squeal round the curve into the short tunnel. The picture is never the same sun, shade, cloud, mountains and river current providing an ever changing kaleidoscope of colour into which the railway fits like a toy.

One more day on the runabout ticket with two narrow gauge lines yet to see. As luck will have it Evan Richards has a signalman colleague at Towyn who sits in chapel with a Mr Edward Thomas – 'something to do with the Talyllyn Railway'. Using Control's telephone he asks if anything is moving on Monday and gets a promise that enquiries will be made at the office over the ironmonger's shop in the High Street. The call back confirms that there is a train at 9.25. Another check with the timetable board shows the morning 'mail' from Pwllheli leaves at 7.28 from Barmouth getting to Towyn at 7.59 and there is an onward train at 10.17 connecting at Dovey Junction for Aberystwyth. This allows plenty of time for a shed visit and to see anything off the Carmarthen branch before making a trip to Devil's Bridge and back. It means chatting up Miss Richards for sandwiches and parental permission for a late return.

Mr Thomas is as good as his word and just after nine an elderly 0-4-0 well tank painted green and with the name *Dolgoch* on its boiler side backs a train of very ancient red painted four wheeled coaches under the road bridge and down into the yard. The whole affair seems very rickety indeed but the driver confirms that passenger trains run three times a day. A ticket to the next station costs 2d then there is a rather rough ride up through the cutting to Pendre shed. A walk through the town still gives plenty of time to catch the 10.17 which comes in behind Dean Goods No 2477 (MCH).

It is only a two minute connection at Dovey Junction but the 10.44 to Aberystwyth, which has come down from Oswestry, is advertised as such and waits for the coast line train which is a couple of minutes late. The station foreman bustles the seven connecting passengers across the island platform and into one of the corridor doors, slams it and stretches out his arm. A green flag, an engine whistle and the train is away first stop Glandyfi. The ride along the north bank of the Dovey estuary to Ynyslas and down the coast through Borth is dull even though it is the old Cambrian main line.

With an hour and a half before the first afternoon train to Devil's Bridge there is time to use the Great Western shed permit valid on presentation of a rail ticket and sixpence. There are a number of engines around including pannier tank No 2708, new Dukedogs Nos 3203 and

One of the most beautiful views in Wales. Barmouth Bridge across the Mawddach estuary was originally opened in 1867; the whole bridge was rebuilt in 1899 to include a completely new swing portion through which an unknown 'Dukedog' 4-4-0 is seen rolling its train of four corridor coaches at the mandatory 10 mph c1955. The trestle section is all timber and in recent years has been attacked by a virulent form of worm which all but closed the bridge and thus the northern section of the coast line. Fortunately remedial action was taken and services resumed including through trains from London and some steam specials.

Company Promotion

Strenuous efforts were made to attract new industries to the depressed areas of South Wales. This was an exercise in which Sir James took the greatest possible interest, personally meeting any important industrialists. Often at the end of a busy day I wondered if I was working for the general manager of a railway or a company promoter. – S. C. Harvey of his years in the late 1930s as personal clerk to Sir James Milne, general manager.

The Great Western built 1923 south bay at Barmouth in 1937. Ex Cambrian Railways 0-6-0, as GWR No 892, has been doing a little shunting and is coupled to a clerestory corridor composite No 7412 built in 1897. Several of the 0-6-0s were working the coast line section at this time including Nos 844, 855, 892, 894 and 896.

3210, Dukes 3264 *Trevithick*, 3272 *Fowey* and 3291 *Thames*, Dean Goods 0-6-0s Nos 2421 and 2464 (MCH), Cambrian 0-6-0s Nos 844 and 855 both (OSW) and 2327 (OSW). Collett 0-6-0 No 2271 (CAR) is getting ready for the 1pm departure for Carmarthen.

The Vale of Rheidol shed has two engines in steam, No 8 just down with the morning train and being prepared for the 2.30pm whilst No 1213, the original Cambrian one, backs down into the track round the side of the station, tucked away as if the GWR is ashamed of it, for the 2pm. It is a fascinating journey with the train seeming to run faster and over better tracks than the Festiniog; it certainly bears no comparison with the Corris! There is a stop for water at Aberffrwd and then a magnificent climb along a rock ledge the train hugging the hillside as No 8 blasts its way up to the summit station. There is something of the main line importance attached to the Rheidol, chocolate and cream coaches, a guard in Great Western uniform and an engine which has most certainly been through Swindon's hands.

The journey back is awful with a dreadful connection at Aberystwyth, those planning the timetable forgetting that some customers come from elsewhere. The Devil's Bridge train gets in at 5.15pm neatly missing the 5.05pm to Machynlleth. The 6.10pm gives an hour and forty minutes wait at Dovey Junction with an arrival back at Barmouth at 9.14pm. The saving grace is the driver of No 896 (OSW) who is persuaded to allow a footplate trip as far as Fairbourne 'if you get in the corner'. The

Although nominally branch line passenger engines the 45XX/4575 2-6-2Ts also worked freight trains on the Cambrian section. No 4518 heads an up goods between Dovey Junction and Machynlleth on 11 May 1949. Quite a substantial load for this line.

Dovey Junction. A desolate spot in the marshes at the head of the Dovey Estuary in August 1939. Duke class 4-4-0 No 3291 Thames has just arrived with a local from Aberystwyth formed most unusually of a two coach 'B' set plus 4 four wheelers. The coast line train is in the opposite platform.

Signal Variety

Led by Brunel, the GWR was perhaps the world's first major user of standardised prefabricated units. But until the end the signal people showed considerable pragmatism in adapting their equipment to suit the circumstances and re-using older signals replaced elsewhere.

While most distant signals had arms of four or five feet, according to the height of the posts, Yeovil Town had one of little more than a foot since space was tight, and there were other such examples. Until the closure of the Barnstaple branch in BR days, the wooden post of the down home at Venn Cross carried its lamps and spectacle glasses half way down the post, enabling the driver to see the lamp though not the arm while still in the tunnel. Throughout the system, signals were designed to fit their location.

Though virtually all signals were carefully maintained, many were reused. For example, some replaced when Paddington was given colour light signalling surviving at Newton Abbot until the abolition of semaphores there in 1988. Circles to indicate a goods line, a large letter S to indicate shunt (eg detaching a vehicle and running forward) and two holes cut out of stop arms (the backing signal authorising the removal of a vehicle from the train's end), calling on arms, and of course a whole variety of route indicator signals . . . all carry the familiar GWR finial they might, but standardised they were not.

thrill of the climb up to Friog and the sparks showering back over the train in the darkness is long to be remembered.

The *Cambrian Coast Express* attaches through coaches from Barmouth at Dovey Junction on summer Saturdays so this is an excellent train for the homeward journey. Just before 9.15am the Barmouth stationmaster dons his pill box hat and supervises the loading of the important train. First class passengers are led to their compartments and most of the comfortable thirds are reserved; it is impossible to get a corner seat unless it is pre-booked. No luggage in advance on *this* trip – the changeable weather has meant that every piece of clothing has been needed right up to today. The platform trolleys are queueing up for the guard's van so it is just as well that the train starts from here. Machynlleth sends a clean Dukedog for this job, turning on the Junction triangle then picking the stock up from the carriage sidings. Today it is No 3200 (MCH) herself, second only to the original hybrid No 3265 *Tre Pol and Pen* rebuilt using the frames of Bulldog 3365 in 1930 and still an Oswestry engine.

There is a 23 minute wait at Dovey Junction for the shunting movements to take place. The Barmouth gets in at 10.16 followed by the Aberystwyth at 10.33 which has another clean Dukedog No 3202 (ABH). By the time this has arrived the Barmouth engine is in the shunting neck allowing the Aberystwyth train to draw forward and back down on to the Barmouth coaches. No 3200 drops back as pilot as the train will now run double headed; Talerddig summit is a killer. They pass the 8.20 from Oswestry at Machynlleth – this is delayed ten minutes on a Saturday to allow for the to-ing and fro-ing at Dovey Junction. Only one minute allowed here as the tablet is already out of the machine and in the signalman's hands on the platform. The two double framers get away well, their exhausts echoing back from the hill behind the shed and over the river.

The load limit up Talerddig for a Dukedog, or indeed for any other Machynlleth engine, is 160 tons and today's train is eleven coaches the absolute maximum. So the fires need to be right and the firemen experienced, easy enough in 1937 when times are hard and most of the top link men over forty. So the engines are ready for a run at the bank once they have come up through Cemmes Road and Commin's Coch Halt to hit the hill at Llanbrynmair. Through the cutting and up round the curve beside the road the two double framers slog up the grade at around 25mph the exhausts reverberating through the mountains as they pass through the final rocks to the lonely crossing at Talerdigg station where the 9.10 from Birmingham to Aberystwyth is waiting in the loop. The train is first stop Newtown (to pick up only) so by now the fireman's arm is beginning to feel the force of collecting another tablet ring on the move. Down now to Carno, over the level crossing, past the Aleppo Merchant Hotel, through Pont Dolgoch and Caersws to Moat Lane the junction for the Mid Wales line to Brecon. There is a small shed on the right as the train runs in and a head out of the window spots Dean Goods 2323 and Cambrian 0-6-0 849 (both OSW and sub shedded here). A crawl through the station and a seven minute run to Newtown where the distant is on for a passenger pick up within a minute of time at 11.36. Smartly away with the uneven beats of the two engines bouncing off the arch of the road bridge then Abermule with its freight only branch to Kerry and memories of that dreadful accident less than two decades back. Welshpool is a welcome relief for the crews who have been watching the water levels anxiously. They draw up twice and get 2,000 gallons in each tender making it a four minute late departure at 12.09. It is double track to Buttington Junction where the old Cambrian main line goes off to Oswestry and there is a hard run to Shrewsbury passing the Shropshire & Montgomeryshire sidings at Hookagate where an ancient LNWR coal engine 0-6-0 lurks in the distance.

Shrewsbury comes only two minutes late but the train runs round the avoiding curve past the LNWR box where the Dukedogs unhook to go on shed to be replaced by No 5064 *Bishop's Castle* almost brand new. Homeward bound after two glorious weeks.

The first 4-6-0s to be seen on the Cambrian were the Manor class following the upgrading of the line to 'blue' route availability. No 7803 Barcote Manor is leaving Machynlleth on 13 May 1949 with the 7.10am Aberystwyth to Shrewsbury train. The signalman at East box is standing on the steps with the tablet for the next section at the ready.

193

Aberystwyth to Carmarthen

The fifty-six miles of single track from Aberystwyth to Carmarthen traversed a countryside of fertile valleys, high mountains and fast flowing rivers, the latter always in close proximity to the railway as it zig-zagged its way south. The line was characterised by sections of stiff climbing, vicious curves and the shortest of passing loops, through the thinly populated territory. The only localities of moderate importance were the then larger villages of Tregaron, Llanybyther and the small market town of Lampeter. There were numerous halts, mainly long distances from the places whose names they carried. The reader may well wonder why the line was ever constructed.

It was a case of Great Expectations. The promoters of the short-lived Manchester & Milford Railway had ambitious dreams of capturing the cotton trade from Lancashire by way of rail to the deep sea harbour at Milford Haven. Their proposed route would have left the Mid Wales line west of Llanidloes to the small village of Llangurig and then through some of the wildest parts of Central Wales to Strata Florida on the edge of Tregaron Bog. The section to Llangurig was actually completed, then abandoned. The next section through the blizzard-swept highlands to Strata Florida proved too costly. To the south the line had already started at Pencader and forged ahead to Lampeter and eventually to Strata Florida. At this point the promoters opted for an easier route to Aberystwyth, which they always had intended to reach by way of a branch near Devil's Bridge and down the valley of the River Rheidol – the course of

Some freight was still routed via the Manchester & Milford in the 1960s. 43XX class 2-6-0 No 7315 leaves Aberystwyth and tackles the 1 in 41 bank over the Afon Rheidol bridge and up the Afon Ystwyth valley with the 9.25am goods to Llandilo Junction (Llanelly) on 5 June 1963.

today's narrow-gauge line – to the then thriving small sea-port with harbour sidings at Aberystwyth.

So the M&M actually only went from Aberystwyth to Pencader, a mere 41 miles. The egg was laid, partly hatched, and finally addled. However, for a brief period the company did operate its own line. In 1906 it was leased to the Great Western which absorbed it in 1911. After 1923, when the Cambrian Railways were absorbed into the GWR, the section as far as Pencader and the Aberayron branch went to the Oswestry District. The remaining section from Pencader to Carmarthen was assigned to the Swansea District.

Between the wars traffic was surprisingly healthy not only on the branch but the two sub branches to Aberayron and Newcastle Emlyn, while the GWR, now firmly established at Aberystwyth, made great improvements with a lot of overdue track renewal and bridge strengthening. The working of the line was shared by Carmarthen and Aberystwyth men; passenger trains took approximately 2 hours 10 minutes to cover the 56 miles. Visitors could relax and enjoy the beautiful scenery; but businessmen who travelled the long way round via South Wales from Paddington naturally found the last lap to Aberystwyth very tedious.

The route was worked by electric train staff and token system. The climbing started at once from Aberystwyth on a very tight curve and after a deep rock cutting followed the River Ystwyth inland via Llanrhystyd Road to Llanilar. Then the line rose abruptly for four miles by some of the toughest climbing on the GWR, steepening at its worst to 1 in 41 with intermediate stops at Trawscoed and Caradoc Falls Halt. The top of the bank was heralded by a short tunnel before the line dropped again at 1 in 41 to Strata Florida with its historic remains of a Roman Abbey. The next section skirted the famed Tregaron Bog, today a bird sanctuary, before reaching the village itself at the extreme end of the vast expanse of marshland. The next 23 miles south ran through varied picturesque scenery twisting alongside the banks

of the River Teify rising and falling via quaint little halts to Aberayron Junction whose signals and points were controlled electrically from Lampeter Box, 1¼ miles to the south.

At Lampeter was a renowned refreshment room, for many years run by a female character who served food and drinks at any time of the day! The zig-zag course along the banks of the ever-growing River Teify through Llanybyther to the fascinating little station of Maesycrugiau with its short passing loop, goods and cattle siding. Below the station lies a famous salmon pool known locally as the 'boiler pool', which contains the remains of an M&M locomotive which blew up. At Pencader Junction, for the Newcastle Emlyn branch, the Swansea District was entered and the most fascinating part of the entire journey began.

The line now fell rapidly at 1 in 80 then 1 in 55 down the rugged valley of the River Gwili, speed limit being 35mph snaking down the gorge, surrounded by high wooded hills and overhanging rocks, the haunt of the protected Red Kite. The tortuous course with check rails on all curves continued down through Conwil and Bronwydd Arms to Abergwili Junction. From that latter point the route suddenly became the Red classification for locomotives over the short remaining distance to Carmarthen. The maximum speed limit on the branch was 40mph. At many of the crossing stations two passenger trains were not allowed to pass, but a goods train could be admitted to a loop to allow the passenger train to run over the main line. In post World War II days the route earned itself the nick-name of the 'Burma Road'.

Locomotive-wise, the first GWR engines to work the branch were the immortal 0-6-0 Dean Goods, some even with copper caps to their chimneys and polished brass domes and safety valves. What a wonderful sight, especially crossing Tregaron Bog in a biting east wind, rattling along no doubt with the storm canopy stretching from their sparse cab roof to the tender, hauling a string of GWR clerestories. They were the real work horses of

the branch for many years; economical, easy to maintain, adaptable. A few 2-4-0 Barnum and Stella classes helped out together with converted 4-4-0 3521 class locomotives. This picture lasted until the early thirties when the latter classes, with the exception of the Dean Goods, were replaced by 4-4-0 Dean Dukes and later still 4-4-0 Duke Dogs and 0-6-0 Collett 2251 classes. As if in anticipation, the branch was raised from the Yellow category to that of Blue just prior to World War II which permitted engines with outside cylinders in that group to work the line, the exception being the 2-8-0 28XX class.

Traffic increased during the war period with heavy troop and munition trains. There were two daily up and down freights known as the 'Saltney Goods', through workings from Llandilo Junction to Saltney outside Chester. These vital trains saw the introduction of 4-6-0 Manor classes, 2-6-0 Aberdare and 2-6-0 Moguls. Once hostilities ceased the latter classes, with the exception of the Aberdares, became regular performers with the addition of the large 2-6-2 81XX tank locos – oddly enough as freight and passenger traffic dropped away. The two little branch lines continued to operate from Aberayron and Newcastle Emlyn, but milk traffic only, passengers and then general freight having ceased with deep local regret. Both branches were originally worked by 0-4-2 Wolverhampton tanks and later the 0-6-0 2021 PTs until, finally, the 74XX PT locos.

As general freight switched to road after nationalisation, milk was the branch's saviour: vast Milk Marketing depots at Pont Llanio between Tregaron and Lampeter, and Green Grove sidings on the Aberayron branch kept things alive. The importance of this traffic was emphasised by Carmarthen diagramming Castle class locos to work the bulk tanks forward to the south. Passenger services on the branch receded to just three up and down trains, on week-days only, each of only two coaches. But summer Saturdays saw the continuance of a time-honoured through service, now linking Swansea and Butlins Camp at Penychain outside Pwllheli in the north. A local stopping train from Aberystwyth to Tregaron on Saturday nights returned as empty stock.

The branch had her moments of drama. In the winter of 1947 the down 5.30pm passenger from Carmarthen encountered a massive snow drift at Lampeter and was buried for three days while the line ahead was totally blocked. The Aberystwyth crew on one of the last Dean Dukes kept the unfortunate passengers warm with steam heating and hot water, while the driver, a natural comedian, nick-named Darkie, kept them entertained at intervals and the notorious refreshment room was open day and night until they were finally rescued. There were often special freight trains but in 1956 a very heavy Royal train worked the branch from Pembroke Dock to Aberystwyth and back, conveying Queen Elizabeth and Prince Philip. The motive power was two immaculate ex-LMS 2-8-0 Stanier 8F locos who coped with the difficult road to perfection, whilst the last remaining Dean Goods (now preserved), No 2516, stood by in attendance with the steam crane. In 1950 railwaymen had their hopes raised when in connection with an oil refinery at Milford Haven an ex-GWR 2-8-0 loco in the 28XX series worked up to Aberystwyth on a clearance test. They found that the class could work over the branch provided alterations to the platforms at several stations were carried out; however, hopes were soon dashed when it was decided the availability of certain other classes in the Blue group did not justify the expense.

The Manchester & Milford Railway, such of it that was built, traversed sparsely populated country and trains usually consisted of two or three coaches hauled latterly by 43XX class 2-6-0s. Here No 6310 on an Aberystwyth to Carmarthen train crosses another at Strata Florida station. A further Mogul is in the goods yard on a down freight.

Akin to the rest of the Oswestry District the Carmarthen branch was a family affair and naturally a good deal of good humour went on up and down the line. One of the best remembered characters was a passenger guard, the late Owen Humphreys, who started his railway life on the old M&M Railway. He was well-known to passengers, especially first class, and would convey drinks for them from the incredible refreshment room at Lampeter. He had the distinction of bringing the last M&M train into Aberystwyth and years later the last GWR, but failed to make the grand slam in BR days due to retirement. Another character was a station master who shall be nameless, with many hobbies, one of which was the removal of teeth, and was known far and wide for this illegal surgery. Such operations were carried out either in the booking office or waiting room without any form of anaesthetic.

Finally, when the Great Doctor announced his proposals for slaughter of our railway system, it was with no surprise that the Carmarthen branch was included. However, no notices of impending doom appearing on her platforms, it was a case of sudden death. Forty-eight hours of torrential rain resulted in the River Ystwyth washing away a bridge to the east of Llanilar and no more trains ran except from Carmarthen in the south to the Milk Marketing depots at Pont Llanio and Green Grove sidings on the Aberayron branch. That was short-lived as the Milk Board went over to road transport and the remaining rails were lifted. Just prior to this the Cambrian section of the Oswestry District had been transferred to the LMR. However, the Carmarthen branch remained Western to the end, the Swansea District then being extended to just short of Aberystwyth. Dieselisation never really came her way and very few BR standard engines ever worked over her rails.

The first station out of Carmarthen, Bronwydd Arms, is the headquarters of today's Gwili Railway, so a picturesque section of 'the branch' survives in preservation.

One man's View

The Great Western and (particularly in steamdays) the Western Region attracted some of the best in railway photographers; names like M. W. Earley, G. H. Soole and Philip Alexander. Of these Alexander had the good fortune to be trained as an architect; he had, and still has, an eye for a well proportioned picture. He has run the gamut of negative sizes, glass plates, 2¼ × 3¼ film, 2¼ × 2¼ film and 35mm and he is one of the few people who have produced quality photographs which can be published commercially with all the print grading right. Most of his pictures are Western Region rather than Great Western but many were taken in the first decade of nationalisation when the railway and its artefacts hardly changed a dot. This selection of his photographs show the Western as it was then, full of character and charm.

Living and working at Chippenham Philip Alexander was able to be 'in the know' with regard to a number of special workings out of Swindon. One of these related to running in turns for locomotives outshopped from the works after general repair when paintwork was fresh and brasswork sparkling. The train was an early afternoon, Bristol to Swindon local which was regularly King or Castle hauled. Here the engine is No 7033 Hartlebury Castle *one of the last batch built in 1950.*

Most of Alexander's prints were made on cream stippled paper to give that extra effect though this does not always reproduce as well as a standard glossy picture. Sadly his 1951 negatives are lost but this print of a permanent way train in Cornwall survives. The scene is St. Austell on 23 September of that year with small wheeled 2-6-2T No 4565 on a Sunday duty. It is very much single line working with sleepers being unloaded prior to track renewal.

Snow has come early in the winter of 1952/53 and the crisp morning sunshine has caught the scene well. Hall class 4-6-0 No 4912 Berrington Hall *nears the summit of Dauntsey bank on 30 November with the 9.35am (SuO) Weymouth to Swindon semi-fast. The exposure was 1/500 at F5 with a X2 yellow filter on HP3. Camera Agfa Isolette.*

Opposite *The North to West line (Shrewsbury–Hereford–Pontypool Road–Bristol or Cardiff) was not one of the most photographed but Philip Alexander paid special attention to the area of Llanvihangel bank and Abergavenny Junction. This shot of a freight at the summit is something rarely recorded – the need, with a loose coupled train, to pin down wagon brakes before descending an incline. The engine is one of the later batch of 28XX 2-8-0s with a side window cab, No 3813.*

Unusual combination. One of the extended bunker 2-8-0 tanks as a 2-8-2T No 7220 with a down goods passing Stoneycombe Quarry siding on 25 March 1950. These 2-8-2 tanks were not regular visitors to the area and the reason for this particular working is not known. Even more unusual is the banker – No 6934 Beachamwell Hall. *The freight is a through fitted one with ventilated vans and cattle wagons as leading vehicles. The exposure was 1/200 at F4.5 with a X4 yellow filter on HP3, glass plate.*

GREAT WESTERN RAILWAY.

TRAIN SERVICE AND OTHER INFORMATION

London and Bristol and the West of England.

WEEK DAYS.

London (Paddington) dep.																
Bath arr.																
Bristol (Temple Meads) „																
Weston-super-Mare „																
Taunton „																
Barnstaple „																
Ilfracombe „																
Minehead „																
Exeter (St. David's) „																
Torquay „																
Plymouth { North Rd. „																
Plymouth { Millbay „																
Falmouth „																
Penzance „																

Penzance dep.																
Falmouth „																
Plymouth { Millbay „																
Plymouth { North Rd. „																
Torquay „																
Exeter (St. David's) „																
Ilfracombe „																
Barnstaple „																
Taunton „																
Weston-super-Mare „																
Bristol (Temple Meads) „																
Bath „																
London (Paddington) arr.																

* Stapleton Road.   b Slip Carriages.   c Wednesdays, Thursdays and Saturdays only.
D Restaurant Cars are provided on these Trains, in some cases for a portion of the journey only.   e Saturday nights and Sunday mornings excepted.   G Saturday nights excepted.   Runs from Plymouth to Paddington on Sunday nights (Monday mornings).   P Via Exeter and L. & S.W. Railway, one class only.   R Rail Motor Car, one class only.   P Runs Fridays and Saturdays only after September 16th.
Barnstaple Junction Station, via Exeter and L. & S.W. Ry.   v Saturday nights (Sunday mornings) only.   One class only from Truro on Sunday morning.
Depart 8.5 a.m. after September 16th, except on Mondays and Saturdays.   On other nights, 1st class Passengers travelling by this
Y Sleeping Car (1st class) from Plymouth to Paddington on Saturdays.   Z Sleeping Car (1st class) on this Train.
Train can hire rugs and pillows from the Guard.

London and Weymouth.

WEEK DAYS.

London (Paddington) dep.									
Yeovil (Pen Mill) arr.									
Dorchester „									
Weymouth „									

Weymouth dep.									
Dorchester „									

P Rail Motor Car, one class only,   e Town Station.

...nce to induce traffic to pass by
RAILWAY.

ADDITIONAL ATTRACTIVE EXCURSIONS

from the
PLYMOUTH AREA
and SELECTED CORNISH STATIONS
MAY, 1959

For details of other Excursion Facilities during the month of May, see separate announcements.

If any of the matches or events shewn herein are cancelled or postponed and notice is given to the British Transport Commission in time to cancel these facilities, the fares paid by intending passengers will be refunded on application.

Children under three years of age, free : three and under fourteen years of age, half-fare, unless otherwise shewn.

NOTICE AS TO CONDITIONS.—These tickets are issued subject to the British Transport Commission's published Regulations and Conditions applicable to British Railways exhibited at their stations or obtainable free of charge at station booking offices.

TICKETS CAN BE OBTAINED IN ADVANCE AT BOOKING STATIONS AND AGENCIES.

Further information will be supplied on application to Stations, Agencies, or to Mr. F. G. DEAN, District Traffic Superintendent, Millbay Station, Plymouth (Telephone Plymouth 62888, Extension 712); or to Mr. E. FLAXMAN, Commercial Officer, Paddington Station, W.2.
Paddington Station,
March, 1959.

BRITISH RAILWAYS

R198 B.R. 35008/6   Printed by Latimer, Trend & Co., Ltd., Plymouth   P11—15

GWR

SUNDAY EXCURSIONS

FROM

PADDINGTON

AND

EALING, etc.

DURING

AUGUST, 1937.

For particulars of Day and Half-Day Excursions during August Bank Holiday Week, see separate pamphlet.

PADDINGTON,
July, 1937.

JAMES MILNE,
General Manager.

GREAT WESTERN RAILWAY.

SEASON PROGRAMME
OF
Excursion Arrangements
INCLUDING
CHEAP WEEK-END BOOKINGS,
AND ALSO
SPECIAL FACILITIES,
Giving SHOP ASSISTANTS and Others
HALF-DAY EXCURSIONS
ON THEIR
EARLY-CLOSING DAYS.

NORTHERN DIVISION
OCTOBER, 1898,
And until further notice.

For any further information respecting the Arrangements shewn in this Pamphlet, application should be made to Mr. T. I. ALLEN, Superintendent of the Line, Paddington Station, W.; to Mr. G. GRANT, Divisional Superintendent, General Station, Chester; or at the respective Stations.

J. L. WILKINSON,
General Manager.

September, 1898.

13

THREE OFFICIALS

MORE than most businesses, the Great Western reaped a great harvest from the loyalty and skill of its staff. Though there was much training on the job, of course tests for the like of enginemen and signalmen on the promotion ladder, and always a correct GWR way of doing things, management was assembled pragmatically rather than through formal training and selection schemes. There was, for example, nothing like the traffic apprenticeship scheme on the LNER. But neither was there a shortage of managers, for once in the GWR's employment few chose to leave, and there are many instances of several generations of whole families devoting themselves to the company and throwing off the occasional bright spark who rose to the senior ranks. Higher education was generally regarded with suspicion rather than seen as an asset.

Most of the officials who rose through the ranks never gave a thought to any other way of doing things than the Great Western one . . . which is no doubt why nationalisation hurt more at Paddington than elsewhere. The Superintendent of the Line was of course all-powerful and much respected, as was the mechanical chief who reigned over Swindon and the other works. But also seen on a pedestal of considerable height were the superintendents of the sixteen divisions into which the system was carved (without the constant boundary changes that all BR administrations have witnessed).

While frequent promotions of staff between them, and God-like edicts from Paddington, ensured an essential unity, district styles varied sharply. The first two of our trio of portraits are of district men. Others who might have been chosen include the district engineer (who saw himself as the superintendent's equal) and the district's chief inspector who breathed authority out on the territory and was always around at times of gala and crisis.

The Chief Clerk

The divisional superintendent was something of a politician, his chief clerk the principal civil servant who made things happen. It naturally varied between divisions, and depended particularly on how long the superintendent had been occupying his chair, but generally the chief clerk wielded immense practical power and it was more important to get his ear than that of the superintendent's generally younger assistant (clearly on his way up but not yet arrived). If you wanted to meet the great man himself, it was to the chief clerk that you applied. If you wanted a train to call at a station especially for you, the wise went to state their case to the chief clerk and hoped they would get the nod.

Safely On Board

Even at Paddington things could go wrong, like the time the Prime Minister, Lloyd George, was shown to his seat by a horse-loading foreman.

A new stationmaster had just been appointed, and not knowing that the PM was routinely driven across the Lawn to the head of platform 2 from which the 11.55 to South Wales departed, asked the foreman to keep an eye out for the great man while he himself went to the station front. This was during World War I, when passengers could still take their horses with them on most expresses.

There being no sign of the PM, the stationmaster wondered if he would have to hold the 11.55; but what about the Torbay Express at noon? Imagine the stationmaster's feelings when the horse-loading foreman came to say there was nothing to worry about as he had already accompanied Lloyd George to his seat and wished him a good journey on behalf of the Great Western Railway.

The PM's sentiments on being handed so far down the Paddington hierarchy are not recorded, but it is known that the horse-loading foreman (renowned for his ability to coax awkward steeds aboard but not for his social graces) was upset at being shouted at by the stationmaster.

Lapworth Invitation

'Come up on the 6.36 Leamington' said Maurice. 'It'll be dark then and the stationmaster gone home. And don't come over 'til I call you from the window. I'm on 2 to 10 so you can get the 9.21 back to Snow Hill.' Thus was the initiation into the working of Lapworth signal box 78 levers in all at the end of the four track section widened from Olton in 1933.

Over the sleepered crossing at the north end of the platform, in through the door marked 'No admittance' and up the wooden steps to yet another door and Maurice Long beaming his head off. 'Don't you walk on my polished floor now – just keep on those newspapers and don't rupture yourself on No 76, it's had more people on the floor than I've had hot dinners.'

There is a light on the booking desk, another over the diagram, the levers sparkle their brilliance; no one in this box touches them without using a duster. On the board above the levers are the block instruments for both main and relief lines to Knowle & Dorridge and the main line south to Rowington Junction where once the tracks bifurcated to Henley in Arden but are now only sidings used for stabling sets of coaches. Above the desk are the telephones used by control and the boxes on either side. Maurice rings each one and tells them guardedly there is a 'helper' – his hand on the instrument keys sends his own inimitable bell signals.

There is a single ring on the up main. Maurice answers it and receives a 3 pause 1, 'Give him 3.1 and pull off 2 and 5: it's the stopper which turns round here at 6.45.' In a couple of minutes a string of lights appear in the distance and the four coach Bir-

continued opposite

The chief clerk had invariably come up through the ranks, was thorough GWR, and known for his reliability and consistent attention to detail. Like most other successful GWR men, he was usually of large stature, and above all he never lost his cool. His boss might occasionally rant and rave, especially at the engineer's unreasonable demands for line closures and speed restrictions, but the chief clerk argued diplomatically and at his most heated would simply imply that the head man would be 'seriously displeased'. If a young reporter had written something that had upset the superintendent, it would be the chief clerk who telephoned to explain the displeasure as though that in itself would affect the newspaper's policy.

In addition to his capacity for detail, the chief clerk had to enjoy or at least tolerate long hours, always being at his desk before the boss arrived and not leaving until after he had gone. He also needed eyes at the back of his head and acute hearing for it was presumed he knew everything. He certainly knew a great deal more than his boss or his boss's assistant and, again like a civil servant briefing his minister, produced briefing notes, stood by to help answer any awkward telephone questions – and discouraged the introduction of undesirable changes. Though he might have a small cubicle of his own, usually as high as it was wide, he spent most of the time in the general office watching, listening, noting. He seldom went on tour and saw much less of the physical railway than his boss, but knew every last detail of its operation. He expected to be shown any exceptional report – including the use of bad language on a guard's log or other item of GWR stationery. Details of delays, mishaps, arguments all came his way.

His network of special relationships gave priority to key men on the job including the district's chief inspector who he would often suggest went out to investigate 'and let me know what you think'. Stationmasters jumped if he telephoned, and the excursion manager and in later days the chief of the control office along with all the commercial representatives and operators anxiously co-operated since promotion prospects depended more upon him than any other two people together. Indeed, if you had a serious personal problem, best to tell the chief clerk soonest – before he got to hear it second hand as surely he would. Only the district engineer and the regional locomotive and running supremo (traction-wise the GWR was carved into fewer and different management units) were treated at arm's length.

The superintendent's tours of his territory were carefully organised by the chief clerk, as were interview boards, presentations of gold watches to long-serving members of staff, and everything else that made the railway tick. It was all done with that mixture of authority and humility for which the civil service used to be famous. Virtually never was the chief clerk's name seen in print, or even internally was he credited with having had a good idea. The good ideas were always those of his boss. But if he disapproved of something the excursion manager was doing, it would amost certainly be stopped; and each time a new timetable came out, he would take private pride in having been instrumental in effecting some improvements for his part of the system.

His own team of clerks logging, charting, calculating, timing, respected his power and his knowledge usually without receiving much personal warmth or encouragement. The paperwork of running the railway was very dreary but gave safe employment especially to unambitious youngsters much in the same way as junior accountancy jobs do today . . . plus the benefit of free and reduced-price travel and belonging to one of the most successful businesses of its day. News of the company's latest exploits certainly enlivened life in the large offices of bare floorboards, sparse furniture, sweating darkly-painted walls and the occasional corner wash basin with only a cold tap. In its day and age it worked magnificently.

The Excursion Manager
In the days when long rakes of carriages spent most of their life in the sidings waiting for summer Saturday and other peak demands, the excursion office had a key role to play and its manager was one of each district's elite, reporting direct to the superintedent. He was expected to earn substantial revenue, beating both last year's achievement and the current year's plan, and through the publicity the excursions produced generally raise the railway's profile. In most districts, for a small extra salary, he indeed handled local public and Press relations.

In many districts the excursion office was detached from the main administration and enjoyed its distinct culture, generally a more jolly one as befitted the nature of its work. In addition to the manager, there was usually one male assistant on his way up and a handful of lady assistants mainly who would never rise above the ranks but might serve a decade or two and know the detail of the job inside out. The manager's own job was many faceted.

There were, of course, two main types of excursion: those by ordinary trains and those by special ones. The vast array of full, half-day and evening fares by ordinary services had to be advertised in the local papers and by handbills and posters, so print buying and checking was a major task. In most towns with a district headquarters there was a jobbing printer part specialising in railway work; indeed some advertised themselves as 'General and Railway Printer', so great was the volume of excursion work. The manager had to get clearance for the fares to be charged and negotiated what trains might be used (most districts broke the rules by allowing a cheap ticket to be used by a particular train earlier than the rest, on the 9.25am when the official 'opening hour' was 9.30, for example), and in the days when the GWR owned half of many bus companies undercutting the road fare could result in a complaint at the joint committee supposed to be encouraging rail-road liaison. The excursion bills naturally detailed between what pairs of towns you could return by the other mode upon what extra payment.

The fun part was undoubtedly organising the special trains. The range was enormous: long pre-season excursions to help city people decide how they were going to spend their summer holiday, specials to every kind of sporting, commercial, artistic and (in the countryside) agricultural occasion, educational specials, Sunday school and works trips, and in

continued

mingham Division suburban set comes past behind the tin-tin-tin of Tyseley's No 4110. 'Leave this to me, I've got to set the road and get him into No 3.' Two pause one to Knowle. Blue and black painted levers are slammed over, the starter is pulled off and the movement begins. For three or four minutes points move, signals clear and the train is in No 3 waiting to go back to Snow Hill at 7.10. It needs to be quick work as the Portsmouth-Wolverhampton is due out of Leamington at 6.50. This is due at Knowle & Dorridge at 7.5, taking a few people into the city for an evening's entertainment.

One bell from Rowington at 6.58 which is acknowledged then four on the trot. The train is accepted and offered on to Knowle & Dorridge and accepted there. Off come signals 73, 75, 76, 78. The line is clear through. Train on line from Rowington again acknowledged and 'pegged up'. We open the window looking down the platform and in a couple of minutes two swinging head-lamps and orange tinted steam appear beyond the station canopy. The engine, an Oxford Star, two down with eleven on roars alongside but below the box. Two to Knowle. 'Watch that tail lamp' calls Maurice.

Two pause one – train out of section back to Rowington. Un-peg the instrument and slam back the levers. Two pause one from Knowle & Dorridge, the Portsmouth is out of the section. The road is set for the 7.10 stopper to Snow Hill. She runs Relief to Bentley Heath then main line to Solihull leaving plenty of time for the 6.10 Paddington not due into Snow Hill until 8.10. This is the next down train and it comes through right time behind No 6026, Stafford Road's *King John*, a magnificent spectacle of steam and sound. – P.B.W.

Lapworth on 8 October 1961 showing the signal box at the end of the down platform. The train is the 4.30pm Sundays only, Wolverhampton to Paddington hauled by King class 4-6-0 No

6029 King Edward VIII (81A). It is being propelled from up to down main line as single line working was in force for engineering work on the up line south of the station.

Horse Provender Stores

'Hay, oat-straw, oats, beans and maize, which are the finished products of the agriculturalist, are the raw material of the provender store,' wrote the *GWR Magazine*, assuring its readers that through the central store (moved from Handsworth to Didcot in 1884) the company's horses had the very best. 'The London horses have 2½ per cent more oats and a correspondingly lower percentage of hay,' surely a form of racist distinction. But in winter town and country horses alike had more beans. In total 6,000 sacks were supplied weekly, a total of 14,000 sacks being in circulation while no fewer than 882 sprinklers of a pioneer type guarded against fire.

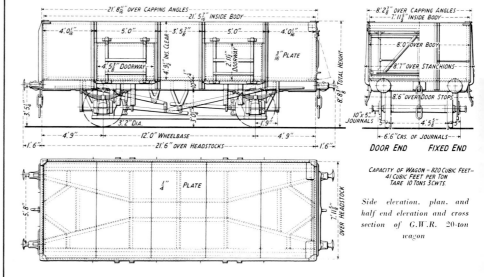

Side elevation, plan, and half end elevation and cross section of G.W.R. 20-ton wagon

204

Great Days Out

Beginning in the mid 1950s the Western Region was host to regular charter trains to the mid Wales coast at Towyn, the terminus of the Talyllyn Railway. They ran on the last Saturday in September for the AGM of the world's first railway preservation operation and were a masterpiece of operation. Starting at Paddington with a variety of specially chosen motive power, including *King George V* and a 47XX 2-8-0, engines were changed at Shrewsbury where the train became double headed via Welshpool, the favourites for this section being a couple of Dukedogs. Occasionally the route was varied via Ruabon where double headed Manors or a Manor and a 45XX tank were used. A real swansong, these trains continued right to the end of steam with *Clun Castle* in 1965 on the Western and two BR Standard class 5 4-6-0s on the Cambrian section.

Each September from 1953 to 1967 the Talyllyn Railway Preservation Society ran a special train from London to convey members to their Annual General Meeting at Tywyn. Whilst the first special utilised ex GWR Railcar No 3, interesting locomotives were used wherever possible thereafter and the route varied between the Cambrian via Welshpool or via Ruabon and Llangollen. The 1964 special is seen at Barmouth Junction/Morfa Mawddach hauled by Manor class 4-6-0 No 7827 Lydham Manor and 2-6-2T No 4555.

King or Castle?

Like most GWR engine men he loved his work, and like many drivers he followed in his father's footsteps. His railway memories went back to when he was five and he listened for his father's private whistle code to tell mother he would soon be home. While he was still at school he saw German bombers attack Newton Abbot just after his father had whistled going through with the Ashburton goods, and cycled down to make sure he was safe.

His own career began in the locomotive works, and a red-letter day was when he was called up in front of his mates to receive the company's thanks from the chief mechanical engineer, F. W. Hawksworth, himself for averting a possible accident. Taking an illicit short-cut home along the down relief, he had seen the track suspended in air following a flash flood. No criticism of him being where he shouldn't, just thanks for prompt action in stopping a train.

Occasionally he fired for his father, and of course often for his father's mates and friends, sharing their enthusiasm and their views on life. He loved working the branch lines (most of the stories in 'West Country Tales' starting on page 181 of *Great Days of the Country Railway* were his) but felt proud when it was his turn to fire the *Torbay Express* running through his home station non-stop, while he waxed lyrical about moonlight nights when the hills were snow-covered on trips on the midnight to Paddington and about memories of the same trip in summer when the sun came up while most of the passengers behind were still asleep.

He switched to diesels happily enough though never lost his love of steam. Though never a full driver, as a passed fireman he was frequently at the controls especially on summer Saturdays. Like

continued opposite

the season ambitious half-day excursions from one holiday region to another as well as the ever-favourite trips from inland cities to the coast for those unable to take a full seaside holiday. Some trains were regulars, repeated for the same event year by year, a careful check made on last season's loading in order to determine how many seats should be provided. Many other trains were requested by organisations (with or without the railway's prompting) and were dealt with courteously and promptly, usually in writing, though the telephone was increasingly used after the mid-1930s and personal callers were always welcome at the excursion office. The vast range of educational excursions, however, had to be sold from each season's 'catalogue'. The Press were encouraged to run features about the amazing value (perhaps two weeks' pocket money for a 500-mile return trip) and headmasters were rewarded with free tickets for their staff (and sometimes families). Free tickets were given for all kinds of purposes: to helpful reporters, trip organisers wanting to come up to the excursion office to discuss details, and anyone who might legitimately encourage traffic. They were of course third-class tickets, the issue of first-class passes being the prerogative of the district superintendent.

Each excursion office was very much its own business centre, though the managers of neighbouring ones (in one case brothers) might co-operate in the filling of some trains, and all arrangements had to be made within the company's overall policy and fare structure. This seldom inhibited local initiative, and many excursion managers became ever more ambitious and, to make sure things ran smoothly, built good personal relations with the operating people.

Though the manager might have his private office, he seldom closed the door even when important customers called to see him, and indeed he seldom took his eyes off his staff or was unaware what was going on in the general office handling an extraordinary range of detail. Walls were covered with the latest offerings, some still in proof stage, and tables piled high with papers of all kinds including scrapbooks of previous season's handbills and records of loadings. Though the district superintendent seldom paid a visit, correspondence with his office was exchanged almost hourly, newspaper and printing staff were ever demanding that the proofs be OK'd, and the operating people telephoning to check how sales were going and would they need to provide a Castle on a strengthened train. Nowhere else were you more conscious of the railway's role in society, and it was indeed to the excursion office that passenger correspondence that could not conveniently be handled elsewhere was passed. One class of letters provided much of the office's laughter: from people saying their conscience had smitten them and paying up for journeys taken without buying a ticket last week or twenty five years ago. 'I know I shall not be able to die in peace until this is off my mind,' came along with 1s 3d 'stolen from the company' by way of a ticketless ride . . . and a detailed explanation of how the 'crime' had been committed.

Relief Stationmaster

Generally he was the least welcome person around, the stranger in the midst of the friendly family of railwaymen that ran most smaller GWR stations. He lacked the local knowledge of the regular stationmaster and could thus easily make a fool of himself, which meant he tended to be defensive and tight, and when his authority was challenged it was all too easy to fall back on the rule book. His was indeed a difficult task, since for example, he must know whether the gangley teenager in the signalbox was a reliable, permanent albeit unofficial helper, or whether he was taking advantage of the regular man's absence to go beyond the 'No unauthorised person' notices. Likewise, had the staff cooked their turns of duty between them for years past or were they taking extra liberty simply because he had appeared on the scene? Every station had its curiosities not quite in accordance with how things had been planned by headquarters, and deciding what to turn a blind eye to and what to insist be regularised was a game that could have one clear loser but no winner.

A lot, naturally, depended on how the relief stationmaster came to be on duty. If the regular man were simply taking his annual fortnight's holiday and everything had been arranged before, then it was fairly plain sailing . . . even more so if it were a return visit. Most relief men tended to keep their head low in such circumstances, making close contact with one member of staff, perhaps the trusted leading porter, and interfering no more than necessary. And indeed stationmasters were not the holders of sinecures. At times the regular man found it hard to keep pace with the paperwork, and with the added element of unfamiliarity the relief was often genuinely hard pressed and in no mood at all to seek trouble for its own sake. Visits to signalboxes were generally brief and showed no curiosity about the frame. When the public came in to complain or make a suggestion, they were encouraged to hold on until the regular stationmaster was back . . . and not unnaturally, sales of things like *Holiday Haunts* (or advertising in it) generally fell away during the interregnum.

But the relief stationmaster might turn up on a Monday morning for a host of other reasons. The regular man might have been promoted or taken ill. He might be on jury service and who knew how long that would last. Worse, he might have been suspended for a breach of the regulations or suspected fraud. The auditors from district office were not feared for nothing; over the years they uncovered prodigious irregularities and outright fraud, hard-pressed stationmasters or their staff perhaps starting on the road to ruin by 'borrowing' a few bob for a day or two until a shortage of tickets or irregularities in the waybills were detected. Like branch bank managers, stationmasters were in a position of trust and the breach of that trust might not be discovered for weeks, months or with great skill even years.

The relief man coming in to replace the regular one suspended under suspicion of course had every reason to be the new broom, and unpleasant that could make life for himself and everyone else. Conversation would be kept to the minimum, fires lit grudgingly, tasks take longer the further they were from the office.

The hardest circumstances were those in which a relief stationmaster

continued

the rest of his Newton Abbot colleagues, he was made redundant, but only after a lot of 'messing us about'. Though the gentlest of men, 'after what they did to us' it was not surprising things went from bad to worse, and though he popped down to the station to see steam resurrected for GWR 150, he never once travelled by train after his enforced retirement.

Until he died very suddenly after leaving me one Friday afternoon, he became my gardener, asking (to find out how hard the day's task would be) whether it would be a King or the Castle turn, and talking about the days when you could be proud to be an engine man and there was always something special to share with your mates. His name was Bob Wyse and he would be proud to see it recorded here. – DStJT.

Stopper

During an engineman's strike on the GWR around 1925, no trains had left Paddington up to 11 o'clock on the first morning. At about that time, a porter climbed up some ladder-steps and started to write in chalk on a blackboard over the door of the stationmaster's office on No 1 platform '11.20am No 4 Platform. ALL STATIONS TO PENZ'. At this, a gasp went up from the onlookers until the porter (a man with some sense of humour) rubbed out 'PENZ' and substituted 'OXFORD'. Nowadays, with so many stations closed the idea of a train stopping at all stations, Paddington to Penzance would not be entirely fantastic but 45 years ago! Royal Oak, Westbourne Park, Acton and all the rest (especially if it was via Bristol). – Pat Hart.

Pre Halt Halt

Before the GWR introduced halts there were a few unstaffed stations, the smallest of which was Wanstrow on the Wells branch between Witham and Cranmore, the section now busy with stone traffic. The platform was a short 24 yards, but in these pre halt days it was thought necessary to provide a waiting room with fire. 'In the winter a platelayer makes a fire, attends to it during the day, and lights the platform lamp when necessary.' Passengers were booked and parcels weighed at the next station.

replaced a regular man who was intermittently ill, perhaps with a condition that was psychologically-based even if only the physical symptoms were being treated. Stationmasters were often lonely, frustrated men working under perpetual strain. The successful could be seen exuding confidence as they walked along their platforms, but the failure rate was high. Promoted from the ranks and with much poorer education than other small-town top people with whom they were meant to be equal and mix, they were often equally ill at ease with the public and their staff and could be seen eating their lunches in strained solitude and count the minutes until that afternoon gap in the train service which allowed time for a quick disappearance to who knew where. The relief man filling in for someone who had been away for four or five weeks for the second time in the year was probably uncomfortable in his lodgings and if it went on much longer he might have to change them anyway. Meantime he knew that everyone was keeping an eye on him. Why was it always at the most distant, least happy station on his beat that he found himself in charge longest? If he were still there next week he would simply have to assume more control and stop things drifting. He felt that customers and staff alike could not see the back of him soon enough for, whether or not they approved of what he did, he stood out as a temporary in the Great Western world that demanded permanence and continuity. Oh for the day he could settle in at his own good station.

Wartime Branch Line

Barnstaple Junction is very not Great Western, peace or war, but after shrieking historic locomotives dash noisily in and out hauling equally ancient rakes of coaches squealing round the Ilfracombe curves, trains are made up and divided, you can detect order being restored as a GW Mogul gently pulls its three coaches into the platform. In later years trains were pooled with Southern stock working to Taunton; not in 1944. The first two coaches, in wartime brown, are non-corridors; the third in fading pre-war chocolate-and-cream is a corridor composite. For many years only non-corridor stock was used on many services but, though the prominent North Devon citizen with a weak bladder has long ceased travelling, his good work in insisting there is at least one lavatory vehicle pays dividends throughout the war and after.

This tea-time service is as much concerned with parcels as passengers and because there is a lot to load we are a couple of minutes down as we start the climb over the Taw and round Barnstaple's suburbs into Barnstaple GW (later Victoria Road). The triangle outside it is still fully signalled, but the crosses on the array of home and distant arms have now been up for years instead of only a winter at a time and, though two of the signalboxes will actually never reopen, there is still a belief that when the war is over some summer expresses will again stop to be divided, the main train for Junction

and Ilfracombe, at least one coach for GW. And indeed that the daily summer restaurant car will again switch trains at South Molton.

It is in fact Friday now, and the down afternoon service from Taunton has been divided, one section unadvertised to Ilfracombe to provide a relief to tomorrow's Ilfracombe-Swansea, the only express, of course summer Saturdays only, running in the war. We should cross the down at Barnstaple GW. After our engine is detached at the buffer, it runs to the loco depot and turns and waters while parcels are loaded and we wait. It should then take us out the way we came toward Junction and back into the bay, to let the down into the main platform. But today there is a military special, nine bogies, mainly LNER sleeping cars with their occupants' names clearly labelled, filling the whole bay. So still only two minutes late we press on.

It is a stiff climb for the first mile but over the summit we momentarily touch the line's limit of 60mph (the fastest anything goes on land around here) before the brakes go on for Swimbridge. We go straight in for the relief down has been waiting ten minutes. On through very rural scenery and past a couple of volcanic-looking peaks (once more this is a popular route in the 1990s, the North Devon link road following the old railway) and into Filleigh, the short remains of the afternoon down freight (most trucks detached at various stations en route from Taunton) waiting in the goods loop. Quite a few packages of the produce of the countryside to be loaded at Filleigh, but the days when there was always a horse box at the ready have passed and Henry Williamson only rarely leaves his rural retreat in the war. A BBC broadcast invariably means a ticket sale.

The starter is at danger so we walk past our locomotive and eventually see another Mogul coming round the curve with seven corridor coaches, no two together with a similar roof profile. They are away before us (only a handful of passengers in unaccustomed wartime luxury) and it is a couple of minutes before the signalman waddles down the platform with the token. Now the prettiest part of the route over Castle Hill viaduct and through lush vegetation before the tunnel and descent into South Molton.

In winter we go into South Molton's up platform because the nation's only rabbit special starts from here and loads conveniently at the down, one van full of rabbits for Cardiff, another for Birmingham. In summer we generally take advantage of the unique signalling allowing up trains through the down: it saves taking several trolley loads of parcels and mail over the tracks. But not today. We are brought nearly to a halt before being let into the up and see one trolley manoeuvred over the crossing ahead of us.

We are already ten late but have to give way to another military special. North Devon is preparing for D Day, and already a rehearsal of PLUTO (pipe line under the ocean) has been brought down the branch to link North Devon with South Wales. General Eisenhower himself has tasted the delights of this badly built-on-the-cheap Devon & Somerset route. The signalman dashes to his box with unaccustomed alacrity and signals the special – distant and all. That means automatic token exchange, and he walks briskly down the platform to set the apparatus. Four down signals all off and the station-master officiously prevents us crossing the track, though it is five minutes before the special thunders through, its locomotive opening up for the climb ahead the moment they have the token. Meanwhile, we have noticed to our surprise that an up freight is waiting in the yard . . . obviously an extra. Five passenger, three freights, Mondays to Fridays in winter the rabbit special, one advertised Summer Saturday extra, are the route's normal wartime ration, and over D Day they will take off one of the passengers. But there are spasmodic outbreaks of all kinds of extras, and with the GW and Southern at perpetual loggerheads as to which through freight should go which way (the competitive arguments of peace now put into reverse) the three freights are seldom enough.

At last we cross the line and the driver of the George Hotel bus providing the link to the hilltop town a mile and a quarter away congratulates himself on waiting – for nearly all of his business is in the up direction. Fridays, however, brings a couple who have been to Barnstaple market since last time they tried to return by bus they were left behind. The small bus also does the town's parcel delivery service under GW franchise. We pay our sixpence and the bus freewheels backwards from its position just under the signalbox as the signalman who has returned from the automatic exchange is ready to take the token to the train we have left. But it is still stationary, twenty two late, as the bus engine starts up and we drive off thinking that it will be some time before the branch is back to normal.

A 73XX 2-6-0 crosses Venn Cross viaduct over the Tone valley with an afternoon train from Barnstaple to Taunton during May 1954. By then non corridor coaches had been superseded by displaced main line corridor stock.

14
A BUSINESS TRIP
WINDSOR TO
SHREWSBURY 1920

Even to the regular traveller Windsor station has that special 'something'; after all it *was* used by Queen Victoria. But today is cold and foggy, with that rawness about it that goes to your bones; so it is straight into the train without bothering to go forward to check the engine number. 8.47 on a March morning is a civilised hour and most of the commuters have long gone so the compartment with the blue-and-white 'smoking' notice stuck on the window is almost empty and there is a corner seat. Open *The Times*, head back on the rectangular antimacassar of perforated linen carefully marked GWR and try to relax. The trip to London, normally pleasant, is full of tension as the chances of getting the 10.15 to Shrewsbury seem slim in this seemingly impenetrable fog. Thank God for ATC. Even with this, the rate of progress is dreadful, station stops longer than usual, signal checks and a constant series of sprints and crawls. But we get into Paddington at 10.10. It is a run down the platform and across the Lawn to No 1 noting that the Windsor engine is a 4-4-2 County tank, No 2242.

In the event there was no cause for worry. Because of fog troubles, nothing comes in until 10.20 when No 1972, an Old Oak saddle tank arrives with twelve 'eights' including a diner. There is plenty of room at the front and time enough to watch one of the 1914 Stars back down; No 4055 *Princess Sophia* is clean but not as sparkling as her earlier sisters would have been pre war. The guard comes up to check his load with the driver: '12 for 362 mate – first stop Banbury'. There are a few unpublishable comments about the weather but the green comes at 10.26.

The guard's optimism loses any reality by Old Oak Common where one can almost feel the inky blackness of the dense dirty fog and the train comes to its first stop. No cause to complain of lack of excitement for detonators are going off somewhere out there in the murk and one gets the impression that a miniature air raid is taking place. Three minutes and the train is away again, sauntering in a despondent sort of way until well past West Wycombe, the pace so poor that speeds fall to just under 20mph on the bank beyond High Wycombe. But here the weather improves and the crew begin to remember that they are heading one of the Great Western's crack expresses and not a pick up goods. No 4055 suddenly wakes up and accelerates in that extraordinary manner that distinguishes the company's new 4-6-0s and there is a maximum of 75mph at Bicester. There is a splash back from the troughs at Aynho, perhaps the fireman was not quick enough in the mist.

Banbury is brighter; the shed on the left hand side just before the

A 4-4-2 'County' tank No 2250, the final loco in the series, built in 1912, approaches Reading West with an up local around 1922. The coaching stock is typical of such trains in the period though the two vans with the intermediate clerestory coach could well be additions to a more normal five coach set. Note the steps at the side of the bogies. Some of the coaches appear to be in crimson lake livery. The splitting distant arm is for Oxford Road Junction, the fixed for Reading General.

Aynho troughs where the Great Western briefly enters Northamptonshire (for about 4 miles). Star class 4-6-0 No 4050 Princess Alice heads a down local on 25 May 1935. Rather surprisingly for 1935 most of the coaches have clerestory roofs and there is a string of vans in the rear.

Public Service

It is the desire of the Company to make the utmost endeavour to satisfy the requirements of the public they cater for so far as it is reasonably practicable to do so. Special staffs are employed to deal with enquiries, and it is earnestly hoped that the fullest advantage may be taken of the arrangements that are in force for supplying information upon any subject connected with railway travel. Such applications addressed to any of the Company's divisional centres or direct to the Superintendent of the Line, GWR, Paddington Station, London, W2, will have immediate attention.

station sports 0-6-0 saddle tank No 1233 from Exeter of all places, 0-4-2 tanks Nos 550 and 218 of Worcester, No 3549, a Didcot 4-4-0 and No 3022 (TYS) a new War Department 2-8-0. In the platform bay is No 1127, a Great Central class 9L 4-4-2 tank, probably off a Woodford local, and as *Princess Sophia* takes a quick gulp of water from the column another GC engine appears, this time class 8 4-6-0 No 181 on a cross country train for Oxford. A quick look out of the window shows that the starter and distant are both off so at least it will be a good run out to Banbury North Junction. A heave on the leather strap and the window shoots up again; the steam heating is working fine so a nap behind *The Times* fits in nicely to Leamington Spa where the sun is coming out at last.

The station buildings at Leamington (like Banbury) seem pretty disreputable, scarcely a tribute to a top line company; sometimes it seems that unless one is travelling over Brunel's old route to the west they don't really care. But there are some fine diversions as this is the end of the suburban service from Birmingham and the terminus of trains from Worcester and Stratford via Hatton. Two secondary passenger classes are visible on the shed as the train runs in Nos 3270 *Earl of Devon* (BAN) and 3346 *Godolphin*; this Bulldog and a couple of suburban 2-6-2 tanks Nos 3901 and 3904 (rebuilt from the Dean 0-6-0 goods) are TYS engines. Nos 2363 and 2369, Dean Goods from Gloucester and Reading plus yet another saddle tank made up the score. Away to the right are the tracks from the LNWR's Avenue station – reached by a subway – and standing just in readable distance, is No 2620, a 19in Goods 4-6-0 from shed 8, Rugby. This sparkles in blackberry black even though it is a mixed traffic engine, putting the Great Western to shame.

Leamington Spa old station in 1926 over a decade before rebuilding. City class 4-4-0 No 3703 Hobart stands in the up platform after working a local train.

Princess Sophia is now blowing off and on the 'right way' gets moving with a vengeance her bark resounding over the yards as she makes for the canal bridge and Warwick to hit the bottom of the 1 in 100 Hatton bank as fast as possible. The weather is still clear and Warwick prison, stark in blue brick, strikes a sombre note. The crew have obviously been this way before as No 4055 passes the Warwick & Birmingham Canal and the Hatton 'Loony Bin' in style to thunder into the summit cutting at 46mph. Speed picks up after Hatton North Junction with a maximum of 70mph by Widney Manor and the twenty two and three quarter miles to Snow Hill takes only a few seconds over twenty five minutes.

Even to someone more used to Reading or Paddington, Snow Hill seems clean and spacious – it should do as it was rebuilt only a decade or so ago. One feels back on the Great Western once again. The train has drawn up well beyond the island platform buildings where the dining car is watered and most of the passengers detrain. Immediately opposite the compartment windows are the bay platforms for the Stourbridge, Dudley and Wolverhampton locals or semi-fasts whilst on the right are two through roads – used mostly for freights including the trip goods from Bordesley Junction to Hockley. In one of the bays at the end of the up platform is the day's station pilot No 4120 *Atbara* (TYS). The

Rowington water troughs were the third set between Paddington and Snow Hill. (Not as frequent as those on the LNW main line but better than the average between sets on the Great Northern.) Star class No 4043 Prince Henry *is heading a train to Birmingham, Shrewsbury, Chester and Birkenhead. The leading coach appears to be a restaurant car which would probably be detached at Wolverhampton.*

213

Snow Hill south end in the throes of rebuilding in April 1911. Saint class 4-6-0 No 173 (renumbered 2973 in December 1912) Robins Bolitho *leaves with a Paddington train.*

Politeness Personified

It is not always remembered how utterly polite many Great Western men were; the only bad language used on many stations came from passengers.

Down in Devon the scene was from the picture book. The evening sun glistened on the autumn leaves and the guard looked benevolently out from his van at the end of a short special of loaded cattle wagons at the sylvan crossing station while the driver and signalman engaged in leisurely conversation.

The only thing was that the starter remained at danger minutes after the signalman had handed up the single line token. 'Neither is going to tell the other,' the guard muttered to a young onlooker. And so it was. While the signalman could not understand why the crew did not get going, they saw the stick firmly on. Neither quite knew how to approach the matter without being critical.

Only the realisation that the special would delay the down passenger at the next station if they did not get started brought resolution.

down bays have 2-6-2 tank No 3908 (WPN STRD) and 2-4-2 tank No 3607 (WOS). In the up carriage sidings are Nos 3916 (TYS) and 3626 (SLO) whilst No 2555 (TYS) comes through on an up trip freight.

Progress through the Black Country is more leisurely and lunch is coming to an end in the dining car which comes off at Wolverhampton. The stewards are cheerful cockneys who joke as they produce bottles of Mitchells and Butlers 'Export' beer lighter and stronger than the Watney dark ales; it goes well with some good roast lamb and surprisingly happily with the rice pudding and shows where the car has been stocked up.

At Wolverhampton Low Level No 4055 is replaced not with one engine but two: No 2902 *Lady of the Lake* (WPN STRD), an early Saint with lever reverse and an elderly Chester Flower class 4-4-0 No 4163 *Marigold*. The pilot seems hardly necessary but the guard intimates that the train is one over the load for a twenty nine and anyway the 'old un's' got to get back. Passing Stafford Road Works there is a bewildering array of engines awaiting repairs or – worse – scrapping. Those doomed included three hoary old 2-4-0s No 211 (an old West Midland engine) and two Chancellor class engines Nos 151 and 155. The luckier ones due for heavy repairs are 0-6-0s Nos 22 (LMTN), 23 (WPN STRD), 316 (STB), and 'Barnum' 2-4-0 No 3218 (WPN STRD). Stafford Road works rarely sees any of the Great Western's big engines.

But now it is time to sort out the papers for this afternoon's meeting: fortunately it will only be an hour or so but needs must. There is little chance to take in what might be on view at Wellington but the shed has a Crewe 4-4-0 No 3267 *Duchess of Teck* and 0-4-2 tank No 1478 (WPN STRD), with a brass dome, is shunting. Because of the short platform the double-headed train has to pull up twice. After what seems a fine run the train rolls round the sharp curve past the tall LNWR signal box with flanges squealing to be under Shrewsbury station's overall roof at 2.10pm, only ten down.

A short meeting with the local manager allows for a good half hour back at the station before catching the 4.35pm back to Birmingham – the 2.35pm Birkenhead-Paddington. This is time well spent for Shrewsbury is home to three companies; the GWR, LNWR and the Cambrian Railways as well as the odd North Stafford visitor. The Great Western produces 2-4-0 No 3251 (WPN STRD) as station pilot, numerous 43XX class Moguls, a couple of Saints Nos 2954 *Tockenham Court* (PPL) and 2977 *Robertson* (WPN STRD), the former off a west to north express, Bulldog No 3366 *Earl of Cork* (SALOP), Nos 3246 (WPM STRD), 1086 (STB), 3837 *County of Gloucester* (SALOP) for the west to north trains, 3342 *Orion* (BAN), 2092 (WPN OXY) and 2108 (SALOP). The Cambrian delights with two 4-4-0s on incoming and outgoing Aberystwyth and coast line trains, Nos 96 (Oswestry) and 11 (from as far away as Pwllheli), the North Stafford an 0-6-0 in No 80. The LNWR, true to form, has some engines on running in turns from Crewe, new Prince of Wales class 4-6-0s Nos 497 and 601 (both

A passengers first sight of Snow Hill. The view from the downside steps looking along the main down platforms Nos 5 & 6. The station pilot, one of the curious inside cylinder 2-6-2Ts 'rebuilt' from Dean Goods 0-6-0s, is attaching a cattle wagon to the train standing in platform 5. Snow Hill suffered some bomb damage during World War II and the ladies waiting room and adjoining rooms on platforms 5 & 1 were demolished. This photograph was taken in July 1927 but the scene would be very similar in 1920 – the date of the chapter.

unnamed), Precursor 4-4-0 No 976 *Pacific* and Experiment No 372 *Belgic* both of shed 30 (Shrewsbury), No 36 *Thalaba* a Jumbo from Buxton (16B), another Precedent No 2006 *Princess* and a Waterloo No 2157 *Unicorn* both (30) ex ROD 2-8-0 No 1949 and a number of 18in goods and saddle tanks. Quite a collection in just on thirty minutes.

The return train is headed by one of Shrewsbury's many Moguls but there is more work to be done; overall the running seems to be good but not brilliant with four minutes lost to Wolverhampton and a further two to Snow Hill which is reached at 5.54pm.

Work out of the way, there is time to break the journey at Birmingham and wend one's way across the Cathedral grounds, down Needless Alley to Stephenson Street and the joint LNWR/Midland station. Not a patch on airy Snow Hill, New Street produces a Renown 4-4-0 No 1902 *Black Prince* (13 – Bushbury), a George The Fifth 4-4-0 on a London, No 132 *S.R. Graves* (10M – Monument Lane) plus numerous tank engines on the North Western side and glistening Midland red 2-4-0s, 4-4-0s and 0-6-4 tanks from Saltley, Derby and Leicester further over the footbridge.

Back to Snow Hill for another 'Export' and some sandwiches in the refreshment room and then the 7.50pm (4.35pm ex Birkenhead) to Paddington which runs via Reading; the engine to Oxford is No 2928

Twenty Dean Goods 0-6-0s were 'rebuilt' into rather unusual inside cylinder 2-6-2Ts between 1907 and 1910 all of which disappeared between 1930 and 1934. Several are noted in this chapter including No 3904 seen here at Snow Hill on a down express freight (if the headlamps are to be believed) in 1929. Flower class 4-4-0 No 4149 Auricula is standing on the line to platforms 11/12 with the twin spires of St Chads Cathedral dominating the background.

Wolverhampton Stafford Road shed with Barnum class 2-4-0 No 3216 outside in February 1936 just prior to withdrawal in May 1936. This is typical of locomotives which would have been seen around Wolverhampton in 1920.

A County class 4-4-0 and an ex West Midland Railway 2-4-0 No 210 (very much rebuilt) leave the down main line platform at Shrewsbury for Birkenhead c1914. Although Shrewsbury was an LNW/GW Joint station the signalling was LNW and Crewe Junction signal box (beyond the County) and the signals are to that company's design.

No So!

During the black out, Maurice and Ivor, two lads returning home from night school, one of them having made a diversion to collect a missing satchel, arranged to rejoin each other on the stopper at West Drayton. The guard was about to blow his whistle before Maurice could find his friend in the darkness, so in panic he shouted 'Ivor! Ivor! Ivor!' whereupon general excitement broke out with people milling around and doors slamming. Which made him shout for his friend the more . . . until an irate, red-faced guard grabbed him and snarled: 'West Drayton, Not Iver'. – From a true story told by Alan Machin.

The Environmental GW

Right from the beginning, one of the characteristics of the Great Western was that it became an attractive and much-painted and later photographed feature of the countryside through which it ran. Important stations were built of local stone, tunnels castellated, viaducts given appropriate finishing touches. Even today we marvel how well Brunel's railway fits into Bath, for example, and that was over a century before planning controls.

Good housekeeping persisted, and even when money could not be so lavishly used as it had been on the Paddington-Bristol route, the railway was still made to harmonise into its surroundings. Great care was taken to make the sores of constructing the new cut-offs heal quickly, and (for example) on the Stratford upon Avon to Cheltenham route the well-built community stations were planted with conifers and lattice tops were fitted to the steel girders of viaducts to give them a more attractive appearance.

Saint Sebastian (OXF). It is now foggy again and hard to see across to the centre roads from platform 12. The train leaves on time and No 2928 picks up speed down through the tunnel under Corporation Street and emerges opposite the new Moor Street terminus out through suburbia and into the blackness of the countryside, the frozen mist curls low alongside the track and the stations are an orange blur in the fog. Signals hold it at Warwick allowing a glimpse of an old double-framed 0-6-0 No 673 (LMTN) used as the Hatton banker. Leamington comes seven minutes later. Once away the fog clears a little but running is harder, even so Banbury is passed at 8.54pm with two minutes made up. No 2928 does well and rolls into Oxford only three down. Off comes the engine and No 2910 *Lady of Shalott* (OXF) backs down, couples and blows up. It then proceeds to put up the best performance of the day with a load of nine 'eights' and a six wheeled van. Didcot, ten and a half miles is passed at 30mph in ten and a quarter minutes, but at this speed the shed on the right is wide open to a quick eye. Outside are 2-4-0s Nos 3501 (DID) (originally a Broad Gauge 2-4-0 tank) and 2214 (DID) with 6ft 6in wheels and probably off the Southampton line plus 0-4-2 tank No 519 (DID) originally a saddle tank built at Wolverhampton in 1868. Reading, forty seven and a half miles, is reached in fifty minutes at 9.59pm dead on time. Past the Reading West/Basingstoke triangle the shed in the middle comes up with yet another ex-War Department Great Central type 2-8-0 No 3028 (RDG) 2-6-0 No 4399 (TYS) and Dean Goods No 2463 (RDG) still with its ROD number painted on the cabsides.

Eight minutes are allowed at the Biscuit Town with the usual interesting collection of engines, Bulldog No 3411 *Stanley Baldwin* (BAN), 2-4-0 tank No 615 (SHL), probably fitted with trip cock apparatus for working the signals on the Underground – 0-6-0 tank No 2757 (RDG) SE&CR class R1 0-6-0 tank No 47 and No 228 an F1 4-4-0 together with an LSWR Adams A12 0-4-2 No 645. The station work is slick, postmen carting mail in their ferocious electric trucks, milk churns rattling on platform trolleys loaded into the front van; somehow a Saint persuades the station staff that it deserves prompt attention.

Refreshed once more from the column and with a crisp clear night No 2910 makes a phenomenal dash for Paddington – covering the thirty six miles in only ten seconds over the thirty six minutes, the five and three quarter miles from Maidenhead to Slough taking four minutes forty five seconds, roaring through the junction at 78mph. Southall shed flashes past with Moguls 4363 (BL) and 4393 (NPT) with 2-8-0 Nos 2854 (WPN OXY) whilst West Ealing has 0-6-0 pannier tank No 2101 still in wartime brown as are many of the motor fitted 0-4-2 tanks. After a round trip of just over twelve hours the Great Western gets the traveller back to his London terminus forty five seconds early at 10.49.20.

The journey back to Windsor is behind 2-4-2 tank No 3601 (PDN) and the day has enabled the enthusiast to see engines of ten different railways including a Great Eastern 0-6-0 No 913, a LB&SC 0-6-2 tank No 452 and two North London 4-4-0 tanks at Acton.

218

Commuters and Steam 1957–64

Keith Grand is the last of the Western Region's general managers to be a Great Western Man and a gust rather than a wind of change is in the air. Regions are getting more autonomy with a little personal identity and chocolate-and-cream coaches are back in Paddington. Something like the old livery is now emerging from Swindon Works; no more black Halls or 51XX tanks; even the 64XX and 14XX auto train engines are green once more. This is, perhaps, the bright evening of steam rather than its twilight.

The Western's biggest suburban business has always been to and from Paddington and round the old Birmingham Division; in each case trains worked principally by 2-6-2 tanks, 41XX, 51XX and 61XX, or with Halls. On the main line east of Reading, Castles if the train is a semi-fast. Take, for example, the 8.02 off Reading (8am in the public timetable) leaving Taplow at 8.29 (public book 8.28) calling at Burnham and then running non stop to Ealing Broadway (8.55-6 to set down only) arriving at Paddington at 9.06.

The commuter arrives at Taplow at 8.21 in plenty of time to see the Dorney Blue bus back up the station approach – a difficult manoeuvre against the flow of traffic, the regulars descend and buy their tickets or SHEW their seasons, flow into the booking hall through a typical GWR portal, pass the collector then move on to the up platform with its well tended flower beds and the footbridge with a wrought iron monogram 'GWR 1882'. At this early stage of the journey the train runs up relief road. The stationmaster, Mr Peppin, has an office

at the Reading end and like his predecessors is always in evidence just before the 8.28 apears. At 8.24 the starter drops and the bell tinkles to announce its departure from Maidenhead. Two more minutes and a shining green Castle hoves into view round the curve beyond the trees to come hissing alongside the bowler-hatted throng. The 8.02 Reading is often a running in turn for some great event, its engines for example appearing on Royal trains with some regularity. Today it is Reading's No 4085 *Berkeley Castle* but modified Halls are also regular performers, 6959 *Peatling Hall*, 6998 *Burton Agnes Hall*, 7903 *Foremark Hall*, 7904 *Fountains Hall* or 7906 *Fron Hall*. No 4085 gets away smartly like the thoroughbred it is; the running needs to be smart to keep well ahead of the 8.10 Reading, a Didcot fast. Once switched to the main line they get a move on, and this morning although there is some thick mist which looks like becoming fog automatic train control makes almost invisible signals as clear to the driver as if it were a bright sunshine. *Berkeley Castle* tears along at well over a mile a minute most of the way to draw into platform 5 at Paddington at 9.15

The mainstay of the Birmingham division local trains were the 2-6-2Ts of the 41XX and 51XX series, shedded mostly at Tyseley, Leamington Spa, Wolverhampton Stafford Road or Stourbridge. No 5185 heads a train of three non-corridors, brake third and 2 coach B set, up Hatton bank on 14 August 1954. Note the headlamp on the centre of the buffer beam, a code which the GWR (and Western Region) often used for local trains in lieu of one lamp at the base of the chimney.

Morning trains from beyond Reading often doubled as commuter trains east of that station. Castle class 4-6-0 No 7010 Avondale Castle *takes an Oxford–Paddington semi-fast through Sonning Cutting on 15 August 1949. Some of the coaches appear to be in wartime all over brown livery.*

exactly. One minute has been dropped on a day when other lines have problems.

On another even foggier morning the commuter travels by the 9.04, known sardonically as the Director's Train. The platform is dark, dank and silent. Then, though not even the footbridge is visible, a familiar sound, the beat of the down *Bristolian*, 8.45 off Paddington approaching at top speed on the down main. With a whistle and a roar the almost invisible heading a blur of orange lighted coaches flies by with uncanny effect; ATC is triumphing once again, the invisible signals giving their audible warnings and encouragements.

It is 4 December 1957 and even though earlier trains have got away well the evening scene is chaos. The 6.38, always the preserve of a 61XX 2-6-2 tank running non stop to Slough is nowhere to be seen and the fog has permeated under Brunel's great roof making the interior of the great terminus almost sepulchral. A packed train stands at each platform but nothing appears to be moving. The first out is the 5.18 all stations down to Reading behind No 6122 which leaves at 7.10 taking two hours to get to Taplow but the passengers arrive safely even though the signal lights are virtually invisible – this very night the Southern suffers the awful Lewisham disaster and Western Region passengers thank their lucky stars for the Great Western's ATC.

From Birmingham's Snow Hill the commuters went north west to Stourbridge, Dudley or Wolverhampton or south east towards Leamington and Stratford. Sometimes they went south east to Worcester via Stratford and Honeybourne. Mostly they travelled behind 41XX or 51XX tanks with their reversing levers standing like sentinels on the driver's side their tops polished as if they were in a well kept signal box. Sometimes the longer distance trains including the Worcesters via Stratford were headed by Halls and, until the demise of Stafford Road's Stars in July 1957, the 7.45 semi-fast from Leamington to Snow Hill going on to Birkenhead was always the preserve of one of these magnificent Churchward engines. Later they were replaced by Halls on this turn.

Although the dmus came early to Birmingham (1957) steam still ran a number of services including the 17.25 Snow Hill to Knowle and Dorridge normally the preserve of one of Tyseley's few remaining 41XX 2-6-2 tanks. But in June 1964 the commuters coming down the wide steps to platform 7 had a surprise. There, as if it were part of her everyday lifestyle was 2-6-2 tank No 4555 resplendent in GWR livery. These were times unbelievable today when local autonomy was still in place and Tom Field the depot superintendent at Tyseley. By now Stanley Raymond was in charge at Paddington and it was he who authorised the sale of this little engine to private purchasers, and its storage on BR property, one of the conditions being that if the railway found a use for it then so be it! Field, although an ex-LNER man who professed no interest in anything unless it was a V2, took kindly to his new acquisition and with Bob Taylor the local operating manager ex-GWR the stage was set.

With her small capacity water tanks No 4555 was not rostered for the Leamingtons or Stratfords, rather the semi-fast Knowle & Dorridge train missing out Bordesley and Small Heath and Tyseley stations. It is a complicated diagram. Light engine Tyseley to Hockley carriage sidings, pick up the stock, to Snow Hill No 7 platform, right away to Acocks Green, Olton, Solihull, Widney Manor, over the crossover to the relief at Bentley Heath and into Knowle and Dorridge. Take water, over into the down sidings, run round and return relief line to Solihull with passenger. Snow Hill, back to Hockley, Snow Hill pilot until early evening and back to shed.

But the great day was the working of the up Pines Express on Monday 24 August 1964 when No 4555 had an adventure of the kind found normally only in railway fiction. Driver Cyril Tolley had taken the engine down from Bordesley Junction to Leamington with a trip goods and with those small tanks it had been a job to make it as they had to shunt at Hatton and Warwick cold store on the way. But by 12.20 they had filled up and were in the shunter's cabin for dinner. At about 13.40 an inspector came over. 'I have a job for you,' he said.

By mid 1964 few, very few expresses over the old Great Western main line were steam hauled, but the Warship class diesel on the Pines had failed and been replaced at Banbury by No 6991 *Acton Burnell Hall* – not in the best of condition. With eleven on the driver had asked for a pilot at Leamington: the 1 in 100 up Hatton was a daunting prospect. Tolley's first questioned whether they could do it with those small tanks, but he told control he would do his best. The express was due in at 13.52 but with the failure was running 25 minutes down. By the time they had coupled on to the train with the Hall leading, it was 14.40 before they got away. They arrived at Snow Hill (24 miles) at 15.08, the same as the booked time for a King in 1939! In a letter amplified by good Black Country language Cyril Tolley said that the only time he had grey hairs was through the platforms 'as she rolled a good bit at speed'. When they got to Snow Hill they looked in the tank and found about a foot of water left. Maurice Long who was the signalman on the late shift at Lapworth, and who had been forewarned of the coming spectacle, swore they passed him at a good seventy.

(Part of this was inspired by the late T. W. E. Roche's *More Great Westernry*.)

After being purchased privately and before being despatched to the Dart Valley Railway small Prairie No 4555 was used by Tyseley shed on various local duties. It is seen here leaving Snow Hill's platform 7 on the 5.25pm to Knowle & Dorridge in June 1964. This was its only passenger working as the small tanks were deemed unsuitable in water capacity to work through to Leamington Spa.

ACKNOWLEDGEMENTS

Once again the preparation of this book has been a team job. Because the two authors have known lines out of Paddington well from boyhood, the majority of the text has come from their two pens. But there had to be additional views: for example, it was important to see what those on the other side of the fence thought of the GWR. Was it really God's Wonderful Railway? Specialist knowledge was also to hand. Ken Jones, for example, spent a lifetime at Swindon Works, Patrick Dalton knew the Aberystwyth–Carmarthen line as his own, and Mike Romans has been a WR man all his working life. Alan Warren, who wrote the pieces on each of the Woodham's yard engines in his successful *Rescued from Barry*, was a certainty for locomotive profiles, while London and Cardiff have been covered by their particular experts, A. A. Jackson and Jim Page. Add to these the usual stalwarts of the consulting team led by Patrick Whitehouse, John Edgington and John Powell (sometimes with his hands tied behind his back) plus a new member David Johnson and we have a whole, and the 'authorship' has real depth.

We should like to thank Richard Hope (as always) of the *Railway Gazette International* for permission to re-use line drawings and information from that journal and its specialist supplements, and the Railway Correspondence & Travel Society for information taken from their various works. The diary of the footplate trip on the Broad Gauge was originally published in *The English Illustrated Magazine in 1892*.

Once again we are in debt to photographers known and unknown as well as to the original publishers of the postcards reproduced; the latter have brought back the colour of the old Great Western. The principal contributors on the photographic side have been Phillip Alexander, Hugh Ballantyne, W. A. Camwell, George Heiron and Patrick Whitehouse as well as the host of others mentioned in the acknowledgements.

The main chapters are based on material supplied as follows: David St John Thomas (Introduction, The Seasonal Great Western, The Sea Wall, Three West Country Journeys, Three Officials); Patrick Whitehouse (A Tale of Four Castles, Snow Hill Days, Cambrian Holiday, A Business Trip to Shrewsbury 1920); Ken Jones (A Day in the Life of 'A' Shop); Alan Warren (Five Locomotive Biographies); A. J. Powell (An Alien View, Fast Work on the Marches); Mike Romans (How Cut Offs Made the Western Great).

'Fillers' between chapters were provided by Alan Warren (No 2937 Clevedon Court, The Railcars); Patrick Whitehouse (Top Dog Underdog, Great Western Cross Country, Commuters and Steam – also based on work by T. W. E. Roche); RCTS (Locomotive Sheds and Allocations January 1938); Jim Page (A Busy Weekend at Cardiff); A. A. Jackson (Great Western London); Keith Richards (Snow Hill's Signalling); David St John Thomas (Taunton, Wartime Branch Line); Patrick Dalton (Aberystwyth–Carmarthen).

The authors are grateful to the following for illustrations. Black and white photographs: P. M. Alexander/Millbrook House Collection (37 upper, 61, 91 lower, 116, 125, 138 lower, 143, 145, 147, 148, 158, 174, 182 lower, 191 upper, 193, 197 both, 198, 199, both, 220); B. J. Ashworth (84); H. Ballantyne (80, 96, 128, 175, 178, 196); G. F. Bannister (113); D. H. Barber FRPS (17); D. S. M. Barrie Collection (135); D. S. M. Barrie/Millbrook House Collection (85 both); City of Birmingham Libraries/Millbrook House Collection (157, 167); Birmingham Post & Mail (49, 160); R. J. Blenkinsop (20, 76, 127); P. F. Bowles (172 lower); F. E. Box/NRM (23); BR/Millbrook House Collection (12, 38, 101, 215); E. D. Bruton/NRM (55); H. W. Burman/Millbrook House Collection (214); W. A. Camwell (136 lower, 137 both, 185); Cawston Collection/NRM (138 upper); Dr. J. A. Coiley (21 upper); C. R. L. Coles (69, 70 lower, 165 lower, 166); E. J. Dew (88); R. J. Doran/D. S. M. Barrie Collection (136 middle); M. W. Earley/Millbrook House Collection (19 lower, 52); M. W. Earley/NRM (16); T. J. Edgington (54, 119, 194, 195); R. K. Evans FRPS (25 upper, 42, 53, 71); D. S. Fish/Millbrook House Collection (172 upper); A. W. Flowers (43, 70 upper, 155, 212, 217 upper); W. L. Good/Millbrook House Collection (213, 216); G. F. Heiron (22, 25 lower, 36, 37 lower, 67, 131, 165 upper); J. R. Hillier/Millbrook House Collection (83); P. Hopkins/Millbrook House Collection (34); M. C. Kemp (209); L & GRP Collection (95); Rev A. H. Malan (29, 30, 31, 91 upper); M. Mensing (142, 157, 169, 177 both, 204); Millbrook House Collection (26 upper, 32 upper, 66, 72, 86 upper, 92, 141, 210 lower); G. W. Morrison (123); National Railway Museum (13 upper, 210 upper); C. F. H. Oldham (21 lower, 168, 219); L. N. Owen/Millbrook House Collection (86 lower); P. W. Pilcher Collection/NRM (217 lower); M. Pope (205); W. J. Probert/Millbrook House Collection (45 lower); Colour Rail (50, 171); P. Ransome-Wallis/NRM (13 lower); R. C. Riley (136 upper); J. H. Russell/BR (46 upper); J. H. Russell (65); K. Sanders (82); G. H. Soole/Millbrook House Collection (162, 163); G. H. Soole/NRM (19 upper); E. Treacy/Millbrook House Collection (44, 45 upper); J. Trounson/Millbrook House Collection (78); Warwick Museum/Millbrook House Collection (146); P. B. Whitehouse ARPS/Millbrook House Collection (4, 14 upper, 24, 26 lower, 32 lower, 41, 59, 75 both, 87, 104, 150, 151, 153, 154, 156, 182 upper, 188, 189, 190, 191 lower, 221); J. R. Whitnall (79); W. H. Whitworth/Millbrook House Collection (115); T. E. Williams/NRM (40, 62).

Colour photographs: P. M. Alexander/Millbrook House Collection (99 lower); H. Ballantyne (15 both); D. H. Barber (98 both); D. Breckon/Courtesy A. R. Hedges (106–7); BR/Millbrook House Collection (102–3, 110 upper); T. Owen/Colour Rail (111 lower); Colour Rail (14 lower, 99 upper, 111 upper); P. B. Whitehouse (14 upper); D. C. Williams/Courtesy Whitbreads (110 lower).

Once more we proudly first publish a new Don Breckon painting, and also use George Heiron's painting as a work of art within the book as well as on the jacket.

Aberdares, 187, *188*, 195
Aberdeen, 88, 97
Abergavenny, 85, 148
Aberystwyth, 43, 87, 88, 114, 184, 189, 190, 194, *194–5*, 196
Afon Wen, 187
Alexander, Philip, 197
Allen, Cecil J., 76, 77, 79
Amalgamation (1923), 9, 39, 43, 85, 184, 194
Andress, Bill, 73, 74, 76, 77
Andoversford, 87
Armstrongs, 7, *11*, 109
Ashchurch, 85
Atlantic Coast Express, 43
Atmospheric system, 90
Auto cars/trains, *41*, 66, 85, 93, 151, 158, 169, 170, *171*, 175, 176, 178, 186, 219
Automatic machines, 152–3
Automatic train control, 11, *32*, 33–4, 39, 112, 139, 211, 219, 220
Avonmouth, 129, 134
Aylesbury, 43–4, 164

Badminton route, 162–4, 169
Banbury, 43, 44, 88, 109, 112, 122, 146, 161, 164, 169, 211–12
Banks, 28, 125, 194; Dauntsey, 62, 126, 148, *199*; Gresford, 83; Hatton, 213, *219*, 221; Hemerford, *52*, 77, *106–7*; Lickey, 74, 148; Llanvihangel, 140–1, *198*; Tigley, 175; Wellington, 29–30, 125
Barmouth, 88, 183, 184, 186–8, *188–90*, 192
Barnstaple, 42, 169, 170, 186, 208
Barnum 2-4-0s, *43*, 88, 195, 214, *217*
Barry, *46*
Basset-Lowke *Count Louis*, 184
Behren, George, 140–1, 152
Bennett, Arnold, 35
Berks & Hants line, 164, 170
Birkenhead, 43, 44, 73–4
Birmingham, 42, 44, 84, 88, 100, 118, 121, 122, 162, 166, 167, 219; *and South Wales Express*, 153, 154; Moor Street, *169*; New Street, 48, 82, 85, 152, 216; Snow Hill, *12*, 48, *49*, 60, *82*, 85, 88, *115*, 129, 146, 149–60, *150–1*, *157–8*, *160*, 213–14, *214–16*, 220–1, *221*
Bishopsteignton, 100
Bodmin, 42–3; Road, 176, *177*
Bookstalls, 151
Brakes, vacuum, 34, 36, 88
Brecon, 87, 112; & Merthyr, *24*, 86, *137*; Beacone, 117
Brent, 175
Bristol, 9, 10, 44, 48, 51, 55, 56, 74, 76, 79–81, 84, 88, 90, 94, 97, 100, 101, 118, 120–2, 125, 126, 128, 129, 134, 146, 148, 161, 162, 164, 167, 169; *Bristolian*, 35, 82, 96, 100, 126, 128, 141, 148, 220; Temple Meads, *19*, *22*, 80, 100, 117, 175
Broad gauge, 6, 27–31, 33, 90; *Amazon*, 27, *31*; *Gooch*, 7; *Great Western*, 27, 77; *Inkerman*, *30*; *Iron Duke*, 7, 29, 30; *Lord of the Isles*, 27; *North Star*, 27, *61*; *Rover*, 29–31; *Timour*, 27, *91*
Brunel, I. K., 9, 27, 33, 65, 89, 100, 116, 167, 192
Bulldogs, 6, 88, 92, *101*, 114, 151,

153, *182*, 212, 215, 218; *A. H. Mills*, 158; *Madras*, *163*; *Meteor*, 155; *Ottawa*, *151*; *Peacock*, 183

Cab layout, *32*, 40
Calne, 118, 119
Cambrian, *26*, 43, 86–8, *86*, *111*, 112, *182*, 183, 186, 187, 189, 190, *190*, 192, 194; *Coast Express*, 114, 127, 129, 192
Cardiff, *37*, 51, 85, 88, 108, 112, 117, 127–35, *132*, 153, 163, 167, 181
Carmarthen, 55, 88, 114, 117, 195, 196
Castle Cary, 88, 90, 94, 97, 118, 121, 164, 169, 170, 173
Castles, 39, 73–83, 88, 92, 94, 117, 121, 122, 124, 126, 148, 193, 195, 219; *Avondale*, *220*; *Carmarthen*, 45; *Chepstow*, *172*, 175, 176; *Clun*, 74, 76–9, *78–9*, 82–3, *82–3*, *110*, *172*, 205; *Denbigh*, 80; *Drysllwyn*, *96*; *Earl Cairns*, *172*; *Earl of Ducie*, 16, 32, 74, 75, 80, 82, *82*; *Eastnor*, 19, 45, *165*; *Fairey Battle*, *37*; *Hartlebury*, *62*, *197*; *Hereford*, *15*; *Monmouth*, *110*; *North Star*, *40*; *Pendennis*, 76, 77, 82–3; *Penric*, *15*, 73–4; *Sudeley*, 77; *Thornbury*, *175*; *Tiverton*, 98; *Trematon*, 17; *Usk*, *71*; *Whittington*, *102–3*; *Windsor*, *138*
Catering, 56, 152
Cathedrals Express, *16*, 73, 122
Caynham Court, 126
Chancellors, 214
Channel Islands, 47, 88, 170
Chapman, W. G., 77
Chard, 42, 169, 170
Cheltenham, 48, 51, 84, 87, 88, 122, 167, 169; & Honeybourne Railway, 167; *Flyer*, 35, 82, 114
Chepstow, 84, 85, 129
Chester, 43, *44–5*, *82*, 109, 116
Chippenham, *41*, 118, 119, 162, 164
Christow, *178*, 179–80
Church Stretton, 142, 144
Churchward products, *6*, 8, 9, *10*, 39, 40, *59*, 60, *101*, *104*, 109, 114–18, *115*, 146 *see also individual headings*
City class, *101*; *Bath*, 7; *Hobart*, *212*; *Truro*, 74, 76, 117
Coal-coaling, 23, 38, 49, 135, *135*, 144, 162
Coleford, *14*, 121
Collett products, 39, *40*, 74, *75*, 88, 114, 118, 121, 124, 187, 190, 195
Commuters, 65–6, 219–21
Cooke, Harold, 74, 76, 79
Cornish Riviera Express, *16*, 92, 94, 97, 120, 121, 123, 125, 127, 146, 148, 170, 173, 174, 176
Cornishman, *40*, 88, 100, 122, *168*, 174, 176
Corris, 184–6, *185*
Corwen, 43, 87, 183
Cotswolds, 74, 87, 88
Coupling, Instanter, 36, 38
Craven Arms, 85, 87, 88, 158
Crewe, 43, *43*, 87, 88
Cross-country, 84–8
Cuneo, Terence, *102–3*, *110*

Cureton, Harry, 73
Cut-offs, 161–72, *161*, *165*

Daffodil Express, 117
Dalton, T. P., 114, 149
Daniels, Driver Albert, *156*, 157
Dartmouth, *172*, 173
Dawlish, *10*, 31, 89, 90, 92, *92*, 93, *95–6*, 100, 120, 168, 174; Warren, 89, 90, 93–5 *passim*
Dean Goods, 74, *101*, 109, 112–14, *113*, 145, 184, 185, 189, 190, 192, 195, 196, 212, *216*
Depots/sheds, 38, 66, *101*, 105, 108; Aberstwyth, *38*; Basingstoke, 116; Bristol (Bath Road), 18, 80, 126, 147; Cardiff (Canton), 112, 123, 127–8, 139, 148; Chippenham, 118, 119; Ebbw Junction, 128–9; Exeter, *101*; Fishguard (Goodwick), 146; Gloucester (Barnwood), 121; (Horton Road), 117, 121, 147; Huddersfield (Hillhouse), *123*, 124; King's Cross, *38*; Ludlow, 112; Marylebone, *38*; Neasden LNER, 23; Neyland, 116–17, *116*; Old Oak Common, 23, 51, *70–1*, 73, 76, 115, 126–9 *passim*; Oswestry, 112, 114; Plymouth (Laira), 78, 115, 122, 125; Pontypool Road, 85, 117, 123, 148; Reading, 147–8; South Lambeth, 66; Southall, 54, 115, 218; Swansea (Landore), 116, 147; Swindon, *15*, 118; Tyseley, 88, *104*, 121, 123, 124, 129, *155*; Vale of Rheidol, 190; Wolverhampton (Oxley), 115, 116, 123, 124; (Stafford Road), 109, 112, 121–2, 146, 147, *217*
Destination boards, *12*, 96–7
Devil's Bridge, 43, 189–90, 194
Devonian, 100
Didcot, 87, 129; Newbury & Southampton line, 42, 87, 88
Dieselisation, 23, 122, 127, 196; multiple units, 56, 118, 120, 220
Districts, 97
Dolgelly, 87, 88, 183, 184, 186
'Dreadnought' coaches, *8*, *42*
Duchesses, 39, 126; *Teck*, 214
Dudley, *54*, 158
Dukes, 184, 186, 190, *191*, 195, 196
Dukedogs', *38*, 88, *182*, 184, 186, 189–90, *189*, 192–3, 195, 205
Dulverton, 187

Earley, M. W., 197
Ebbw Vale, *136*
Elsden, Arthur Hammond, *156*, 160
Excursions, *11*, 51–3, 89, 117, 121, 128, 129, 148, *200*, 203, 205, 206
Evesham, 48, 74
Exeter, 42, 90, 100, 115, 120, 121, 129, 146, 168, 173–5 *passim*; St Davids, 31, 90, 93, 97, *98*, 100, 174, *174*; St Thomas, 17, 174
Experiment *Belgic*, 216

Fairlies, 187
Fares/rates, 54–5, 129, 167, 203
Falmouth, 90, 97, 176
Festiniog, 184; Railway, 186, 187
Field, Tom, 220
Fiennes, Gerard, 73
Fishguard, 47, 51, 116, 117, 135, 146, 167

Flowers, 214, *216*
Flying Dutchman, 7, 27, 29, *30*
Folkestone, 118
Forest of Dean, *14*, 84, 85
France, 9, 84, 112, 115
Freight, 47, 48, 66, 97, 118–19, 163, 167, 178, 185, *194*, 195
Frome, 168

Gloucester, 51, 84, 85, 117, 118, 121, 123, 161, 162; Railway Society, 114
Golden Valley, 43, 162
Gooch, Sir Daniel, 27, 163
Goods trains, *24*, *26*, *37*, 47, 48, *52–3*, *69*, 74, 88, 90, *99*, 112–14, 118–19, 135, *135–6*, *191*, *194*, 195, 196, 199 *see also* Dean; yards, 66, 90, 118, *172*, 185
Grand, Keith, 219
Granges, 39, 116, 121; *Hewell*, *158*; *Leaton*, *177*; *Woolston*, 121–4, *123*
Great Bear, The, 60
Great Central, 10, *21*, 43–4, 164, 166, 212
Green Don, 73
Gwili Railway, 196

Halls, 39, *49*, *71*, 88, 121, 123, 140, 148, 219, 220; *Acton Burnell*, 221; *Beachamwell*, *199*; *Berrington*, *199*; *Broome*, *177*; *Brownsholme*, *157*; *Campion*, *25*; *Capel Dewi*, 77; *Capesthorne*, *45*; *Eydon*, *157*; *Farnley*, *138*; *Glasfryn*, *22*; *Hagley*, *96*; *Kingsthorpe*, 74; *Lilford*, *131*; *Marwell*, *169*; *Soughton*, *99*; *Trematon*, 58, 64; *Trevor*, *52*; *Westwood*, 158
Halts, 119, 179, 194, 208
Hancock, Jack, *59*, 73, 74, 76, 80
Harvey, S. C., 190
Hart, Pat, 117, 207
Hawksworth, F. W., 39, 118, 206
Hay on Wye, 43, 87
Helstone, *23*
Hereford, 44, 55, 84, 85, 87, 88, 112, 117, 122, 129, 141, *142*, 147, 148, 153
Higby, driver, 80
Higgins R. W., 124
High Wycombe, 164, 166
Holiday traffic, 17, *25*, 35, 49, *49*, 50, 51, 89, 122 *see also* Excursions
Huddersfield, *123*, 124
Humphreys, Owen, 196
Hurricane, 27

Ilfracombe, 170, *171*, 208
Instructions, engineering, 180–1

Jubilee, 146; *Straits Settlements*, 45
Jumbo *Thalaba*, 216
Junctions: Aberayron, 195; Abergavenny, *37*, *138*; Abergwili, 195; Ashendon, 164, 166; Aynho, 164, 166, *210*, 211; Bala, 87, 179, 183; Barmouth, 183, 184, 187, *205*; Barnstaple, 208; Buildwas, 85, *88*; Buttington, 193; Cogload, 78, 94, 164, 170; Cowley Bridge, 78; Curry Rivel, 164; Dovey, 87, 183, 184, 186, 189, 190, *191*, 192; Dr Day's Bridge, *25*, 80; Exeter City Basin, 168, 179; Filton, 134; Foxhall, *21*; Hatton North, 212; Honeybourne, 74, 75, 84, 122, 167; Llandillo, 167,

195; Longhedge, 67; Lydney, 84; Kemble, 88, 119; Moat Lake, 87, 112, 184, 192; Old Oak Common West, 164, 166; Pencader, 194, 195; Pengam, *131*; Pontsticill, *24*, *137*; Severn Tunnel, 84, 97, 112; Smethwick, 85; Stourbridge, 85, 153, 154, *154*, 157, 167; Subway, Westbourne Park, *8*; Swindon, 53; Three Cocks, 86, 87; Westerleigh, 167; Worle, *30*; Yate South, 167

Kerry, 112, 114, 193
Kidderminster, 85, 112, 153
King, L., 124
Kingham, 51, 74, 84, 87, 88
Kings, *16*, 39, 88, 92, 94, *106–7*, 115, 124–6, 141, 148, 155; *Edward II, 106–7, V, 153, VI, 65, VIII, 204*; *George I*, 158, *II, 20, V*, 59, 128, 153, 205; *Henry V, 111, VI, 98*, 124–9, *125, 127–8*; *James II, 165*; *John, 203*; *Richard I, 16*; *William IV, 151*
Kingswear, 96, 115, *172*, 173
Knowle & Dorridge, 220–1

Lampeter, 194–6 *passim*
Langport, 88, 164, 173
Lavington, 77, 164, 169
Leamington Spa, *20*, 44, 129, 156, 157, 212, *212*
Ledbury, *46*, 85
Liskeard, 115, 176
Liverpool, 96; 100
Llandovery, 43
Llanelly, 112, 122, 167–8
Llangollen, *11*, 87, *182*, 183
Lloyd George, David, 201
LMS, 33, 42–5 *passim*, 48, 53, 85, 87, 100, 135, 139, 146
LNER, 20, 23, 43, 55, 97, 201
LNWR, 33, 85, 87, 112, 135, 153, 162, 167, 212, 215, 216; LSWR, 88
Lode Star, 65
London, 56, 65–72, 101, 115; Transport, 65–7 *passim, 72, 166*
Long Maurice, 202–3, 221
Loop lines, 48, 51, 129, 162, 166, 167
Lostwithiel, 176, *177*
Luggage in advance, 49, 50, 63

Machin, Alan, 218
Machynlleth, 87, 114, 183–7 *passim, 193*
Malan, Rev. A. H., 27–31
Manchester, 96, 100, 128; & Milford Railway, 194, *194*, 196
Manors, 39, *87*, 116, *193*, 195, *195*, 205, *205*
McNaught, 73–4
Midland, *11*, 44, 45, 85, 86, 88, 135, 167, 216; & South Western Junction Railway, 51, *85*, 87
Milk, 47, 122, 128, 195, 196
Milford Haven, 187, 194, 196
Milne, Sir James, 190
Minehead, 169, 170
Minffordd, 184, 186, 187
Moguls, *14*, 44, 50, 61, 85, 88, *95*, 114–18, *115–16*, 140–6, *142*, 155, 183, *188*, *194*, 195, *196*, 208, 209, 215, 216
Monmouth, 55, 85

Nantymoel, *137*
Nationalisation, 23, 24, 33, 117, 120, 121
Narrow gauge, 184, 187
Neath, 105, 135, 167

New York, 100
Newbury, 48, 56, 87
Newcastle, 51, 84, 88, 98, 100; Emlyn, 195
Newport, 84, 85, 105, 109, *110*, 117, 122, 128, 129, 135
Newquay, 97, 122, 176
Newton Abbot, 27, *31*, *36*, 51, 90, 93, 95, 96, 100, 125, 126, 168, 171, 173, 175, 178, 192, 206
Newtown, 183, 192
Nock, O. S., 78, 126

Oswestry, 112, 114, 193
Oxford, 42, 55, 56, 74, *99*, 123, 129, 147, 161, 164, 166

Pacifics, *15*, 39, 120, 127
Paddington, 7, 23, 48, 51, 65–7, *66–8*, 76, 77, 90, 93, 94, 97, 100, 120–3, 125–9 *passim*, 134, 147, 148, 163, 164, 169, 176, 192, 194, 211, 218–20 *passim*; Bishop's Road, 65, 67, 70
Paignton, 94, 96, 100, 128, 173
Patchway, 162, *162*
Patney & Chirton, 164
Penzance, 88–90 *passim*, 96, 97, 122, 123, 129, 146, 169, 176
Pines Express, 221
Platforms, 179; tickets, 149, 171
Plymouth, 9, 44, 74, 76, 77, 79, 90, 93, 94, 96, 97, 100, 115, 120–2 *passim*, 125, 126, 128, 129, 146, 148, 176
Police, railway, 156
Pontypool, 53, 87, 88, 184, 187, 196
Portland Dockyard, 120
Portmadoc, 186, 187
Ports to Ports Express, 51, 84, 88
Postal trains, *13*, 146
Powell, C. W., 176
Precedent *Princess*, 216
Precursor *Pacific*, 216
Prince of Wales, 83; class, 215
Princes Risborough, 143, 166
Pryce Owen, guard, 185–6
Pwllehli, 53, 87, 88, 184, 187, 196

Railcars, *5*, *14*, 54–6, *54–5*, 66, 67, 85, 88, *88*, 93, 108, 151, 154, 155, *154–5*
Railtours, 114, 117, 120, 129
Raymond, Stanley, 220
Reading, *14*, 42, 51, 55, 56, 93, 116, 117, 140–1, 147, 148, 164, 166, 170, 218
Red Dragon, *111*, 122
Refreshment rooms, 60, 195, 196
Renown *Black Prince*, 216
Reservations, seat, 95, 173, 192
Restaurant cars, *8*, *25*, 51, 93, 95–6, *95*, 214
Rheidol, Vale of, 184, 190
Roach, driver, 77–9
Roads, 179
Roche, T. W. K., 221
Royal Duchy, 76, 127, *175*
Royal trains, *19*, 120, 126, 138, 176, 196
Ruabon, 87, 88, 183, 187
Ruislip, *10*, 69, *166*

Safety, 9, 11, 39, *71*, 126–7
Saints, 10, *10*, 60, 88, 92, *122*, 140–2, 146–8, 154, 156, 214, 215; *Bride of Lammermoor, 143; Clevedon Court, 140–8, 147–8; Fawley Court, 145; Helena, 32*, 156, *168; Lady of the Lake, 10*, 156, 214; *Robins Bolitho,*

214; Taplow Court, 42; William Dean, 10
Salisbury, 42, *42*, 88
Saltash, 92, *102–3*, 115, 176
Scilly Isles, 51, 118
Seasonal traffic, 17, 47–56 *see also* Holiday traffic; Specials
Shrewsbury, 44, 84, 112, 114, 122, 123, 126, 128, *145*, 146, 147, 158, 193, 215, *217*
Signals, *8*, *13*, *20*, 23, 28, 29, *30*, 35–6, *36–7*, 39, *68*, 85, 92–4, 97, *101*, 130–1, *133*, 134, 152, *153*, 159–60, *160*, *174*, 186–7, 192, *193*, *217*; boxes, 34, *34*, 39, 51, 92, 130, 131, 134, 159–60, *160*, 202–3, *204*, *217*
Skelsey, fireman Walter, *156*, 157
Sleepers, 51, 118, 121
Slip coaches, *21*, 121, 170
Slough, *19*, 51
Soole, G. H., 197
South Molton, 48, 187, 208, 209
South Devon Railway, 89, 90
Southampton, 87, 167
Southern, 42, 43, 88, 100, 152, 186, 209, 220
Specials, 49–53, 73, 76–82, *96*, 97, *110–11*, 114, *119*, 122, 128, 129, 134, 148, 203, *205*, 206, 208
Speed, 16, 35, 54, 74, 76–82, 97, 100, 181, 195
Staff, 18, 33, 201, 218; apprentices, 60, 62, 159–60; chief clerk, 201–3; excursion manager, 203, 206; fireman, 29, 30, 41; stationmaster, 18, 34, *53*, 74, 156, 160, 176, 185, 196, 201, 219; relief, 206–8; superintendent, 18, 201, 202; ticket collectors, 57, 149, 152, 156, 158, 171; works, 57–65 *see also individual headings*
Standard 4-6-0s, 205
Stanier, William, 33, 39; products, 39, 187, 196
Stars, 10, *13*, *19*, 60, 122, 146, 220; *British Monarch, 99; Glastonbury Abbey, 19*, 158; *Knight of the Garter, 13*; *Prince Henry, 213*; *Princess Alice, 210*; *Maud, 166*; *Sophia, 211*
Starcross, 31, 100
Steele, Keith, 160
Stella class, 195
Stourbridge, 112, 153, 154
Strata Florida, 194, *196*
Stratford upon Avon, 10, 84, 88, 100, 122, 129, *168*
Swansea, 55, 84, 116, 122, 129, 135, 181, 196; District Line, 167
Swindon, *26*, 85, 87, 88, 121, 123, 162, 170 *see also* Works

Taff Vale Railway, *135–6*
Talerddig, 183, 184, 192
Talyllyn, *86*, 87, 184; Railway, 184; Preservation Society, 114, 205
Tanks, 151, 152, 154, 214, 218, 220; 0-4-2s, *41*, 85, 88, 118, 120, 121, 139, 178, *178*, *185*, *195*; 0-6-0s, *11*, *24*, *26*, 35, *62*, *70*, *72*, *86*, 88, *111*, 115, 118–21, *119*, *131*, 152, *171*, *178*, 186, 187, 190, *190*, 195, 218; 0-6-2s, *135–6*, 218; 2-6-2s, *23*, 59, *70*, *84*, 88, *88*, *91*, 109, *136*, *138*, 156–8, *156*, 187, *191*, 195, *197*, 214, 219, *219*; 2-6-4s, 187; 2-8-2s, 152, *199*; 4-4-2s, 7, *8*; Prairie, 64, *104*, *128*, 173–5, 221; Saddle, 154, 185
Taunton, 29, 77, 90, 118, 120, 121, 148, 164, 169–71, *171*, 186

Taylor, Bob, 220
Teignmouth, 28, 31, 89–93 *passim, 91*, 97, 100, 120, 121, 174; Teign Valley, 178
Tenbury Wells, 85
Tender, *26*, 39, 60
Tewkesbury, 85
Thomas, Campbell, 185–6
Tidworth, 87
Timetable, 92–4, 118, 120–1
Tolley, driver Cyril, 221
Torbay, 35, 90, 93; *Express*, 92, 94, 97, *98*, 120, 125, 170, *172*, 206
Torquay, 90, 94, 173
Totnes, 90, 175
Towyn, 114, 184, 189, 205
Training, 124, 201
Tregaron Bog, 194, 195
Trench, Louis, 33
Trewin, J. C., 118
Truro, 97, 146, 176
Tunnels, 28, 89, 92; Alderton, 163; Box, 28, 30; Campden, 74; Chipping Sodbury, 163; Dinmore, 143; Greenway, 173; Mutley, 77, 176; Parsons, 6, 92; Sapperton, 162; Severn, 49, 117, 161, 162, *163*; Somerton, 164; Whiteball, 28, 30–1, 78, 170
Tylwych, *86*
Tyseley, *153*, 156, *167*

Valves, piston, 40, 62; poppet, 126
Viaducts, 117, *135*, 183, *209*

Wales, *26*, 43, 44, 51, 55, *86*, 108, 112, 114, 117, 118, 183–96 *see also* Cambrian; South, 18, *24*, 43, 84, 85, 88, 100, 114, 116–18, 121, 127–35, *135–7*, 146, 161–4 *passim*, 167, 190, 194; & Bristol Direct Railway, 162–3, *165*
Walking tickets, 63–4
Warwick, 43, 156; North – line, 33, 85, 88, 100, 122, 167, *167*, 169, *169*, 170
Watering, 35, *111*, *145*, 152, 193
Wellington, 29–30, 85, 88, 112, 158, 170, 214
Welshpool, 183, 193, 205
Westbury, 77, 88, 125, 147, 164, 168, 173
'West Coast Joint Service', 73
Weymouth, 10, 44, 48, 55, 56, 88, 112, *119*, 120, 147, 164, 173; Wiltshire, 87–8, 119–20; Somerset & Weymouth route, 164
Winchester, 42, 88
Windsor, 51, 211, 218
Wolverhampton, *53*, 67, 69, 100, 105, 109, 115, 116, 123, 126, 154, 156, 158, 161, 167, 170, 214
Worcester, 55, 73–4, 84, 85, 88, 105, 112, 116, 122, 123, 129, 153, 161, 162; Shrub Hill, *11*, *45*, 74, *80*
Works, 117, 120, 214; Swindon, *11*, *15*, 36, 39–40, 53, 57–65, *59*, *61–2*, *65*, *68*, 112, 116–18, 122, 125, *128*, 129, 219
World War I, 39, 112, 115, 201; II, 56, 92, 100, 112, 117, 119, 122, 148, 168, 184, 195, 208–9
Wyatt, M. D., 65
Wyse, Bob, 206–7

Yards, 27, 90, 129, 163
Yeovil, 42, 88, 120, 164, 169, 170, 192